Regional Hidden Places

Cambs & Lincolnshire
Chilterns
Cornwall
Derbyshire
Devon
Dorset, Hants & Isle of Wight
East Anglia
Gloucs, Wiltshire & Somerset
Heart of England
Hereford, Worcs & Shropshire
Lake District & Cumbria
Lancashire & Cheshire
Lincolnshire & Nottinghamshire
Northumberland & Durham
Sussex
Thames Valley
Yorkshire

National Hidden Places

England
Ireland
Scotland
Wales

Hidden Inns

East Anglia
Heart of England
Lancashire & Cheshire
North of England
South
South East
South and Central Scotland
Wales
Welsh Borders
West Country
Yorkshire
Wales

Country Living Rural Guides

East Anglia
Heart of England
Ireland
North East of England
North West of England
Scotland
South
South East
Wales
West Country

Published by: Travel Publishing Ltd, 7a Apollo House, Calleva Park, Aldermaston, Berkshire RG7 8TN

ISBN 1-904-43418-5

First published 1991, second edition 1994, third edition 1997, fourth edition 1999, fifth edition 2002, sixth edition 2005

All information is included by the publishers in good faith and is believed to be correct at the time of going to press. No responsibility can be accepted for errors.

Foreword

The *Hidden Places* is a collection of easy to use travel guides taking you in this instance on a relaxed but informative tour of the *Peak District and Derbyshire*. The *Peak District National Park* was the very first of Britain's National Parks covering an area of 540 square miles. The *Dark Peak* covering north Derbyshire and small parts of Cheshire and South Yorkshire is an area of windswept moorland, steep river valleys and impressive crags. Futher south is the *White Peak* a limestone-based undulating green landscape criss - crossed by miles of dry stone walls and gently flowing rivers whilst to the west can be found the beautiful valleys and rivers of the *Dales* as well as the *Staffordshire Moorlands*. In contrast the rest of Derbyshire offers the visitor an intriguing mix of villages and towns packed with cultural and industrial heritage and should certainly not be missed.

This is the 6th edition of a *Hidden Places* title including the Peak District and Derbyshire and the guide has been fully updated. In this respect we would like to thank the many Tourist Information Centres in the Peak District and Derbyshire for helping us update the editorial content.

Our books contain a wealth of interesting information on the history, the countryside, the towns and villages and the more established places of interest. But they also promote the more secluded and little known visitor attractions and places to stay, eat and drink many of which are easy to miss unless you know exactly where you are going.

We include hotels, inns and bed and breakfast accomodation, restaurants, public houses, teashops, historic houses, museums, gardens, and many other attractions throughout the area, all of which are comprehensively indexed. Most places are accompanied by an attractive photograph and are easily located by using the map at the beginning of each chapter. We do not award merit marks or rankings but concentrate on describing the more interesting, unusual or unique features of each place with the aim of making the reader's stay in the local area an enjoyable and stimulating experience.

Whether you are visiting the area for business or pleasure or in fact are living in the Peak District and Derbyshire we do hope that you enjoy reading and using this book. We are always interested in what readers think of places covered (or not covered) in our guides so please do not hesitate to use the reader reaction forms provided to give us your considered comments. We also welcome any general comments which will help us improve the guides themselves. Finally if you are planning to visit any other corner of the British Isles we would like to refer you to the list of other *Hidden Places* titles to be found at the rear of the book and to the Travel Publishing website at www.travelpublishing.co.uk.

Travel Publishing

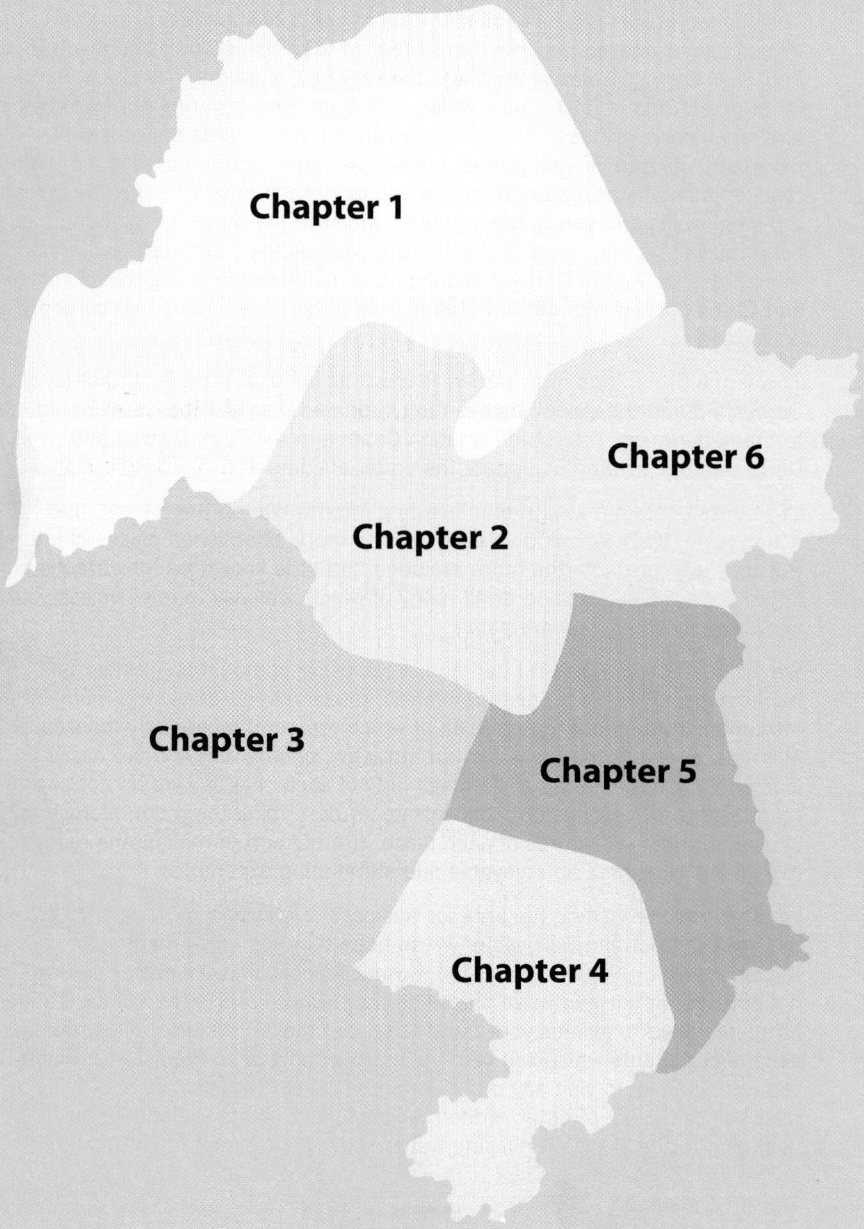

Chapter 1

Chapter 6

Chapter 2

Chapter 3

Chapter 5

Chapter 4

Contents

PLACES TO STAY, EAT AND DRINK

Lime Tree Park Holidays, Buxton, Derbyshire	1	Self Catering	p6
The White Lion, Buxton, Derbyshire	2	Pub	p6
Café Nats & The George, Buxton, Derbyshire	3	Inn with Food & Café with Accommodation	p8
Buxton Museum & Art Gallery, Buxton, Derbyshire	4	Museum	p10
The Cat & Fiddle Inn, Macclesfield Forest, Cheshire	5	Pub with Food	p12
Fools Nook Inn, Sutton, Cheshire	6	Pub with Food	p12
Jolly Carter, Chapel-en-le-Frith, Derbyshire	7	Pub with Food	p14
Kings Arms Hotel, Chapel-en-le-Frith, Derbyshire	8	Hotel	p15
The Old Hall Inn, Chinley, Derbyshire	9	Pub, Food & Accommodation	p16
The Shady Oak, Whaley Bridge, Derbyshire	10	Pub with Food	p17
The Torrs, New Mills, Derbyshire	11	Pub, Food & Accommodation	p18
Pack Horse Inn, New Mills, Derbyshire	12	Pub, Food & Accommodation	p20

● Denotes entries in other chapters

1 Buxton and the Dark Peak

Situated right at the centre of England, the Peak District and surrounding area is truly a microcosm of the country. It divides the rugged north from the softer pastoral countryside of the south. There are spectacular rock formations, windswept moorlands, undulating pastures, picturesque villages and historic churches and castles. The Romans have left their roads and the remains of their forts and baths, there are Saxon and Norman churches and the Civil War raged through the area leaving a trail of destruction. Mainly agricultural for hundreds of years with some coal mining and ironworks, the industrial revolution transformed the area as mills, mines and works sprang up everywhere. As the population of the towns grew, the factory and mine owners built houses for the workforce, churches and grand civic buildings and left a rich legacy of Victorian architecture.

The first of Britain's National Parks, The Peak District itself covers an area of 540 square miles close to the large industrial conurbations of middle England. The National Park is scattered with the remains of ancient settlements. The northern area of the Peak District National Park, known as the Dark Peak or High Peak is a landscape of moorlands and deep valleys edged with escarpments of dark sandstone and shale.

PLACES TO STAY, EAT AND DRINK

● Denotes entries in other chapters

Black Tor & Loose Hill, High Peak

many pleasant walks and magnificent stately homes for visitors to enjoy. Derbyshire was at the forefront of the Industrial Revolution and its history is recorded in the Industrial Museum at Derby. It is reflected too in many of the villages with their rows of 18th and 19th century workers' cottages. To the northeast of Derbyshire is the heart of the coal-mining area, which prospered during the 19th and early 20th century. Sometimes overlooked, this part of Derbyshire is well worth exploring for its industrial architecture alone.

On the southern edge of the Peak District, the undulating pastures and crags of the Staffordshire Moorlands are ideal places to walk, cycle or trek. It is a mixture of charming villages, historic

The rugged Millstone Grit moorlands and crags enclose the softer limestone plateau of the White Peak like a horseshoe. The southern section of the Peak District is the beautiful Dovedale. The River Dove is a famous fishing river, first mentioned in Izaak Walton's *The Compleat Angler*, in 1653. The River Manifold too has wonderful scenery including the beautifully preserved estate village of Ilam. The ancient custom of well-dressing is found mainly in these limestone areas of Derbyshire, where the streams frequently disappear through the porous rock.

The Amber Valley, the Erewash and the Trent Valley, to the east and south of Derbyshire, although not part of the National Park, have

Rolling Hillsides of the Peak District

market towns, ancient farms and relics of the Industrial Revolution including the reservoirs of Rudyard and Tittesworth, originally the water supply for the Midlands, now peaceful havens for wildlife and leisure.

The Dark Peak, or High Peak, is not as foreboding as its names might suggest. These high moors are ripe for exploring on foot, and a walk from the Kinder Reservoir will lead to the western edge of Kinder Scout. This whole area is really a series of plateaux, rather than mountains and valleys, with the highest point on Kinder Scout some 2,088 feet above sea level. In this remote and wild area the walker can feel a real sense of freedom - however, it is worth remembering that the moors, with their treacherous peat bogs and unpredictable mists which can rise quickly even in summer, should not be dismissed as places for a casual ramble.

To the eastern side of this region are the three reservoirs created by flooding of the upper valley of the River Derwent. Howden, Derwent and Ladybower provide water for the East Midlands but their remote location, along with the many recreational activities found there, make them popular places to visit. The Derwent dam is particularly famous as the site of practice exercises for the Dambusters of the Second World War. Even those who have not visited the area before will be familiar with some of the place names, as they feature heavily in winter weather reports. Snake Pass (the A57), one of the few roads that runs through this northern section of the National Park, is often closed during the winter; even in spring, conditions can deteriorate quickly to make driving hazardous.

Buxton

With a population of barely 20,000 the elegant Georgian town of Buxton is nonetheless the largest settlement within the boundaries of the Peak District National Park. (The second largest town, Bakewell, has fewer than 5,000 inhabitants.) Referred to as the heart of the Peak District, Buxton, like Bakewell, is right on the divide between the Dark Peak and White Peak areas of the National Park. A large part of the White Peak lies between the two towns. Buxton is also England's highest market town, at 1,000 feet above sea level and provides a wealth of things to do. Buxton's gracious architecture can be attributed mainly to the 5th Duke of Devonshire, who hoped to establish a northern spa town that would rival, and possibly surpass, the attractions of Bath. In both locations it was the Romans who first exploited the healing waters of apparently inexhaustible hot springs as a commercial atmosphere. The Romans' name for Buxton was *Aquae Arnemetiae* - The Spa of the Goddess of the Grove. The waters still bubble up at Buxton, always maintaining a constant temperature of 82 degrees F (28 degrees C). Go on, drink a glass – Buxton water is reputed to be particularly pure and especially effective at mitigating the

Lime Tree Park Caravan and Camping Holidays

Dukes Drive, Buxton, Derbyshire SK17 9RP
Tel/Fax: 01298 22988
e-mail: limetreebuxton@dukes50.fsnet.co.net
website: www.ukparks.co.uk/limetree

A premier 4-Star caravan and camping park, **Lime Tree Park** occupies a 17-acre site. The scenic location – in the heart of the Peak District in its own valley on the edge of Buxton – is ideal for discovering the magnificent Derbyshire countryside.

There are eight quality caravans available to hire, along with a wood lodge that sleeps up to four people, and two apartments that sleep four and six respectively. Each caravan has two to three bedrooms and sleeps up to six. All are available from March to October, with short breaks offered off-season (March to June and September to October). Facilities include shower blocks, adventure playground, TV lounge with pool table, launderette, shop and payphone.

The site also welcomes tourers and campers, with room for up to 70 touring caravans, hard and soft standing pitches and electric hook-ups. The camping area can accommodate up to 70 tents. Tourers and campers have access to all facilities on site.

The White Lion

Spring Gardens, Buxton,
Derbyshire SK17 6BZ
Tel: 01298 23099

The White Lion public house is a distinguished establishment located in a traffic-free precinct in Buxton town centre, close to all of the town's amenities including the Opera House. The convenient location makes this an ideal place to enjoy a refreshing drink while sightseeing or shopping, and proves to be popular with locals and visitors alike. Occupying a listed building, it dates back in parts to 1661 and was originally a coaching inn. Inside there is a traditional feel, with the spacious interior divided into three bars, including one with pool tables, football table and wide-screen satellite TV.

The Tap Room is cosy, welcoming and furnished with an eye towards comfort – it is a relaxing place where guests can enjoy the many offerings of the bar. There are two real ales kept on tap – Marston's Pedigree and Bitter – together with a good selection of lagers and a variety of wines, spirits and soft drinks. Owner Ann Smith has run the pub since 1996 and brings a wealth of experience to her work, as well as offering every guest a genuinely warm welcome. Open all day every day.

The Crescent, Buxton

As with many places, the coming of the railway to Buxton in 1863 marked the height of popularity of the town. Nothing, however, could be done to alter the harsh climate, and the incessant rainfall meant that the Duke's dream of making Buxton the 'Bath of the North', was never truly realised.

symptoms of rheumatism. Countless rheumatism sufferers are on record attesting that the balmy Buxton water has helped to soothe their symptoms – Mary, Queen of Scots, a political prisoner detained at nearby Chatsworth but allowed out on day-release to Buxton, was among them. The people of Buxton also say that it makes the best cup of tea possible, and collect bottles of it to take home.

In the 18th century, the 5th Duke of Devonshire commissioned the building of **The Crescent** to ensure that visitors would flock here. Designed by John Carr of York, the building is similar to the architecture found in Bath and, after suffering from neglect, underwent a huge restoration programme. Next to The Crescent, the Thermal Baths are now the Tourist Information Centre, and the former town house of Bess of Hardwick and her husband the Earl of Shrewsbury, where Mary Queen of Scots stayed when she visited Buxton, is now the Old Hall Hotel.

Among the other notable architectural features of the town are **The Colonnade** and the Devonshire Royal Hospital. They were originally built as stables for hotel patrons of The Crescent and, after their conversion by the 6th Duke in 1858, the largest unsupported dome in the world was built to enclose the courtyard in 1880.

The attractive **Buxton Opera House** was designed and built in 1903 by the renowned theatre architect, Frank Matcham. Gertrude Lawrence, Gracie Fields and Hermione Gingold all played here and on one memorable occasion, the famous Hollywood screen stars Douglas Fairbanks and Mary Pickford were in the audience to watch the Russian ballerina, Anna Pavlova. However, in the 1930s it was the cinema which virtually wiped out live performances for many years, apart from an annual pantomime and a handful of amateur performances. Restored in 1979 to its grand Edwardian style, it once again hosts live performances. The

Café Nats and The George

Café Nats: 9/11 Market Street, Buxton,
Derbyshire SK17 6JY
Tel/Fax: 01298 23969
The George: The Square, Buxton,
Derbyshire SK17 6AZ
Tel/Fax: 01298 24711

Two premises in the heart of Buxton well worth seeking out are **Café Nats** and **The George**, both owned by Sue and Mike Jordan. They have been in the trade in Buxton for over 30 years, and their experience shows in the excellent hospitality they offer all their guests.

Café Nats is open Monday to Saturday from 10 a.m. to 10 p.m.; 10 a.m. to 3 p.m. on Sundays (closed Bank Holidays). Handsome and attractive, the décor is a happy marriage of traditional and modern. Here guests can enjoy a drink, light snack or full meal, from a superb menu of hearty favourites and more innovative dishes. As a member of the new Peak Cuisine group, wherever possible all ingredients are sourced locally to create the tempting range of dishes on offer. Booking advised for evenings.

The café also boasts five ensuite guest bedrooms. The rooms are cosy and comfortable, and available all year round.

The George stands close to Buxton Opera House and dates back in parts to the 1600s, and occupies part of an impressive four-story stonebuilt building. While the first president of the then-new USA, George Washington, once stayed here, it was of course not named for him but, more traditionally, for the king on the throne at its inception. The interior is warm and welcoming, with traditional features such as exposed stonework walls, low beamed ceilings and handsome fireplaces. Open all day, every day for ale, the George features in the Good Beer Guide. There are six real ales available, with Pale Rider the regular here, complemented by changing guest ales, most of which come from micro-breweries. The George also serves food at weekday lunchtimes until 3 p.m. and weekend lunchtimes until 4; food can also be served in the evenings by prior arrangement.

This convivial inn hosts regular live music twice a week – please ring for details.

The Opera House, Buxton

Buxton Opera Festival is one of Britain's best-known and largest opera-based festivals and, since 1994, the International Gilbert & Sullivan Festival has been held here. Throughout the rest of the year its comprehensive and popular programme has won it a well-deserved reputation nationally and internationally.

The Opera House stands in 23 acres of ornamental gardens in the heart of Buxton. The attractive **Pavilion Gardens** have a conservatory and octagon within the grounds - antique markets and arts shows are often held here, and it is a very pleasant place to walk at any time of year. Laid out in 1871 by Edward Milner, with money donated by the Dukes of Devonshire, the 23 acres include formal gardens, serpentine walks and decorative iron bridges across the River Wye. The conservatory was reopened in 1982 following extensive renovation; there is also a swimming pool filled with warm spa water.

Pavilion Gardens, Buxton

St John the Baptist church was built in Italian style in 1811 by Sir Jeffrey Wyatville. That same year Wyatville laid out The Slopes, the area below the Market Place in Upper Buxton. The grand Town Hall was built 1887—1889 and dominates the Market Place. Further down Terrace Road is the **Buxton Museum** (see panel on page 10), which reveals the long and varied history of the town and its surrounding area. As well as housing an important local archaeology collection, the Museum also has a fine collection of Ashford Marble, Blue John ornaments, paintings, prints, pottery and glassware.

Buxton Museum and Art Gallery

Terrace Road, Buxton, Derbyshire SK17 6DA
Tel: 01298 24658 Fax: 01298 79394
e-mail: buxton.museum@derbyshire.gov.uk
website: www.derbyshire.gov.uk/libraries

Explore the Wonders of the Peak through seven time zones. Discover when sharks swam in warm 'Derbyshire' seas; when lions and sabre tooth cats terrorised mastodons. Meet the Roman Legionaries, and the scientists unravelling the history of Earth. An audio tour, 'Time Moves On', helps to enhance your visit.

For art lovers, enjoy intricate Ashford Black Marble inlay and Blue John ornaments, and a regular programme of exhibitions, featuring work by national and local artists, photographers and craftworkers. Activities for all the family accompany the exhibitions. The museum welcomes visits from school parties. Accessible for disabled, local parking (pay & display), shop, toilets and nearby tearooms.

It is not known for certain whether well-dressing took place in Buxton before 1840, though there are stories that Henry VIII put a stop to the practice, but it has certainly been a part of Buxton's cultural calendar since the Duke of Devonshire provided the townsfolk with their first public water supply at **Market Place Fountain**. From then on, High Buxton Well (as the fountain came to be called) and St Anne's Well were decorated sporadically. In 1923 the Town Council set about organising a well-dressing festival and carnival that continues to this day. Every year on the second Wednesday in July, this delightful tradition is enacted.

St Anne's Church, built in 1625, reflects the building work here before Buxton's 18th century heyday when limestone was the most common construction material rather than the mellow sandstone that dominates today.

Buxton is surrounded by some of the most glorious of the Peak District countryside. These moorlands also provide one of the town's specialities - heather honey. Several varieties of heather grow on the moors: there is ling, or common heather which turns the land purple in late summer; there is bell-heather which grows on dry rocky slopes; and there is cross-leaved heather which can be found on wet, boggy ground.

The town is also the starting point for both the Brindley Trail and the Monsal Trail. Covering some 61 miles, the Brindley Trail, which takes its name from the famous canal engineer, leads southwest to Stoke-on-Trent, while the Monsal Trail, beginning just outside Buxton at Blackwell Mill Junction, finishes at Coombs Viaduct near Bakewell, some 8 miles away.

Around Buxton

To the west of Buxton lies **Axe Edge**, the highest point of which rises to 1,807 feet above sea level. From this spot on a clear day (and the weather here is notoriously changeable) the panoramic views of Derbyshire are overwhelming. Just beyond, at 1,690 feet above sea level, the **Cat and Fiddle Inn** is the second highest pub in England. Axe Edge Moor, which receives an average annual rainfall of over 4 feet, is strictly for hardened walkers. It should come as no surprise that this Moor is the source of several rivers which play important roles in the life of the Peak District. The River Dove and the River Manifold, which join at Ilam, rise not far from one another; the River Wye rises above Buxton to join the Derwent further south; the River Goyt, a major source of the Mersey, rises to the west of Axe Edge.

The entire length of the River Goyt can be walked, from its source to its confluence with the River Etherow to the north and just outside the boundaries of the National Park. Once marking the boundary between Derbyshire and Cheshire (which now lies just to the west), a walk along the Goyt takes in sections of the riverbank as well as the Errwood and Fernilee reservoirs before leaving Derbyshire just north of New Mills. Although the two reservoirs look well established and very much part of the landscape, they are relatively recent additions: the Fernilee was opened in 1938 while the Errwood was flooded in 1967.

Those who venture to Errwood Reservoir will be surprised to see rhododendrons growing near the banks of a man-made lake. They once stood in the grounds of Errwood Hall, which was built in the 1830s for the Grimshawe family. The house was demolished before the Reservoir was flooded, but the gardens were left to grow wild. Not far away can be seen the strange-looking **Spanish Shrine**. Built by the Grimshawes in memory of their Spanish governess, it is a small stone building with an unusual beehive roof.

The highest point in this area is Shining Tor, overlooking Errwood Reservoir and standing some 1,834 feet above sea level. To the north is **Pym Chair**, the point at which an old packhorse road running east to west crosses this gritstone ridge. An old salters' route, it was used for transporting salt from the Cheshire plains across the Peak District moorlands to the industrial and well-populated areas of south and west Yorkshire.

During the 19th century, the Goyt valley with its natural resources of both coal and water developed rapidly into one of the nation's major textile production centres. In order to service this growth, the valley also developed an intense system of transport, including canals and railways. The rugged terrain that had to be negotiated has made for some spectacular solutions to major engineering difficulties.

Also to the west of town on Green Lane is **Poole's Cavern,** so called for 'The robber Poole', who supposedly lived in the cave in the 15th century. It is a

The Cat & Fiddle Inn

Buxton Road, Macclesfield Forest,
Cheshire SK11 0AR
Tel: 01298 23364
e-mail: cat-and-fiddle@tiscali.co.uk

Midway between Buxton and Macclesfield on the A537, within Macclesfield Forest and the Peak District National Park, **The Cat & Fiddle Inn** stands 1,690 feet above sea level and looks over thousands of acres of unspoilt countryside in every direction.

A popular stop-off point for walkers, cyclists, motorists and day-trippers, this justly famous inn is run by Guy Danner, who has been here for two years and is ably assisted by daughters Abi and Emily. Open every day but Thursday, the inn serves three real ales from the Robinsons brewery range: Unicorn, Olde Stockport and a regularly changing guest ale. In addition there's a good selection of lagers, cider, wines, spirits and soft drinks.

Food is available all day – booking is advised at weekends and for larger parties. Main courses include steaks, roast beef, Cumberland sausage, steak and ale pie, roast chicken and other traditional favourites together with moussaka, cauliflower bake and a selection of sandwiches and jacket potatoes. A range of chef's specials are served as well as the regular menu and a varied children's menu is also available.

Fools Nook Inn

Leek Road, Oakgrave, Sutton, Macclesfield,
Cheshire SK11 0JF
Tel: 01260 252254

Adjacent to the main A53 Macclesfield-to-Leek road, about three miles south of Macclesfield, The **Fools Nook** is believed to take its unusual name from its proximity to Gawsworth Hall (National Trust), the last premises in England to retain a Court Jester. After eight years running a licensed premises in the Netherlands, leaseholders Kathryn and Tim took over here early in 2004. Closed Monday evenings, this convivial and welcoming inn is open every other session weekdays and all day at weekends.

There are two real ales – Boddingtons and Bombadier – together with a changing guest ale and a good complement of lagers, cider, stout, a full wine list, spirits and soft drinks. Excellent food is served at lunch (12 – 2.30) and dinner (6 – 8.30), with a menu and specials board of steaks, duck, salmon, seafood, chicken and vegetarian dishes using the freshest local ingredients. Tim is the chef, and among his specialities are authentic curries.

natural limestone cave, which was used by tribes from the Neolithic period onwards. Archaeological digs have discovered Stone Age, Bronze Age and Roman artefacts near the cave entrance. Mary, Queen of Scots visited and the 'chair' she used is still in evidence, and pointed out during the regular tours of the cave on offer. The spectacular natural formations in the cavern include a large stalactite called the 'Flitch of Bacon' and the 'Poached Egg Chamber', with blue grey and orange formations, coloured by manganese and iron soaking down from the lime-tips above.

Poole's Cavern

Above the cavern and about 20 minutes' walk away is **Grin Low Country Park** and the prominent folly and scenic viewpoint, built in 1896, known as **Solomon's Temple**.

North of Buxton

Taxal

5 miles NW of Buxton off the A5004

Overlooking the Goyt Valley, Taxal is home to the church of **St James**, in which can be found a series of fascinating memorials - the earliest to William Jaudrell, who died in 1375, and Roger Jaudrell, a soldier at Agincourt.

West of Taxal are **Windgather Rocks**, a gritstone outcrop popular with trainee rock-climbers. East of the village is the elegant and gracious **Shallcross Hall**, dating back to the 18th century.

Combs

3 miles N of Buxton off the A6

Combs Reservoir southwest of Chapel-en-le-Frith is crossed at one end by Dickie's Bridge. 'Dickie' is said to have resided at a farm in Tunstead where he was known as Ned Dixon. Apparently murdered by his cousin, he nevertheless continued his 'working life' as a sort of guard-skull, alerting the household whenever strangers drew near. Various strange occurrences are said to have ensued when attempts were made to move the skull.

On Castleton Road just a few miles northeast of the town, the **Chestnut Centre** is a fascinating wildlife conservation centre, popular with children and adults alike. It is famed for its otters, with award-winning otter and owl enclosures set along an extensive circular nature trail, which meanders through some historic wooded parkland.

Chapel-en-le-Frith

4 miles N of Buxton off the A6

This charming town is often overlooked by travellers on the bypass between Buxton and Stockport, but it repays a closer look.

In 1225 the guardians of the High Peak's Royal Forest purchased land from the Crown and built a chapel here, dedicating it to St Thomas à Becket of Canterbury. A century later the chapel was replaced with a more substantial building; further modernisation took place in the early 1700s. The building of the original chapel led to the foundation of the town and also its name, which is Norman French for 'chapel in the forest'. Although the term 'forest' suggests a wooded area, the frith or forest never really existed, but referred to the Royal Forest of the Peak, hunting grounds which extended over much of north

The Kings Arms Hotel

Market Place, Chapel-en-le-Frith,
Derbyshire SK23 0EN
Tel/Fax: 01298 812105
website: www.kingsarms@tiscali.co.uk

Set in the heart of Chapel-en-le-Frith, four miles north of Buxton off the A6, **The Kings Arms Hotel** is a marvellous 17th century former coaching inn offering visitors and locals the very best in facilities and hospitality. Leaseholder Sally and her daughter Kelly have been here since late in 2001. Ably assisted by bar manager Leigh, they offer all their guests a warm welcome and great food, drink and accommodation. Distinctive and impressive inside and out, the interior boasts a wealth of warm wood panelling and very comfortable seating.

Open from midday every day, the real ale here is Marstons Pedigree, along with a good selection of draught keg ales, lagers, cider, stout, wines, spirits and soft drinks.

Simon the chef whips up superb meals daily between 11 a.m. and 9 p.m. Guests choose from the menu and specials board from a range of delicious beef, pork, chicken, seafood and vegetarian dishes.

This excellent inn also has 10 attractive and comfortable guest bedrooms, including family rooms.

Derbyshire during the Middle Ages.

A curious legacy has been passed down allowing owners of freehold land in the district the right to choose their vicar. The interior of the church boasts 19th century box pews and a monument to 'the Apostle of the Peak', William Bagshawe of nearby Ford Hall, a Non-Conformist minister of the late 17th century, who was forced to resign his ministry for refusing to accept the Book of Common Prayer.

In 1648 the church was used as a gaol for 1,500 Scottish prisoners and the dreadful conditions arising from such close confinement caused unimaginable suffering. Their ordeal lasted for 16 days and a total of 44 men died.

Chapel Brow is a steep and cobbled street lined with pictuesque little cottages leading down from the church to Market Street. An ancient market town, the cross still stands in Market Square, as do the town's stocks. This is the true centre of Chapel, surrounded by a variety of old inns and buildings.

Chinley

6 miles N of Buxton off the B6062

This small north Derbyshire village lays claim to the superb **Chinley Viaducts**, a masterpiece of Victorian engineering. Chinley Station was once an important railway junction, as the railway lines

The Old Hall Inn

Whitehough, Chinley, High Peak SK23 6EJ
Tel: 01663 750529
e-mail: anncapper@hotmail.com

The hamlet of Whitehough is found via Chinley off the B6062 or via the sign on the B5470 at Chapel-en-le-Frith. It is worth seeking out **The Old Hall Inn**, a historic premises attached to Whitehough Hall: the present structure dating back to the 16th century. The interior is comfortable and welcoming, while the superb beer garden (part of the main Hall) is a simply wonderful place to enjoy a relaxing drink. Michael and Ann Capper have been the owners here since 1979 and the inn is open seven days a week offering traditional cask ales. Food is the big draw here, served Monday to Saturday 12pm-2pm, 5pm – 9pm and Sundays midday to 7pm. The excellent range of dishes include tempting delights such as home-made steak and Guinness pie, home roast ham, stilton chicken and chargrilled steaks and much more.

The inn also boasts four superior ensuite guest bedrooms, comfortable, attractive and available all year round.

from Derby to Manchester and Sheffield linked up here. Chinley Chapel dates back to the late 17th century, looking deceptively like an ordinary house from the outside.

Buxworth

6½ miles N of Buxton off the B6062

Once known as Bugsworth, before the villagers got tired of the jokes and changed the village's name in 1929, Buxworth is the site of the terminal basin for the **Peak Forest Canal**, finished in 1800. The village is popular with visitors attracted by the historic Bugsworth Basin, where limestone and lime were brought down from the works up at Dove Holes to be transported by canal barge. The limestone was carried in small horse drawn wagons on the Peak Forest Tramway, which was operated in part by the force of gravity. The wagons were rolled down the track to the Basin full and then pulled back up empty by horses. The basin was not used after 1926 but reopened in 1999 thanks to the efforts of the Inland Waterways Preservation society.

Buxworth used to have several public houses. Nowadays there is one Inn, the Navigation, and a war memorial club known as 'Buggy Club', where sixteen year old members are allowed with parental permission to buy alcohol at the bar.

Whaley Bridge

6 miles N of Buxton off the A5004

This small industrial town at the gateway to the **Goyt Valley** grew up around the coal-mining and textile industries. Both have now gone, but the **Peak Forest Canal** flowing through the town remains very much the centre of activity.

The 'bridge' of the village's name crosses the River Goyt, on the site of what may once have been a Roman crossing.

Many of the old warehouses in Whaley Bridge have been restored and converted to meet the needs of the late 20th century and, where once narrow boats transported goods and raw materials to and from the town, boats can be hired to those who want to explore the delights of the waterways in the area.

The **Toddbrook Reservoir** was built in 1831 to be a feeder for the Peak Forest Canal. The wharf here is dotted with picturesque narrowboats.

Just outside Whaley Bridge is the curiously shaped ridge known as **Roosdyche**, a natural feature running up towards Eccles Pike. The great scoop taken out of the hillside was the result of glacier erosion, though its distinctive shape gave rise to the theory that it was once a racecourse for Roman chariots.

Above Roosdyche is **Bing Wood**, a charming name until the true meaning of Bing is revealed - it means 'slag heap'

THE TORRS

34 Market Street, New Mills,
Derbyshire SK22 4AE
Tel/Fax: 01663 747847

A quite outstanding inn located in the heart of the High Peak, **The Torrs** has been known in its time as The Crown and The Bee's Knees, but took on its new name at the time it was completely refurbished in 2001. This sensitive and tasteful conversion has made the inn a comfortable and welcome retreat where you can enjoy great food, drink and accommodation. Leaseholders Dave and Sue have taken the inn from strength to strength, thanks in part to Sue's long experience in the hotel trade. They came to the inn in late 2002, and it's their first venture in the licensing trade. They've made the place come to life, and are popular with locals and visitors alike.

Dating back to 1884, the inn's refurbishment left intact lovely original features such as the wood-panelled walls, open fire and warm ambience. It is cosy and comfortable, and the friendly staff offer a high standard of service.

Open all day every day, the bar stocks a good selection of keg draught bitters, lagers, cider, stout, wines, spirits and soft drinks – something to quench every thirst. Food is served at breakfast (8 – 11.30 a.m.) most days, as well as every lunchtime and in the evenings up to around 8 p.m. Guests choose off the menu from a selection of traditional favourites. Sue does the cooking, using the freshest ingredients to create delicious home-cooked dishes to order. Monday is curry night, which has proved justly popular with discerning diners.

In the way of entertainment, the inn hosts a disco on Friday and Saturday nights from 8 p.m. until 2 a.m., and Sundays are karaoke night from 8 until 12.30.

This fine inn also offers three comfortable and attractive ensuite guest bedrooms. Guests can stay on a room-only or bed-and-breakfast rates. The inn makes an ideal base from which to explore the many sights and attractions of the region, which include Buxton, many picturesque villages and some great walking. During the lifetime of this guide Dave and Sue hope to add three more bedrooms.

The Goyt Valley

- a name that hearkens back to the locality's prominence during the 19th century in the coal industry.

Lyme Park

8 miles NW of Buxton off the A6

Lyme Park is an ancient estate, now in the hands of the National Trust, and was given to Sir Thomas Danyers in 1346 by a grateful King Edward III after a battle at Caen. Danyers then passed the estate to his son-in-law, Sir Piers Legh, in 1388. It remained in the family until 1946, when it was given to the Trust. Not much remains of the original Elizabethan manor house; today's visitors are instead treated to the sight of a fantastic Palladian mansion, the work of Venetian architect Giacomo Leoni. Not daunted by the bleak landscape and climate of the surrounding Peak District, Leoni built a corner of Italy here in this much harsher countryside. Inside the mansion there is a mixture of styles: the elegant Leoni-designed rooms with rich rococo ceilings, the panelled Tudor drawing room, and two surviving Elizabethan rooms. Much of the three-dimensional internal carving is attributed to Grinling Gibbons, though a lot of the work was also undertaken by local craftsmen.

As well as the fantastic splendour of the mansion, the estate includes a late 19th century formal garden. The 17-acre Victorian garden is laid out with impressive bedding schemes, a sunken parterre, an Edwardian rose garden, Jekyll-style herbaceous borders, a reflection lake, a ravine garden and Wyatt conservatory. The garden is surrounded by 1400 acres of medieval deer park of moorland, woodland and parkland, including an early 18th century hunting tower. Lyme featured as 'Pemberley' in the 1995 BBC film of Jane Austen's novel *Pride and Prejudice*.

The grounds now form a country park owned and managed by the National Trust and supported by Stockport Metropolitan Borough Council. Though close to the Manchester suburb of Stockport, the estate lies wholly within the Peak District National Park.

New Mills

9 miles N of Buxton off the A6015

Situated by the River Sett, New Mills takes its name from the Tudor corn mills

Pack Horse Inn

Mellor Road, New Mills, High Peak SK22 4QQ
Tel: 01663 742365 Fax: 01663 741674
e-mail: info@packhorseinn.co.uk
website: www.packhorseinn.co.uk

Situated just out of New Mills on the Mellor Road, the outstanding **Pack Horse Inn** stands high up overlooking acres of scenic countryside in the High Peak. This former coaching inn dates back to the first years of the 18th century. For the past 24 years it has been family-run by the Crosslands. John and Beryl, ably assisted by their son Mark and his partner Rose, make every guest's visit an enjoyable one. The décor and furnishing are supremely attractive and comfortable, with traditional features that make the inn cosy and welcoming.

Open every session weekdays and all day at weekends, there are always four real ales to sample – Tetleys plus rotating guest ales, many of which are from micro-breweries. An average week sees the inn host up to 10 real ales in all.

Excellent food is available Monday to Friday at lunch (12–2) and dinner (6–10 p.m.), Saturdays midday until 10 p.m. and Sundays midday until 9 p.m. Mark is the chef, ably assisted by Beryl, and creates a tempting range of dishes for the menu and specials board, with an additional menu on Sundays for roasts. Bar meals, main courses and mouth-watering puddings include favourites such as steak sandwiches, fillet of salmon, home-made steak and kidney pie, lamb cutlets, mushroom and red pepper stroganoff, Bakewell tart and syrup sponge all cooked and prepared to perfection. The wine list is very good.

There are 12 ensuite guest bedrooms, with a good mixture of different-sized rooms, two of which are on the ground floor. A hearty breakfast is included in the price.

To the rear is a large extension, soon to be finished, which will incorporate a new kitchen, new dining room and additional bedrooms.

that once stood on the riverbanks. Later, in the 18th and 19th centuries water power was used to drive several cotton-spinning mills in the town and, as New Mills grew, the textile industry was joined by engineering industries and the confectionery trade. There is still a rich legacy of this industrial heritage to be found in the town. The Torr Mills featured on the millennium series of postage stamps issued by the Post Office. The elevated **New Mills Millennium Walkway**, built on stilts rising from the River Goyt, sits directly opposite the Torrs Mill. The walkway answered public demand for a route through the impassable gritstone **Torrs Gorge**. The gorge is an area of exceptional natural beauty and unique industrial archaeological heritage. The 175-yard-long steel walkway is fixed to the rock face and adjoining railway retaining wall at a height of about 20 feet from the base of the 100-foot deep gorge.

The Little Mill at Rowarth still retains a working water wheel, although the mill building is now a well-known public house. Opposite the library is the Police Station, where the ringleaders of the 'Kinder Trespassers' were kept in the cells, following their arrest in 1932, after the mass public trespass on Kinder Scout. Although it is now a private house, the site is identified by a plaque on the wall. The trespass was a significant factor in the creation of National Parks, to allow public access to the countryside.

The serious walker or stroller can use New Mills as a starting point for various way-marked walks. The Goyt Valley Way leads south to Buxton via Whaley Bridge and the Goyt Valley north to Marple. There are local signposted walks below the Heritage Centre and the **Sett Valley Trail** follows the line of the old branch railway to Hayfield and then on to Kinder Scout. Opened in 1868, the single track line carried passengers and freight for over 100 years. However, by the late 1960s much of the trade had ceased and the line closed soon afterwards. In 1973, the line was reopened as a trail and is still used by walkers, cyclists and horse riders and it takes in the remains of buildings that were once part of the prosperous textile industry. Kinder Scout is a high gritstone plateau, rising steeply from the surrounding ground to a height of around 600 metres. The edges are studded with rocky outcrops and crags and the highest point at 631 metres is Crowden Head. This is also the highest point in the **Peak District**.

Hayfield

9 miles N of Buxton off the A624

This small town below the exposed moorland of **Kinder Scout** was once a staging post on the pack-horse route across the Pennines. The old pack-horse route went up the Sett valley and by Edale Cross, where the remains of an old cross can still be seen, down to Edale by Jacob's Ladder. Some ancient cottages still survive around the centre of the old village, and some local farmhouses date from the 17th century.

Hayfield is a popular centre for exploring the area and offers many amenities for hillwalkers. Like its neighbour New Mills, Hayfield grew up around the textile industry, in this case wool weaving and calico printing. Many of the houses were originally weavers' cottages. A curious building can be found in Market Street on the left of a small square known as Dungeon Brow. Built in 1799 this was the town's lock-up and was referred to as the New Prison. However, the stocks in front of the building appear to be somewhat newer than the prison itself.

At the other end of the Sett Valley Trail, the old station site has been turned into a picnic area and information centre. The elegant Georgian parish **Church of St Matthew** is a reminder of this Pennine town's former prosperity. **Bowden Bridge Quarry** was the starting point for the famous 'Mass Trespass' on Kinder Scout and is now a car park with public toilets and a Peak Park camp site opposite.

Three miles northeast of the town is **Kinder Downfall**, the highest waterfall in the county, where the River Kinder flows off the edge of Kinder Scout. In low temperatures the fall freezes solid - a sight to be seen. It is also renowned for its blow-back effect: when the wind blows, the fall's water is forced back against the rock and the water appears to run uphill! There are not many natural waterfalls in Derbyshire, so Kinder Downfall appears on most visitors' itineraries. Not far from the bottom of the fall is a small lake known as **Mermaid's Pool**. Legend has it that those who go to the pool at midnight on the night before Easter Sunday will see a mermaid swimming in the dark waters.

Charlesworth

12 miles N of Buxton on the A626

On the western edge of the Pennines, Charlesworth has many old and typically Pennine cottages. Three storeys tall, they were built as weavers' cottages. Apart from the 1849 mock-Gothic parish church of St John the Baptist

there is also a Catholic church, built primarily for the Irish immigrants working in the nearby mills, which stands at the edge of the village in a lovely position near the banks of the River Etherow.

Glossop

13 miles N of Buxton off the A624

At the foot of the Snake Pass, Glossop is an interesting mix of styles: the industrial town of the 19th century with its towering Victorian mills and the 17th century village with its charming old cottages standing in the cobble streets. Further back in time, the Romans came here and established a fort now known as **Melandra Castle**, but probably then called Ardotalia. Built to guard the entrance to Longdendale, little survives today but the stone foundations. The settlement developed further as part of the monastic estates of Basingwerk Abbey in north Wales and the village received its market charter in 1290, but subsequently there was a decline in its importance. Little remains of Old Glossop except the medieval parish **Church of All Saints**.

Planned as a new town in the 19th century by the Duke of Norfolk, the original village stood on the banks of the Glossop Brook at the crossing point of three turnpike roads. The brook had already been harnessed to provide power for the cotton mills, as this was one of the most easterly towns of the booming Lancashire cotton industry. Many still refer to the older Glossop as Old Glossop and the Victorian settlement as Howard Town, named after the Duke, Bernard Edward Howard.

Dinting

13 miles N of Buxton off the A624

The impressive **Dinting Viaduct**, built to carry the main Sheffield to Manchester railway line, stands 120 feet high. The village church of the Holy Trinity was built in 1875 in Victorian Gothic style and has a tall and elegant spire.

Hadfield

14 miles N of Buxton off the A624

The small village of Hadfield is the terminus of the **Longdendale Trail,** which follows the line of the former Manchester to Sheffield railway line and is part of the Trans-Pennine Trail. It is now a safe, traffic-free trail for biking and walking. Its level sandy surface makes it suitable for wheelchair users and less agile people, as well as for families with small children and pushchairs. **Old Hall** in The Square is the oldest building in the village, built in 1646. The Roman Catholic Church of St Charles was built in 1868 by Baron Howard of Glossop; members of the Howard family are buried here.

The Longdendale Trail continues eastward from here. Longdendale itself is the valley of the River Etherow, and is a favourite place for day-trippers. Along the footpath through this wild and desolate valley there are many reminders of the past, including **Woodhead Chapel**, the graveyard of which has numerous memorials to the navvies, and

The Chieftain

Green Lane, Hadfield, Derbyshire SK13 2DT
Tel: 01457 860213
e-mail: d.smith@31btinternet.com

The Chieftain is an impressive inn open all day, every day for great food, drink and hospitality. Real ales from the Hydes Brewery include Hydes Bitter and Hydes Mild, together with a good variety of lagers, cider, stout, wines, spirits and soft drinks. The interior is handsome and welcoming, open plan with raised areas for dining and for games.

Excellent home-cooked food is served Monday to Thursday at lunch (12–2) and dinner (5.30–8.15) and throughout the day (midday to 8.15 p.m.) Friday, Saturday and Sunday. Guests choose from the menu and specials board from a range of tempting dishes made with locally-sourced ingredients whenever possible. Specialities include sirloin steaks, spicy chicken baguettes (as a snack or main course), minted lamb, salmon fillet and peppered pork.There's also a children's menu.

To find this excellent inn, turn off the main A628 towards Glossop then, before you reach the impressive Dinting Viaduct, turn left (signposted Hadfield and Longdendale Trail) and, after a short distance, turn left again into Green Lane and follow this road; The Chieftain stands on your left.

their families, who died in an outbreak of cholera in 1849 while working on the Sheffield to Manchester railway line.

North East of Buxton

From Glossop, the A57 East is an exhilarating stretch of road, with hair-pin bends, known as Snake Pass. The road is frequently made impassable by landslides, heavy mist and massive snowfalls in winter but, weather permitting, it is an experience not to be missed. For much of the length of the turnpike road that Thomas Telford built across Snake Pass in 1821, the route follows the line of an ancient Roman road, known as **Doctor's Gate**, which ran between Glossop and a fort at Brough. The route was so named after it was rediscovered, in the 16th century, by Dr Talbot, a vicar from Glossop. The illegitimate son of the Earl of Shrewsbury, Talbot used the road with great frequency as he travelled from Glossop to his father's castle at Sheffield.

Edale

8 miles NE of Buxton off the A625

In the valley of the River Noe, Edale marks the start of the **Pennine Way**. Opened in 1965, this long-distance footpath follows the line of the backbone of Britain for some 270 miles from here to Kirk Yetholm, just over the Scottish border. Though the footpath begins in the lush meadows of this secluded valley, it is not long before walkers find themselves crossing the wild and bleak moorland of featherbed Moss before heading further north to Bleaklow. Many travellers have spoken of Derbyshire as a county of contrasts, and nowhere is this more apparent than at Edale. Not only does the landscape change dramatically within a short distance from the heart of the village, but the weather - as all serious walkers will know - can alter from brilliant sunshine to snowstorms in the space of a couple of hours.

Fields in the Valley, Edale

The village, in the heart of dairy-farming and stock-rearing country, began as a series of scattered settlements that had grown around the shepherds' shelters or bothies. The true name of the

Ye Olde Cheshire Cheese Inn

How Lane, Castleton, Hope Valley S33 8WJ
Tel: 01433 620330 Fax: 01433 621847
e-mail: kslack@btconnect.com
website: www.cheshirecheeseinn.co.uk

Deep in the heart of the Peak District National Park, near the Market Place in the beautiful village of Castleton, which is famous for the nearby caverns of Speedwell, Peak and Blue John, as well as Peveril Castle, **Ye Olde Cheshire Cheese Inn** occupies a striking building dating back to 1660. It is a truly lovely inn with half-timbered walls and a myriad of flower-filled window boxes and hanging baskets. Inside guests can sit beside the fire accompanied by black oak beams and a wealth of gleaming brass. More than just a place to enjoy great food and drink, the inn also offers some of the best accommodation in the area, making a perfect base from which to explore the region.

Owners Ken and Angie Slack have been here since 1993, and have nearly 30 years' experience in the trade. Ably assisted by bar manager Gary and Neil, the chef, they offer all their guests superior hospitality. Ken, known locally as 'The Mayor' for his place as chair of the area's Chamber of Commerce, is a font of knowledge about sights and attractions in the region.

Within the inn there are 10 beautifully appointed ensuite guest bedrooms, with tv and tea- and coffee-making facilities, and competitively-priced tariffs all year round. All the rooms are individually styled, beautifully decorated and comfortable. Some even have four-poster beds! Over the road there are four superior, newly constructed ensuite rooms and also a state-of-the-art gymnasium for guests. Angie is a qualified fitness instructor and can provide expert advice and information.

Open all day, every day for ale, the three real ales here are Worthington, Stones and a changing guest ale, together with a comprehensive selection of wines, spirits, lager, cider, stout and soft drinks. Food is served daily from midday until 8.30 p.m. The restaurant seats 74, and there

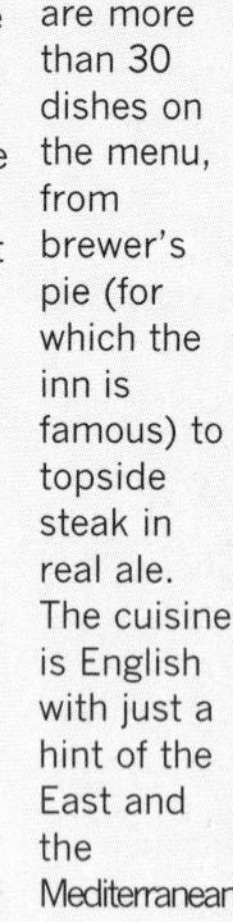

are more than 30 dishes on the menu, from brewer's pie (for which the inn is famous) to topside steak in real ale. The cuisine is English with just a hint of the East and the Mediterranean thrown in.

village is actually Grindsbrook Booth, but it is commonly known by the name of the valley. Tourism first came to Edale with the completion of the Manchester to Sheffield railway in 1894, though at that time there was little in the way of hospitality for visitors. Today there are several hotels, camping sites, a large Youth Hostel and adventure and walking centres.

Castleton

Not far from the village is the famous **Jacob's Ladder**, overlooking the River Noe. Nearby is the tumbledown remains of a hill farmer's cottage; this was the home of Jacob Marshall, who some 200 years ago cut the steps into the hillside leading up to Edale Cross.

Castleton

8 miles NE of Buxton off the A625

Situated at the head of the Hope Valley, Castleton is sheltered by the Norman ruin of Peveril Castle (built by Henry II in the 1170s) and is overlooked by Mam Tor. Approaching Castleton from the west along the A625, the road runs through the **Winnats Pass**, a narrow limestone gorge. Thought to have been formed under the sea, from currents eroding the seabed, the gorge has been used as a road for centuries and is still the only direct route to the village from the west.

Originally laid out as a planned town below its castle, the shape of the village has changed little over the years and it has become a popular tourist centre. The mainly 17th century church of St Edmund was heavily restored in 1837, but retains its box pews and a fine Norman arch, as well as a Breechers Bible dated 1611.

On Oak Apple Day, 29th May, the ancient ceremony of Garlanding takes place and after the Garland has been paraded though the streets, it is hoisted to the top of Saint Edmund's Church tower. The ceremony celebrates the ending of winter, and the restoration of Charles II to the throne in 1660 after the rule by the parliamentarians.

The Garland is a wooden frame, with bunches of wild flowers attached and a small 'Queen's' wreath of garden flowers on top. The 'King', dressed in Stuart costume, with the garland on his shoulders tours the village on horseback

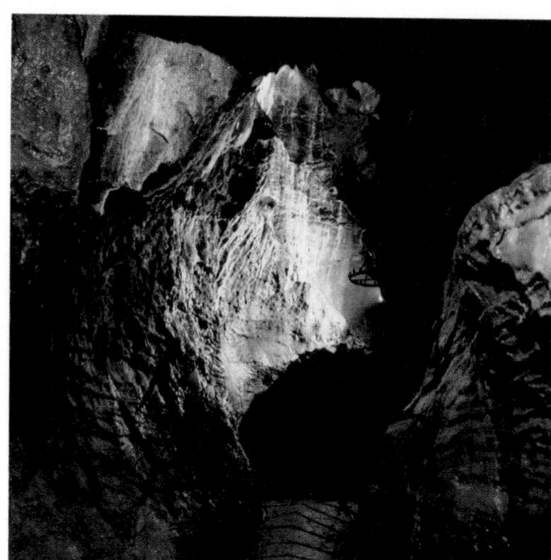

Blue John Caverns, Castleton

followed by a procession and a band. At the end of the ceremony the garland is left on the top of the tower of St Edmunds Church to wither and the Queen's wreath is placed on the war memorial. **Castleton Village Museum** in the Methodist Church School Room has a collection of Garland memorabilia, including a King's costume worn 200 years ago.

The hills to the west of Castleton are famous for their caves. The **Blue John Mine and Caverns**, which have been in the hands of the Ollerenshaw family for many years, are probably one of Derbyshire's most popular attractions. Amazing trips down into the caves themselves can be made. During these trips, as well as seeing the incredible natural beauty of the caverns and the unique rock formations, there are collections of original 19th century mining tools. Above ground, in the gift shops, various items can be bought made with the distinctive Blue John fluorspar with its attractive purplish veining.

The village's **Ollerenshaw Collection** of huge vases and urns made with the same unique stone is open to the public. Once prized by the Romans, it is said that Petronius paid the equivalent of around £40,000 for a wonderfully ornate vase carved from the stone. It is said that in a fit of petty-mindedness he preferred to smash the vase rather than relinquish it to the **Emperor Nero.**

At the bottom of Winnats Pass only 1000 metres (0.6 miles) from the centre of the village, lies **Speedwell Cavern.** It is a very gentle walk along the road to this former lead mine, which used boats on an underground canal to ferry the miners and iron ore to and from the rockface. The mine had a short life: it started up in 1771 and, following an investment of £14,000, closed in 1790 after only £3,000 worth of iron ore had been extracted. The cave can only be explored by underground boat, and visitors can follow the same boat journey as the miners, in the company of a guide. This underground canal is about 800 metres long finally reaching a glorious cavern with a huge subterranean lake known as the Bottomless Pit.

Peak Cavern, reached by a delightful

Peveril Castle Ruins

re-enact the process of making rope. One ropemaker's cottage still exists. Recently the cave was used by the BBC, who filmed an episode of *The Chronicles of Narnia* series here. Over the years successive Kings and Queens would entertain deep within the belly of the cave, which would be festooned with candles and other open flames - visitors can see the ledge on which the Royal musicians would perch. Peak Cavern was originally known as The Devil's Arse, though the Victorians - ever fastidious - felt this was 'inappropriate' and changed it to the name it carries today.

Above Peak Cavern is **Peveril Castle** with its spectacular views over Castleton and the surrounding countryside. The Castle, originally called Castle of the Peak, was built as a wooden stockade in 1080 by William Peveril, illegitimate son of William the Conqueror. Later rebuilt in stone, the keep was added by Henry I in 1176. It was originally about 60 feet high and faced with gritstone blocks, which still remain on the east and south sides and still dominates the view across Castleton. The foundations of the Great Hall and kitchens can be seen

riverside walk, has the widest opening of any cave in Europe. Up until the 17th century, little cottages used to stand within the entrance. The ropemakers who lived in these tiny dwellings used the cave entrance for making rope, the damp atmosphere being a favourable environment for rope making. Bert Marrison, the last rope maker in Castleton, worked here. His ashes, along with some of his tools, are buried here. The ropewalk, which dates back some 400 years, can still be seen and guides

inside the courtyard. It remains the only surviving example of a Norman castle in Derbyshire, and is among the best preserved and most complete ruins in Britain.

Mam Tor

No description of Castleton would be complete without a mention of **Mam Tor**. The name means 'Mother Hill', and locally the Tor is referred to as "Shivering Mountain", because the immense cliff face near the summit is constantly on the move owing to water seepage. It was used as a hill fort in the late Bronze Age or early Iron Age and a climb to the top of the ridge shows what a splendid vantage point it provides over the surrounding landscape, in particular of the two diverse rock formations, which differentiate the White (limestone) Peak from the northern Dark (gritstone) Peak.

Halfway up Losehill, midway between Castleton and Hope, visitors can find the 300-year-old gritstone-built Losehill Farm, nicknamed **Crimea Farm** during the Crimean War, and still known as such locally. It is a traditional working farm, which combines agriculture with education, conservation, recreation and traditional rural crafts. The Weaving Shed houses displays of fleeces from rare breed sheep and goats. There is spinning and other craft work in progress such as paper-making and natural dyeing. There is a farm trail, which takes in bottle-fed lambs, kids and calves, free-ranging hens, ducks and geese, playful Pygmy goats, rare breed Golden Guernseys and angora goats.

Hope

9 miles NE of Buxton off the A625

Hope gets its first mention in AD 926 as the site of a battle won by King Athelstan. By the time of the Domesday survey of 1086, the parish of Hope had extended to embrace much of the High Peak area and included places such as Buxton, Chapel-en-le-Frith and Tideswell. It remained one of the largest parishes in the country until the 19th century, though a market charter was not granted it until 1715. Hope lies at the point where the River Noe meets

Woodroffe Arms

1 Castleton Road, Hope, Derbyshire S33 6SB
Tel: 01433 620351

Situated in the charming and lovely village of Hope, close to many of the Peak District's many attractions, particularly the well-known mines and caverns, **The Woodroffe Arms** is a traditional country inn that dates back in parts over 400 years. It took its name from a wealthy landowner, who was then Lord of the Manor. Tenants Catherine and David have been here only a short time, but bring a wealth of enthusiasm and many plans for the future. This former coaching inn is open all day, every day for ale, with two real ales – Timothy Taylor Landlord and a changing guest ale – together with a range of lagers, cider, stout, wines, spirits and soft drinks.

Catherine cooks up a good variety of excellent dishes served every day between midday and 9 p.m., with something to suit everyone's taste in abundant portions. The no-smoking restaurant is housed in the new conservatory and has a very pleasant and relaxed ambience. The inn also boasts five cosy and very comfortable ensuite guest bedrooms.

Peakshole Water, which takes its name from its source in **Peak's Hole,** better known as Peak Cavern.

The parish **Church of St Peter** was built at the beginning of the 13th century; the only part remaining from the original church is the Norman font. The Latin inscription on a chair in the north aisle reads (in translation) 'You cannot make a scholar out of a block of wood' and is said to have been carved for Thomas Bocking, the vicar and schoolmaster here during the 17th century. His name also appears on the fine pulpit; his Breechers Bible is

Hope Valley

Shatton Hall Farm Cottages

Shatton Hall Farm, Bamford,
Hope Valley S33 0BG
Tel: 01433 620635 Fax: 01433 620689
e-mail: ahk@peakfarmholidays.co.uk
website: www.peakfarmholidays.co.uk

Outstanding accommodation is yours to be had at **Shatton Hall Farm Cottages**. Owners Angela and James Kellie have lived here since 1966, and have been providing excellent self-catering accommodation since 1980. Their first visitors all those years ago return every year – a real testament to the comfort, charm, peace and relaxation on offer here.

The three lovely stonebuilt cottages – Paddock Cottage, Orchard Cottage and the

Hayloft – have been given a four-star rating. Each has its own garden or terrace and is tastefully furnished, mainly in old pine, has central heating and is well equipped for four people in double and twin bedrooms (Orchard Cottage and the Hayloft also have sofa beds). These charming cottages also boast fully equipped kitchens, bath with shower and spring-fed water supply. Videos, cots and high chairs are available, and there's a guests' laundry room and pay phone nearby. Paddock Cottage looks out over the valley below and features a cosy living room with wood-burning stove. Well-behaved dogs allowed by prior arrangement. The Hayloft's bedrooms are on the ground floor, with a spacious oak-beamed living room upstairs. Orchard Cottage also has a beamed living room and access to the garden and, as its name suggests, orchard. Garden furniture and barbecues are provided for all three, and you can also order 'freezer meals' of local produce and 'breakfast packs' to save you the labour of preparing meals during your stay.

The properties stand in 100 acres of scenic land that includes an ancient woodland that attracts many varied types of wildlife. There's also a lake stocked with trout for a bit of fishing. For the energetic there's a full-sized hard-standing tennis court. Another fantastic feature onsite is Townfield Barn, which hosts a summer programme of instruction in landscape and botanical art, wild flower, medicinal plants and fungi, creative willow and working with clay. Expert instruction is on hand in a truly inspirational setting. The cottages are also, of course, conveniently located for many of Derbyshire's leading attractions.

The cottages are available all year round, and there's an online booking system available – please visit the excellent website for more details.

displayed nearby. From the outside, the squat 14th century spire gives the church a rather curious shape; in the churchyard can be found the shaft of a Saxon cross.

The **Hope Agricultural Show** is held every year on August Bank Holiday Monday.

Brough

9 miles NE of Buxton off the A6187

At the village of Brough can be seen remains of the earthworks of the Roman fort of Navio. At the confluence of the River Noe and Bradwell Brook, this small, rectangular fort was built in AD 158 to control the Romans' lead mining interests in the area. The site was excavated in the early 20th century.

Bamford

11 miles NE of Buxton off the A6187

This charming village situated between the Hope Valley and Ladybower Reservoir, stands at the heart of the Dark Peak below Bamford Edge and close to the Upper Derwent Valley Dams. When the Derwent and Howden Dams were built in the early years of the 20th century, the valley of the Upper Derwent was flooded, submerging many farms under the rising waters. The 1,000 or so navvies and their families were housed at Birchinlee, a temporary village which came to be known locally

The Snake Pass Inn

Snake Road, Bamford, Hope Valley S33 0BJ
Tel: 01433 651480 Fax: 01433 651061
e-mail: info@snakepassinn.freeserve.co.uk
website: www.snakepassinn.freeserve.co.uk

The Snake Pass Inn is situated along the road that gives the inn its name. This famous inn dates back to the early 19th century and stands amid hundreds of acres of scenic countryside, close to the Ladybower Reservoir in the beautiful Peak District National Park.

Local farming couple John and Sandra Atkin took over in July of 2003 and have given the place a new lease of life. Open all day for ale, the real ales here are John Smiths and Theakstons, along with a rotating guest ale.

Delicious food is served Monday to Saturday from midday to 9 p.m., and Sundays from midday until 5.30. Booking required at weekends and on Bank Holidays. Among their specialities are fish dishes, while at certain times of the year they produce their own lamb (as the couple still engage in farming as well as running the inn).

This outstanding inn also boasts eight ensuite guest bedrooms for bed and breakfast in the main building, as well as four apartments in the adjacent former coach house. Two of the apartments are on the ground floor. All of the accommodation is supremely comfortable and attractive.

Ladybower Reservoir

as 'Tin Town', for its plethora of corrugated iron shacks. During the Second World War the third and largest reservoir, the **Ladybower**, was built. This involved the inundating of two villages — Derwent and Ashopton. Many buildings were lost including ancient farms and Derwent Hall dating from 1672 and made into a youth hostel in 1931. The spire of the Parish church was visible at first, but was demolished in 1947. The dead from Derwent's church were re-interred in the churchyard of St John the Baptist in Bamford. The living were re-housed in Yorkshire Bridge, a purpose-built hamlet located below the embankment of the Ladybower Dam. A viaduct was built to carry the Snake Road over the reservoir at Ashopton and another for the road to Yorkshire Bridge. The packhorse bridge at Derwent, which had a preservation on it, was moved stone by stone and rebuilt at Slippery Stones at the head of the Howden Reservoir. There is a Visitor Centre at **Fairholmes** (in the Upper Derwent Valley), which tells the story of these 'drowned villages'.

The **Derwent Dam**, built in 1935, was the practice site for the Dambusters, who tested dropping their bouncing bombs here.

Bamford's **Church of St John the Baptist** is unlike any other in Derbyshire. Designed in 1861 by famous church architect William Butterfield, it has a slender tower and an extra-sharp spire. Also worthy of note, particularly to lovers of industrial architecture, is **Bamford Mill**, just across the road by the river. This cotton mill, built in 1820, retains its huge waterwheel and also has a 1907 tandem-compound steam engine. Like many cotton mills of its time, the original mill burnt to the ground just 10 years after it was erected. The mill standing today was its replacement. It ceased to operate as a cotton mill in 1965 and was used by an electric furnace manufacturer until a few years ago. It has now been converted into flats. The village lies in the heart of hill-farming country, and each Spring Bank Holiday Bamford plays host to one of the most famous of the Peak District Sheepdog Trials, which draws competition from all over the country.

Along the A57 towards Sheffield, the road dips and crosses the gory-sounding **Cutthroat Bridge**. The present bridge dates back to 1830, but its name comes from the late 16th century, when the body of a man with his throat cut was discovered under the bridge which then stood here.

Hathersage

12 miles NE of Buxton off the A625

The name Hathersage comes from the Old English for 'Haefer's ridge' - probably a reference to the line of gritstone edges of which the moorland slopes of **Stanage Edge**, overlooking the town to the east, is the largest. It is surrounded by spectacular tors, such as Higgar Tor, and the ancient fortress at Carl Wark. Several of the edges were quarried for millstones for grinding corn and metals.

It is difficult to know whether to classify Hathersage as a large village or a small town. In either event, it is a pleasant place with interesting literary connections. Charlotte Brontë stayed at Hathersage vicarage in 1845, and the village itself appears as 'Morton' in her novel *Jane Eyre*. The name Eyre was probably gleaned from the monuments to the prominent local landowners with this

Stanage Edge

The Little John Inn

Station Road, Hathersage, Hope Valley,
Derbyshire S32 1DD
Tel: 01433 650225 Fax: 01433 659831

As its name tells us, **The Little John Inn** – and the picturesque village of Hathersage in which it is found – has associations with the legend of Robin Hood. Owner Stephanie Bushell has created a hostelry of great character which is popular with both locals and visitors alike. It is a handsome stone building which dates from the 19th century, and inside many period features have been retained. There's a bar, a no-smoking lounge and an excellent, roomy restaurant. The inn also has extensive accommodation available, from cottages and apartments to ensuite rooms. Bookings are taken for one night or more.

This is just the place to have a relaxing, enjoyable drink or a meal after a day walking on the high moors. Head Chef Richard Mosley creates great food which is served Monday to Thursday at lunch (12 – 2) and dinner (6 – 10), Fridays and Saturdays 12 – 10 and Sundays 12 – 8.30. On Bank Holiday Sundays these hours are extended to 12 – 10, and Bank Holiday Mondays from 12 – 7. The varied and comprehensive menu makes use of only the finest, freshest ingredients for each dish. If you have a real hunger, try the Robin Hood/Little John Mixed Grill, an enormous plateful which is every bit as much a legend in these parts as Robin himself! Booking is advised for Saturday evening and Sunday lunch.

The inn has also won awards for its ale, and carries a good selection of real ales at the bar, plus draught bitter, stout, lager, cider, wines, spirits and soft drinks. Later in the week and at weekends there are up to five rotating guest ales, all from micro-breweries.

The accommodation comprises six ensuite rooms and two charming cottages – Loxley and Squire Cottage, which sleep four. Stephanie offers all her guests a very warm welcome – and she'll dare you to order and finish that mixed grill!

surname, which can be seen in the village church of St Michael and its churchyard.

The Eyre family has been associated with this area for over 800 years. Legend has it that the family were given their name by William the Conqueror. During the Battle of Hastings, so it is said, William was knocked from his horse and, wearing his now battered helmet, found it difficult to breathe. A Norman, Truelove, saw the King's distress and helped him take the helmet off and get back on his horse. In gratitude the King said that from thenceforth Truelove would be known as 'Air' for helping the King to breathe. Later the King learned that Air had lost most of a leg in the battle, and made arrangements that Air and his family were cared for and would be granted land in this part of Derbyshire. The name became corrupted to Eyre over the years, and the family's coat of arms shows a shield on top of which is a single armoured leg. The 15th century head of the family, Robert Eyre, lived at Highlow Hall. Within sight of this Hall he built seven houses, one for each of his seven sons. **North Lees** was one, which Charlotte Brontë took as a model for Rochester's house, Thornfield Hall. It is one of the finest Elizabethan buildings in the region - a tall square tower with a long wing adjoining and the grounds are open to the public. Another was **Moorseats**, where Charlotte Brontë stayed on holiday and used as the inspiration for Moor House in *Jane Eyre*.

In Hathersage churchyard lie the reputed remains of Little John, Robin Hood's renowned companion. Whether or not the legend is to be believed, it is worth mentioning that when the grave was opened in the 1780s, a 32-inch thighbone was discovered. This would certainly indicate that the owner was well over seven feet tall.

Until the late 18th century Hathersage was a small agricultural village with cottage industries making brass buttons and wire, until in 1750 a Henry Cocker started the Atlas Works, a mill for making wire. By the early 19th century it had become a centre for the manufacture of needles and pins. Though water power was used initially for the mills, by the mid-19th century smoke from the industrial steam engines enveloped the village. The fragments of dust and steel dispersed in the process of sharpening the needles destroyed the lungs of the workers, reducing their life expectancy to 30 years. The last mill here closed in 1902, as needle making moved to Sheffield, but several of the mills still stand, including the Atlas Works.

Hathersage has a superb outdoor swimming pool, open to the public at certain times throughout the summer holidays.

The Robin Hood

Greaves Lane, Little Matlock,
Sheffield S6 6BG
Tel: 0114 234 4565 Fax: 0114 234 4581
e-mail: robinhood.loxley@virgin.net

The Robin Hood is a true hidden gem. Found in the tiny hamlet of Little Matlock, it is reached by turning off the main A57 (before you reach Sheffield) at the signpost for the village of Stannington. By following this road for a couple of miles you come to a left turn for Myers Grove Lane – then, after a short distance, turn right into Greaves Lane, which will lead you straight to The Robin Hood.

The premises date back some 200 years and in its early days was known as The Rock. It takes its present name from the long-held belief that Robin Hood was from these parts – and indeed in many of the extant stories about him he is called Robin of Loxley, which is the ancient name (still used) for this part of the region. Standing in its own grounds with an adjacent paddock where can be found outdoor seating, swings, slides and a barbecue area, since December of 2003 this Free House has been family run – three generations of the Ayres family can be found working here in various roles.

Open every session throughout the week and all day at weekends, there are always two real ales here to be sampled. Both are guest ales, rotated regularly.

Quality food is served Wednesday to Sunday and Bank Holiday Mondays at lunchtime (12 – 2) and every day in the evenings (5 – 8) in the winter months, while in summer there is food available all day and every Sunday hosts a carvery served between 1 and 4 p.m.

Keeley is the licensee; his mum Bridget is the cook. Guests choose from the specials board for an assortment of mouth-watering dishes. One speciality here is the home-made meat-and-potato pie, cooked to Grandma Phyl's own recipe. The menu changes weekly – and at times daily – to make the best use of the freshest produce available locally. The Sunday carvery offers guests a choice of four roast joints and up to 15 different vegetable side-dishes.

During the lifetime of this edition it is hoped that this fine inn will also be able to offer bed and breakfast accommodation – please ring for details.

The Travellers Inn

Four Lane Ends, Oxspring, Sheffield S36 8YJ
Tel: 01226 762518

On the edge of the Peak District alongside the A629 Huddersfield-to-Sheffield Road at Oxspring, **The Travellers Inn** is a welcoming and convivial public house enjoying quite outstanding views over the National Park.

Set on part of the Trans-Pennine Way, the inn dates back to the first years of the 18th century and began life as a farmhouse where beer was brewed. It became an inn some 90 years later. Known locally as The Fours because it stands at the crossroads of four lanes, it is very much a family-run inn.

Tenants Ron and Sue Speed, ably assisted by their son Scott, a qualified chef, have been here since 1996. They are friendly and warm hosts who do their best to ensure that every guest enjoys the best food, drink and hospitality they can offer.

The interior boasts a wealth of wood panelling, and is tastefully furnished and decorated. Open every session Monday to Friday and all day at weekends, the real ale here is Tetleys, complemented by a good range of draught and keg bitters, lagers, cider, stout, wines, spirits and soft drinks.

Scott whips up delicious food every day – Monday to Friday 12 – 2 and 5.30 – 9.15, Saturdays 12 – 4 and 7 – 9.15, and Sundays 12 – 6.15. The menus and specials board offer a selection of tempting delights such as triple-tail scampi, chicken breast, California ham, steak pie, half-shoulder of lamb, full rack of barbecued ribs, super jumbo cod and poached salmon, together with a selection of steaks. On Sundays guests can choose from six starters and six main courses for the traditional lunch. Booking is advised on most days and essential on Sundays at this justly popular place. The restaurant is no-smoking.

East Edges of the Dark Peak

Froggatt

5 miles N of Bakewell off the B6054

Nearby **Stoke Hall**, situated high above the Derwent Valley, was built in 1755 for Lord Bradford and was later leased to Robert Arkwright, son of Sir Richard Arkwright, who lived here while he managed the Lumsford Mill at Bakewell. The Hall is now a hotel and restaurant, but remains home to a ghost, said to have been haunting the building for well over 100 years. The ghost is claimed to be that of a maid at the Hall who, while pining for a soldier fighting overseas, was brutally murdered. Her employers at the Hall were so shocked by this that they built a memorial to her in the front garden. However, the memorial was seen to move not long after it had been erected, and so it was rebuilt in a quiet corner of the estate, where it remains undisturbed.

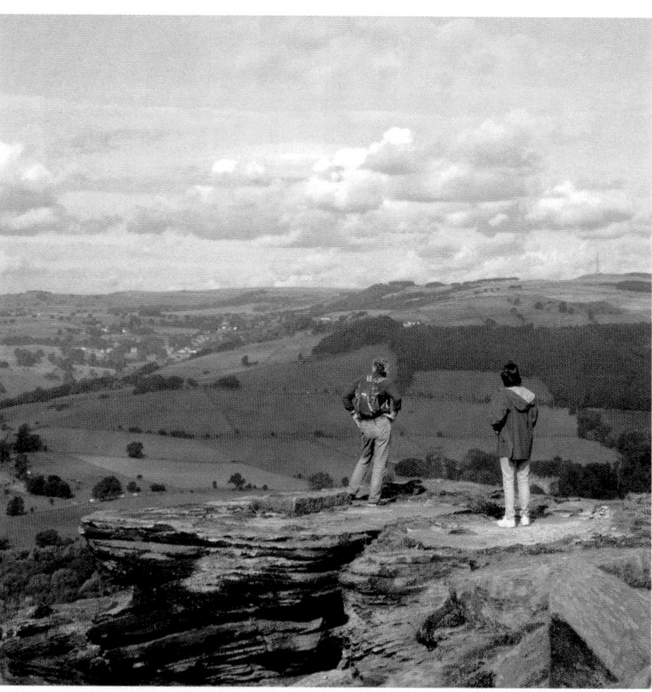

Froggatt Edge

Curbar

5 miles NE of Bakewell off the A623

Curbar is a hillside village very close to Calver. It grew up up around the crossing point of the River Derwent on the old turnpike road.

Although it is Eyam that is famous as the Plague Village, many communities suffered greatly at the hands of this terrible disease. During the height of the infection bodies were interred away from the centre of the village, and usually as quickly as possible, to prevent the spread of the disease. Many of the graves were left unmarked, but at Curbar the **Cundy Graves** (dating from 1632) can be seen on the moors above the village and below the Wesleyan Reform Church.

Missionaries used to be trained at Cliffe college, Curbar in the 19th century. It is now a college of Sheffield University, sponsored by the Methodist Church and operates as a training centre and a conference centre. Interesting older features of the village include a circular pinfold or stock compound on top of Pinfold Hill, where stray animals were kept until claimed by their owners, a covered well and circular trough, and an unusual village lock-up with a conical roof. The coarse gritstone ridge of **Curbar Edge**, which shelters the village, is popular with rock climbers.

Calver

4 miles NE of Bakewell off the A623

Recorded as Calvoure in the *Domesday Book*, evidence of an early Anglo Saxon settlement was found when skeletons were discovered in limestone rock in 1860. It is a pleasant stone-built village, situated by the River Derwent, with a pleasing 18th century bridge, which no longer carries the main road over the river. Calver is home to one of the most sinister buildings known to television viewers with long memories. The handsome, though austere, **Georgian Cotton Mill**, which is now converted into luxury flats, was the infamous Colditz Castle of the television series of that name.

Baslow

4 miles NE of Bakewell off the A619

Standing at the northern gates to Chatsworth, Baslow has for centuries been closely linked with the affairs of the Cavendish family. The village has three distinct parts – Bridge End, the oldest part around the church, Over End, a residential area to the north of the village and Nether End, next to the Chatsworth Estate. The village is unusual in having thatched cottages rather than the more traditionally tiled, slate or gritstone shingled roofs. Though most houses in the area were thatched they are much less common today and give the village a very distinctive air. The village **Church of St Anne**, beautifully situated by the River Derwent, has a squat broach spire that dominates the village. The church has an unusual clock face, added to commemorate Queen Victoria's Diamond Jubilee in 1887, that is well worth a second glance. The idea of a local man, Dr Wrench, instead of the usual numerals the clock face has 'Victoria' and '1897' around the edge. An ancient Saxon cross can also be found in the churchyard. Inside the church another unusual feature is preserved: the whip that was used to drive stray dogs out of the church during services.

The key building in the village is the Cavendish Hotel, which was originally known as the Peacock Hotel when it was

Avant Garde of Baslow & The Garden Café

Hollingworth House, Calver Road, Baslow, Derbyshire DE45 1RD
Tel/Fax: 01246 583888
Cafe Tel: 01246 582619
e-mail: avantgarde@btopenworld.com
website: www.avantgarde-of-baslow.co.uk

Open seven days a week from 10 a.m. to 5 p.m., **Avant Garde of Baslow & The Garden Café** can be found just a short drive from Chatsworth House on the A623 through-road in the centre of Baslow. There are two establishments here: Avant Garde with a range of stylish items for the home and garden, and the Garden Café. The café is a real gem, created by Linda and John Lowen in 2000. In this short time it has become a very popular eatery attracting regular customers from the surrounding area and beyond.

Open daily from 9 a.m. until 5 p.m., the regular menu offers a fine selection of home-made dishes. The range includes breakfasts, light meals, sandwiches, salads, drinks, cakes and much more. The surroundings are charming and the service is excellent, all resulting in the café having been awarded Best Tea and Coffee House of 2001/2 by both Derbyshire County Council and the English Tourist Board. On Friday and Saturday evenings the café opens as a restaurant, serving a seasonal menu of delicious dishes which are sure to tempt every palate. A sample from the excellent menu includes steak garni, wild mushroom risotto, fresh cod and chicken breast in sweet and sour sauce. It is essential to book for evening meals in advance.

Adjacent to the café, Avant Garde, open daily from 10 a.m. to 5 p.m., is the place to find an impressive range of handsome gifts and homeware, and has been featured many times in *Country Living* magazine. Here you will find all sorts of delightful items, ranging from furniture and wicker baskets to vases and artificial flowers, books and giftwrap. It's well worth a visit either for a gift for a friend, or a treat for yourself.

in the ownership of the Duke of Rutland. The Hotel passed into the hands of the Duke of Devonshire in the 1830s and also changed its name to reflect its new owner. Extensively restored in the 1970s, the Hotel is famous for the 10 miles of trout fishing it offers along the banks of the Derwent and Wye rivers.

Baslow sits beneath its own Peakland 'edge', which provides fine views across the Derwent Valley towards Chatsworth House. From the **Eagle Rock,** a 6 metre high block of gritstone on Baslow Edge, to the north of the village, there are wonderful views. Climbing to the top of this isolated rock was a test for every young Baslow man before he married. It is here that Dr Wrench, in 1866, erected the Wellington Monument to celebrate the Duke's victory at Waterloo and to counterbalance the monument to Nelson on Birchen Edge not far away.

Baslow has two very fine bridges over the Derwent. The **Bridge End Bridge,** which is near the church, was built in 1603 and features a tiny tollhouse with an entrance only 3½ feet high. It is the only bridge across the Derwent, which has never been destroyed by floods. The bridge at Nether End is a neighbour of one of the few thatched cottages in the Peak District.

PLACES TO STAY, EAT AND DRINK

Bolehill Farm, Bakewell, Derbyshire (24) B&B and Self Catering p48

Wyes Waters Tea Rooms, Bakewell, Derbyshire (25) Tea Rooms p50

Haddon Hall, Bakewell, Derbyshire (26) Visitor Attraction p51

Chatsworth House, Edensor, Derbyshire (27) Visitor Attraction p52

The Maynard, Grindleford, Derbyshire (28) Hotel p56

Ye Olde Bowling Green Inn, Bradwell, Derbyshire (29) Pub, Restaurant & Accommodation p58

Bluebell Cottages, Cressbrook, Derbyshire (30) Self Catering p62

Wellhead Farm, Wormhill, Derbyshire (31) B&B p66

The Bulls Head, Monyash, Derbyshire (32) Pub, Food & Accommodation p69

Biggin Hall Hotel, Biggin-by-Hartington, Derbyshire (33) Hotel p70

The Packhorse Inn, Crowdecote, Derbyshire (34) Pub, Food & Accommodation p71

Denotes entries in other chapters

2 Bakewell, Matlock and the White Peak

This region of the Derbyshire Dales, sometimes also known as the Central Peak and occupying the central area of the Peak District National Park between the two major towns of Ashbourne and Buxton, is less wild and isolated than the remote High Peak area. The limestone plateau of the White Peak was laid down in a tropical sea over 300 million years ago, along with the fossilized remains of countless tiny sea creatures. The two main rivers, the Wye and the Derwent, which both have their source farther north, are, in this region, at a

Park & Gardens, Matlock

PLACES TO STAY, EAT AND DRINK

Denotes entries in other chapters

River Wye, Bakewell

more gentle stage of their course. Over the centuries, the fast-flowing waters were harnessed to provide power to drive the mills situated on the riverbanks; any walk taken along these riverbanks will not only give the opportunity to discover a wide range of plant and animal life, but also provide the opportunity to see the remains of buildings that once played an important part in the economy of north Derbyshire. The landscape of the White Peak is gentler than the dark brooding peat moors and sharp gritstone edges of the Dark Peak. Sheep graze on rolling pasture land criss-crossed by miles of dry stone walls.

The town of Bakewell lies in the White Peak and, although to the northeast of the town lie the eastern edges of the Dark Peak, most of its surrounding villages are in the White Peak. It is the only town in the Peak District National Park.

Bakewell

Bakewell, the only town in the Peak District National Park, dominates the area and close to it are two of the most magnificent stately homes in Britain, Chatsworth House and Haddon Hall. The vast Chatsworth estate straddles the River Derwent east of Bakewell, but the influence of the Cavendish family extends much further and few villages in the surrounding area have escaped.

The only true town in the Peak District National Park, Bakewell attracts many day-trippers, walkers and campers as well as locals who come to take advantage of its many amenities. The beautiful medieval five-arched bridge spanning the River Wye is still in use today as the main crossing-point for traffic.

A stonebuilt town set along the banks of the River Wye, Bakewell enjoys a picturesque setting among well-wooded hills. With only 4,000 inhabitants it is nevertheless generally acknowledged as the capital of the Peak District National Park.

However, for most people it is a dessert that has made the name of Bakewell so famous, but please remember it is referred to locally as a *pudding* and most definitely not as a tart! Its invention is said to have been an accident when what was supposed to have been a strawberry tart turned into something altogether different. The cooking mishap took place in the kitchens of the Rutland Arms Hotel, which was built in 1804 on the site of an old coaching inn. Mrs Greaves, the mistress, instructed the cook to prepare strawberry tart and the cook, instead of stirring the egg mixture into the pastry, spread it on top of the jam. The result was so successful that a Mrs Wilson, wife of a Tallow Chandler, where candles were made, saw the possibility of making the puddings for sale and obtained the so-called recipe and commenced in a business of her own. Several businesses in the town claim to have the original recipe. Although it's a delightful tale, a more likely explanation is that Bakewell pudding originated as a type of 'transparent' pudding, popular in the 18th century, in which a layer of fruit or jam was covered with a mixture of sugar, butter and eggs and then baked. These puddings were usually baked in a dish without pastry. Eliza Acton's recipe for Bakewell pudding without pastry first appeared in 1845 in 'Modern Cookery'. By 1861 Mrs Beeton's recipe had a puff pastry case. Almonds weren't used either in the original Bakewell pudding, although either almond essence or ground almonds feature in most modern recipes.

Bakewell

The novelist Jane Austen reputedly stayed at the Rutland Arms in 1811 and it featured in her book *Pride and Prejudice*, while Bakewell itself is said to appear as the town of Lambton.

Bakewell's situation has always made it the ideal place for a settlement and, as well as being home to the Romans, an Iron Age fort has been discovered close by. Another reason for the popularity of the town was the existence of 12 fresh water springs which gave the town its

Bolehill Farm

Monyash Road, Bakewell,
Derbyshire DE45 1QW
Tel: 01629 812359
e-mail: info9@bolehillfarm.co.uk
website: www.bolehillfarm.co.uk

Standing in 2 acres of gardens and 18 acres of pastureland the impressive **Bolehill Farm** occupies a very scenic location just outside Bakewell. It has eight self-catering cottages and in the main house owners Chris and Shirley Swaap offer superb bed and breakfast accommodation in two ensuite guest bedrooms that look out over the Lathkill Valley. One room is a double, the other a king-size. Both are available all year round except Christmas Day and New Year's Day. The seasonal price includes a hearty and delicious breakfast.

The charming collection of stonebuilt buildings are in the heart of the Peak District National Park. A peaceful haven some 150 metres from the road, they make an excellent base from which to explore the many sights and attractions of the region.

Chris and Shirley have been here since 2003. They have carefully refurbished and redecorated the cottages to a high standard of quality and comfort. New kitchens, baths, carpeting and central heating have now been installed throughout each cottage. Former farm buildings, the cottages are set around a central courtyard and date back to the early 19th century. Available all year round, four of the cottages are on the ground floor. Rated between 3 and 4 stars by the ETC, four cottages sleep two; one sleeps five; one sleeps up to six; the rest sleep four. Most can also accommodate a cot for young babies. Each is airy, spacious and bright, with modern amenities happily married to traditional features such as the brickbuilt fires and exposed beamwork.

Short breaks are available out of season – and sometimes in high season, please ring for details. Guests can enjoy walking, cycling, fishing and more. The area offers a good choice of pubs, restaurants and tea rooms, excellent shopping and weekly markets.

No smoking.

Pudding Shop, Bakewell

name - *well* means 'bath spring'. This Old English name is also said to mean 'Badeca's spring', and is a reference to the warm, iron-bearing springs which rise in and around the town.

The market town for this whole central area of the Peak District, markets were held here well before the granting of a charter in 1330. In fact, its importance during the 11th century was such that, as recorded in the *Domesday Book* of 1086, Bakewell had two priests. Monday is now Bakewell's market day and the cattle market, one of the largest in Derbyshire, is an important part of the area's farming life.

The annual **Bakewell Show**, held every summer, started in 1819 and has gone on to become one of the foremost agricultural shows in the country. Across the River Wye stands the enormous Agricultural and Business Centre, where the livestock market takes place.

The large parish **Church of All Saints** was founded in Saxon times, as revealed by the ancient preaching crosses and stonework. Its graceful spire, with its octagonal tower, can be seen for miles around. One of the few places in Derbyshire in the *Domesday Book* to record two priests and a church, the churchyard and church itself contain a wonderful variety of headstones and coffin slabs and, near the porch, a most unusual cross. Over 1,200 years old, it stands an impressive 8 feet high. On one side it depicts the Crucifixion, on the other are the Norse gods Odin and Loki. The west front is still essentially Norman. Most of the eastern end of the church, the south transept, and the chancel date from the 13th century. The decorative font is early 14th century, as are the chancel stalls, which have interesting misericords. The Vernon Chapel in the south aisle has impressive monuments to 'The King of the Peak', Sir George Vernon of Haddon Hall, who died in 1567, and also to Sir John Manners, who died in 1584, and his wife Dorothy Vernon - these latter two feature in one of the great romantic legends of the Peak District.

Behind the church is the lovely **Old House Museum**, housed in a building on Cunningham Place which dates back to

Holme Bridge, Bakewell

It was extended during the early 17th century and, at one time, the building was converted into tenements by the industrialist Richard Arkwright for his mill-workers. Now established as a folk museum, it houses a fascinating collection of rural bygones.

1534. It is thought to be the oldest house in Bakewell. This beautiful building escaped demolition and has been lovingly restored by the Bakewell Historical Society and now displays its original wattle and daub interior walls.

The town is full of delightful, mellow stone buildings, many of which date from the early 17th century and are still in use today. The **Old Town Hall**, famous as the scene of the Bakewell riots, is now a clothing shop whilst the Bakewell Visitor Centre is housed in the late 17th century Market Hall. Few buildings remain from the days when Bakewell was a minor spa town, but the **Bath House**, on Bath Street, is one such building. Built in 1697 for the Duke of Rutland, it contained a large bath which was filled with the spa water and kept at a constant temperature of 59 degrees Fahrenheit.

Traditionally well-dressing flourished in the town in the 18th century, when Bakewell had aspirations to become a fashionable spa. However, the recent revival dates back only to the 1970s, when the British Legion - with the help of the well-dressers of Ashford in the Water - dressed the warm well at Bath House. Today, all five wells are dressed on the last Saturday in June.

There is little evidence of industry in the town, which is not very surprising

Haddon Hall

nr. Bakewell, Derbyshire DE45 1LA
Tel: 01629 812855 Fax: 01629 814379
e-mail: info@haddonhall.co.uk
website: www.haddonhall.co.uk

Only a mile to the south of Bakewell down the Matlock Road, on a bluff overlooking the Wye, the romantic **Haddon Hall** stands hidden from the road by a beech hedge. The Hall is thought by many to have been the first fortified house in the country, although the turrets and battlements were actually put on purely for show. The home of the Dukes of Rutland for over 800 years, the Hall has enjoyed a fairly peaceful existence, in part no doubt because it stood empty and neglected for nearly 300 years after 1640, when the family chose Belvoir Castle in Leicestershire as their main home. Examples of work from every century from the 12th to the 17th are here in this treasure trove.

As with all good ancestral homes, it has a family legend. In this case the story dates from the 16th century when Lady Dorothy Vernon eloped with Sir John Manners. Many feel this legend was invented by the Victorians, partly because there is no historical evidence to back the claim that the two eloped together during a ball and also because neither the steps nor the pretty little packhorse bridge across the Wye, over which Dorothy is supposed to have escaped, existed during her time. However the small museum by the gatehouse tells of their romantic journey, as well as the history of the Hall.

Little construction work has been carried out on the Hall since the days of Henry VIII and it remains one of the best examples of a medieval and Tudor manor house. The 16th century terraced gardens are one of the chief delights of the Hall and are thought by many to be the most romantic in England. The Hall's splendour and charm have led it to be used as a backdrop to television and film productions including *Jane Eyre*, *Moll Flanders* and *The Prince and the Pauper*. Nikolaus Pevsner described the Hall as "The English castle par excellence, not the forbidding fortress on an unassailable crag, but the large, rambling, safe, grey, loveable house of knights and their ladies, the unreasonable dream-castle of those who think of the Middle Ages as a time of chivalry and valour and noble feelings. None other in England is so complete and convincing."

The Hall's chapel is adorned with medieval wall paintings. The kitchens are the oldest extant part of the house, and feature time-worn oak tables and dole cupboards. The oak-panelled Long Gallery features boars' heads (to represent Vernon) and peacocks (Manners) in the panelling.

considering Bakewell is surrounded by farming country, but the remnants of **Lumford Mill** can still be seen. Originally built in 1778 by Sir Richard Arkwright as a cotton spinning mill, over 300 hands, mainly women and children, were employed here. Badly damaged by fire in 1868, the Mill has been rebuilt and it is used as offices today. Here can also be found a very fine example of a low-parapeted packhorse bridge across the Wye, dating from 1664. Holme Hall to the north of town dates from 1626. This Jacobean hall faces the water-meadows of the Wye.

North of Bakewell

Edensor

2 miles E of Bakewell off the B6012

This model village (the name is pronounced Ensor) was built by the 6th Duke of Devonshire between 1838 and 1842 after the original village had been demolished because it spoilt the view from **Chatsworth House** (see panel below). Unable to decide on a specific design for the buildings, as suggested by his architect Paxton, the Duke had the

Chatsworth House

nr Edensor, Derbyshire
Tel: 01246 565300 Fax: 01246 583536
e-mail: visit@chatsworth.org
website: www.chatsworth-house.co.uk

On the Outskirts of the village lies the home of the Dukes of Devonshire, **Chatsworth House**, known as the "Palace of the Peak", is without doubt one of the finest of the great houses in Britain. The origins of the House as a great showpiece must be attributable to the redoubtable Bess of Hardwick, whose marriage into the Cavendish family helped to secure the future of the palace.

Bess's husband, Sir William Cavendish, bought the estate for £600 in 1549. It was Bess who completed the new House after his death. Over the years, the Cavendish fortune

continued to pour into Chatsworth, making it an almost unparalleled showcase for art treasures. Every aspect of the fine arts is here, ranging from old masterpieces, furniture, tapestries, porcelain and some magnificent alabaster carvings.

The gardens of this stately home also have some marvellous features, including the Emperor Fountain, which dominates the Canal Pond and is said to reach a height of 290 feet. There is a maze and a Laburnum Tunnel and, behind the house, the famous Cascades. The overall appearance of the park as it is seen today is chiefly due to the talents of "Capability" Brown, who was first consulted in 1761. However, the name perhaps most strongly associated with Chatsworth is Joseph Paxton. His experiments in glasshouse design led him eventually to his masterpiece, the Crystal Palace, built to house the Great Exhibition of 1851.

Edensor

cottages and houses in the new village built in a fascinating variety of styles. The village church was rebuilt by Sir George Gilbert Scott; in the churchyard is buried the late President Kennedy's sister Kathleen, who had married into the Cavendish family. Both she and her husband, the eldest son of the 10th Duke, were killed during the Second World War. The original village of Edensor lay nearer to the gates of Chatsworth House; only Park Cottage remains there now.

Pilsley

2 miles NE of Bakewell off the A619

This is a relatively new village created by the Duke of Devonshire after he had demolished Chatsworth village to make way for his mansion house and estate. It is now the estate workers who help the villagers dress four wells to coincide with the village fair in mid-July, a custom revived in 1968. The Shire Horse Stud Farm, built by the 9th Duke of Devonshire in 1910, has been converted into a variety of craft workshops and a farm shop.

Hassop

3 miles N of Bakewell off the B6001

This little village is dominated by its fine Roman Catholic **Church of All Saints,** which dates from 1818. It was built by the Eyre family who, as well as being devout Catholics, also owned some 20 manors in the area. Hidden behind a high wall is one of the Eyre manor houses, **Hassop Hall**. Dating from the 17th century, the Hall was garrisoned for the King by Thomas Eyre during the Civil War and it remained in the family until the mid-19th century when there were a series of contested wills. The Hall is now a private hotel and restaurant and it contains a lead mine shaft in its cellars.

To the south of the village is Hassop Station, built in 1863, to serve the Duke of Devonshire at Chatsworth House and not for the convenience of the villagers. Now situated along the **Monsal Trail**, the station building is a bookshop.

Great Longstone

3 miles NW of Bakewell off the B6465

An attractive stonebuilt Peak District

village nestling below Longstone Edge, **Longstone Hall**, built in 1747 of red brick, was the home of the Wright family (who now live at Eyam Hall). The present Hall replaced a much larger Elizabethan building which is said to have been similar in style, but bigger, than the present Eyam Hall. The 13th century village church has a particularly fine roof, with moulded beams, that dates from the 15th century. In the nave is a plaque placed to commemorate the work of Dr Edward Buxton when, in the 1820s and aged 73 years, he treated the whole village against an outbreak of typhus.

Stoney Middleton

4 miles N of Bakewell off the A623

This village, known simply as "Stoney" locally, is certainly well named as, particularly in this part of **Middleton Dale**, great walls of limestone rise up from the valley floor. Further up the Dale there are also many disused limestone quarries as well as the remains of some lead mines. Not all industry has vanished from the area, as this is the home of nearly three-quarters of the country's fluorspar industry. Another relic from the past also survives, a shoe and boot-making company operates from the village and is housed in a former corn mill.

An ancient village, the Romans built a bath here and the unusual octagonal village church was built by Joan Padley in thanksgiving for the safe return of her husband from the field of the Battle of Agincourt in the 15th century. The lantern storey was added to the Perpendicular tower in 1759. Stoney Middleton has preserved its village identity and character and also partakes in the custom of well-dressing, when two wells around The Nook are dressed in late July/early August.

Higher up the dale from the village is the dramatically named **Lover's Leap**. In 1762, a jilted girl, Hannah Badderley, tried to jump to her death by leaping from a high rock. Her voluminous skirts, however, were caught on some brambles and she hung from the ledge before gently rolling down into a sawpit and escaping serious injury.

Eyam

5 miles N of Bakewell off the B6521

Pronounced 'Eem', this village will

Maypole Dancing, Stoney Middleton

Cottages at Eyam

forever be known as the **Plague Village**. In 1666, a local tailor received a bundle of plague-infected clothing from London. Within a short time the infection had spread and the terrified inhabitants prepared to flee the village. However, the local rector, William Mompesson, persuaded the villagers to stay put and, thanks to his intervention, most neighbouring villages escaped the disease. Eyam was quarantined for over a year, relying on outside help for supplies of food which were left on the village boundary. Out of a total of 350 inhabitants, only 83 survived.

An open-air service is held each August at Cucklet Delf to commemorate the villagers' brave self-sacrifice, and the well-dressings are also a thanksgiving for the pureness of the water. Taking place on the last Sunday in August, known as Plague Sunday, this also commemorates the climax of the plague and the death of the rector's wife, Catherine Mompesson.

The village itself is quite large and self-contained, and typical of a mining and quarrying settlement. An interesting place to stroll around, there are many information plaques documenting events where they took place. Eyam Museum tells the story of the heroic sacrifice and the **Church of St Lawrence** houses an excellent exhibition of Eyam's history.

Also inside the Church are two ancient coffin lids; the top of one of the lids is known as St Helen's Cross.

Born in Derbyshire, St Helen was the daughter of a Romano-British chief and the mother of Emperor Constantine. She is said to have found a fragment of the cross on which Jesus was crucified. In the churchyard is the best-preserved Saxon cross to be found in the Peak District, along with an unusual sundial which dates from 1775.

The home of the Wright family for over 300 years, **Eyam Hall** is a wonderful, unspoilt 17th century manor house that is now open to the public. As well as touring the house and seeing the impressive stone-flagged hall, tapestry room and the magnificent tester bed, there is also a café and gift shop. The Eyam Hall Crafts Centre, housed in the farm building, contains several individual units which specialise in a variety of unusual and skilfully-fashioned crafts.

Grindleford

6 miles N of Bakewell off the B6521/B6001

This is one of the smallest Peak District villages and from here, each year in July, there is a pilgrimage to **Padley Chapel** to commemorate two Catholic martyrs of 1588. The ruins of ancient Padley Manor House, found alongside the track bed of the old railway line, are all that remain of the home of two devout Roman Catholic families. It was from here that two priests, Robert Ludlam and Nicholas Garlick were taken, in the 16th century, and sentenced to death, in Derby, by hanging, drawing and quartering. The then owner of the house, Thomas Fitzherbert, died in the Tower of London three years later while his brother died at Fleet Prison in 1598.

In 1933, the charming chapel seen today was converted from the still standing farm buildings.

To the northwest of the village is the **Longshaw Country Park**, some 1,500 acres of open moorland, woodland and the impressive Padley Gorge. Originally the Longshaw estate of the Dukes of Rutland, the land was acquired by the National Trust in the 1970s. At the heart of the country park, is the Duke's former shooting lodge.

Abney

8 miles NW of Bakewell off the A625

Abney, and the neighbouring hamlet of

Longshaw Country Park

Abney Grange, are isolated settlements guarding the upper reaches of the Highlow Brook on Abney Moor. First recorded as *Habenai* in the *Domesday Book*, Abney was at that time owned by William Peverel, William the Conqueror's son and creator of Peveril Castle at Castleton.

Abney is very popular with walkers, and with the Derbyshire and Lancashire Gliding Club located at the ridge end at Camphill, overlooking Bradwell Dale.

To the east of the village, **Highlow Hall** is a fine, battlemented manor built in the 1500s by the Eyre family. It features an attractive gateway and a stone dovecote.

Bradwell

9 miles NE of Buxton off the B6049

Usually abbreviated in the unique Peak District way to 'Bradder' - Bradwell is a charming little limestone village sheltered by Bradwell Edge. At one time this former lead mining community was famous as the place where miners' hardhats - hard, black, brimmed hats in which candles were stuck to light the way underground - were made; thus these hardhats came to be known as Bradder Beavers. It owes its fortune to the lead mining industry of the 18th and 19th centuries, though among other items manufactured in Bradwell include coarse cotton goods, telescopes and opera glasses. It was also the birthplace of Samuel Fox, the 19th century inventor of the folding-frame umbrella. His house is marked with a plaque and lies just off the main street. The centre of the village, which lies above the stream south of the main road, is a maze of narrow lanes with tiny cottages. Though most of the village dates from the lead mining era, Bradwell had been occupied in Roman times. A narrow street called Smalldale follows the line of the Roman road between Brough and Buxton. Near the New Bath Hotel, where there is a thermal spring, the remains of a Roman Bath were found. Legend has it that Bradwell was also once a Roman slave camp, to serve the lead mines. During

Ye Olde Bowling Green Inn

Smalldale, Bradwell, Hope Valley S33 9JQ
Tel: 01433 620450 Fax: 01433 620280

Tucked away in Smalldale, in the village of Bradwell, **Ye Olde Bowling Green Inn** is a delightful former coaching inn dating back to the 16th century. Retaining its original bow windows, the whitewashed exterior is set off with climbing roses, hanging baskets and shrub borders in a lovely show of colour.

The inn is larger inside than might at first be expected, and many of the rooms enjoy panoramic views in all directions.

Owners Angela and Glyn, ably assisted by their daughters Carolyn and Tina, have only been here since July of 2004 but have many years' experience in the trade. They are very knowledgeable about the area and are happy to share this knowledge with their guests, to help them have the best possible experience of the region. There's a long-established tradition of friendly service and a welcoming atmosphere at this Free House, where the bar stocks a choice of four real ales – Stones and Tetleys are the regulars, together with two rotating guest ales – as well as a good choice of lagers, cider, stout, wines, spirits and soft drinks. There are two superb restaurants (one no-smoking); each seats up to 32 diners. Meals can also be taken in the snug, the lounge and, on fine days, on the outdoor patio/beer garden area. Food is available Monday to Saturday at lunch (12 – 2) and dinner (6 – 9), and from midday to 7 p.m. on Sundays. Angela and Carolyn do the cooking, creating an impressive selection of dishes for the menu and specials board. The freshest ingredients are used to prepare meals such as roast of the day, steaks, wild mushroom lasagne, chicken tikka masala, home-baked ham and much more. There's also a children's menu. Booking advised at weekends.

This superb inn also boasts six charming and comfortable ensuite guest bedrooms, housed in an adjacent former farm building that has been tastefully renovated to offer every comfort. There are five doubles and one twin; three rooms are on the ground floor and feature French windows and a patio area. The tariff includes a hearty and delicious breakfast.

the period of struggle that followed the Romans' departure, the mysterious fortification to the north of the village, known as **Grey Ditch**, was built. It may have been constructed to defend Bradford Dale and the village against the Hope Valley. A different local legend speaks of Bradwell as the scene of the hanging of the Saxon King Edwin. The local name 'Eden Tree' is said to stem from this. Today it is more famous for producing the delicious Bradwell's Home-made Dairy Ice Cream.

A key attraction here is the massive **Bagshawe Cavern**, a cave reached by a descending flight of 98 steps through an old lead mine. For the more adventurous caving trips are made available.

A mile south of the village is the mid-16th century **Hazlebadge Hall**. One of several manors of the Vernon family, whose main seat was at Haddon Hall, their coat of arms can be seen above the upper mullioned windows. The house dates from 1549 and was part of Dorothy Vernon's dowry to her new husband, John Manners.

On the Saturday before the first Monday in August, four wells are dressed in the village. Although wells were dressed even at the turn of the 20th century, the present custom dates back only to 1949, when the Bowling Green Well was dressed during Small Dale Wakes. The village has its own particular method for making the colourful screens, section by section, so that the clay does not dry out.

Ashford in the Water

1 mile NW of Bakewell off the A6

Not exactly in the water, but certainly on the River Wye, Ashford is another candidate for Derbyshire's prettiest village. It developed around a ford that spanned the river and was once an important crossing place on the ancient Portway. Originally a medieval packhorse bridge, **Sheepwash Bridge** crosses the Wye, with overhanging willows framing its low arches. It is one of three bridges in the village, and a favourite with artists. There is a small enclosure to one side that provides a clue to its name, as this is still occasionally used for its original purpose - crowds gather to witness sheep being washed in the river to clean their fleece before they are shorn. The lambs would be penned within the enclosure and the ewes, left on the other side of the river would conveniently swim across, getting a good wash in the process. Sheepwash Bridge is older than Mill Bridge which is dated 1664.

So-called Black Marble, actually a highly polished grey limestone from quarries and mines near the village, was mined nearby for some considerable time, and particularly during the Victorian era when it was fashionable to have decorative items and fire surrounds made from the stone. It was also exported all over the world. Once a thriving cottage industry, Ashford Marble, as it was known, was inlaid with coloured marbles, shells and glass.

River Wye, Ashford in the Water

1950, of the 10th Duke of Devonshire who never resided at Chatsworth. To the south of Ashford is another manor House, **Ashford Hall** overlooking a picturesque lake on the river Wye. Owned by the Dukes of Devonshire, it was built in 1785 to a design by Joseph Pickford of Derby. It was occupied by the family for a time, but was sold in the early 1950s. It now belongs to the Olivier family.

The great limestone parish **Church of the Holy Trinity**, largely rebuilt in 1871 but retaining the base of a 13th century tower, has a fine Ashford marble table on show as well as a tablet to the memory of Henry Watson, the founder of the marble works who was also an authority on the geology of the area. Several of the pillars within the church are made of the rare Duke's Red marble, which is only found in the mine at Lathkill Dale owned by the Duke of Devonshire. The church also boasts a Norman tympanum, complete with Tree of Life, lion and hog, over the south door. Hanging from the roof of Ashford's church are the remains of four 'virgin's crantses' - paper garlands carried at the funerals of unmarried village girls.

Near the village is **Churchdale Hall**, which dates from the 18th century and is part of the vast Chatsworth estate. It was also the home, until his death in

Ashford is perhaps most famous for its six beautifully executed well-dressings, which are held annually in early June. After a break of many years the custom of well-dressing was briefly revived at Sheepwash Well in 1930, though this revival petered out until the arrival in the village of an enthusiastic vicar in the 1950s when the well-dressings became an annual custom once more. Rather than adhering strictly to the custom of depicting scenes from the Bible, the well-dressers of Ashford have pictured such unusual themes as a willow pattern to celebrate the Chinese Year of the Dog, and have also paid tribute to the Land Girls of the First World War. The village also has a pleasant range of mainly 18th century cottages, and a former tithe barn.

Monsal Head

3 miles NW of Bakewell off the B6465

Monsal Head is a renowned, and deservedly so, beauty spot from which there are tremendous views - particularly over **Monsal Dale**, through which the River Wye flows.

Viaduct, Monsal Dale

Wardlow

6 miles NW of Bakewell off the B6465

At a crossroads near Wardlow Anthony Lingard was hanged in 1812 for the murder of a local widow. He was the last felon to hang in the county, and his execution drew an enormous crowd - so much so that the local lay-preacher at Tideswell found himself preaching to virtually empty pews. Determined not to waste this opportunity to speak to so large a congregation, he relocated to the gibbet in order to give his sermon.

Litton

6 miles NW of Bakewell off the A623

Situated in the Wye Valley, Litton is a typical example of a Peak District limestone village. Though the oldest house dates from 1639 - many of the buildings have date stones - most date from the mid-18th century, a time of prosperity for the area when the local lead mining industry was booming. As well as strolling around the village taking in the typical architecture of the Peak District found here, the ancient patterns of the small, stone-walled fields can also still be seen here.

The young apprentices at **Litton Mill**, unlike those at nearby Cressbrook Mill, experienced very harsh conditions. The Mill still stands, beside the Wye Mill stream, and is said to be haunted by the ghosts of the orphans who were exploited as cheap labour.

Cressbrook

5 miles NW of Bakewell off the B6465

Clinging to the slopes of the Wye Valley, the village cottages of Cressbrook are found in terraces amongst the ash woodland. The handsome **Cressbrook Mill**, built in 1815, is still partly in use;

Bluebell, Butterfield and Badger - cosy cottages in the heart of the National Park

Trinity House, Cressbrook,
Derbyshire SK17 8SX
Tel/Fax: 01298 872927
e-mail: jan@cosycotts.com
website: www.cosycotts.com

Butterfield Cottage

Tucked away in the villages of Cressbrook and Tideswell (four and six miles northwest of Bakewell respectively) are three superb holiday cottages that make a perfect base for exploring the many sights and attractions, including the lovely and tranquil surrounding countryside, of the area.

All three are supremely cosy, luxurious and comfortable, filled with exquisite traditional features yet offering every modern convenience. Facilities include washer/dryers, log-burners, gas central heating and kitchens fitted with full facilities. These traditional stonebuilt cottages are brimming with character and charm. All rooms are tastefully furnished with good quality furniture and antiques, and boast marvellous walks right from the door. The cottages are maintained by the owner who lives nearby.

Bluebell Cottage is located in Church Street, Tideswell. It's a 17th-century property that began life as a pub called The Miners Arms. This cottage sleeps up to eight people and is available all year round (from Fridays). The inviting beamed sitting room has plenty of comfortable seating around a stone fireplace, while the oak refectory dining table seats eight comfortably. The walled garden is gated and has a small wildlife pond, paved areas, flower beds and seating. The stone outbuilding is ideal for storing bikes. A public footpath lies between the cottage and garden and leads within minutes to lovely walks in the glorious countryside.

Butterfield Cottage is also in Tideswell, on Condliff Terrace. It dates back to the 1700s, sleeps six in three bedrooms and is available all year round (from Saturdays). It also boasts sunny private, secure gardens with patio furniture and barbecue.

Badger Cottage is located at Top Cottages, Cressbrook. It's Grade II listed 18th-century and was awarded (May 2004) a prestigious Greenwatch Conservation Award for the careful restoration of the cottage. It sleeps six in three bedrooms and is available all year round (from Saturdays). This mid-terrace cottage commands superb views along Monsal Dale. There is a pretty cottage garden with stepped path to the front of the cottage and a secure paved rear patio with table and chairs and a barbecue.

Children and pets very welcome. Short breaks available.

Badger Cottage

Bluebell Cottage

the apprentice house, used to house the pauper children from London and elsewhere who worked long hours in the mill, also exists. The owner of the Mill, William Newton, saw that the apprentices were treated well. The stretch of the River Wye between Cressbrook and Litton mills is known as Water-Cum-Jolly Dale. Cressbrook's well-dressing takes place during the first week in June.

Tideswell

8 miles NW of Bakewell off the B6049

One of the largest villages in the area, Tideswell takes its name from a Saxon chieftain called Tidi. Over 900 feet above sea level, the surrounding countryside offers many opportunities to wander, stroll, or take a leisurely (or energetic) hike through some varied and impressive scenery.

Known as the 'Cathedral of the Peak', the magnificent 14th century church of **St John the Baptist** has a wealth of splendid features. The tower is impressive, the windows are beautiful, there is a fine collection of brasses inside and the 'Minstrel of the Peak', William Newton, is buried in the churchyard. Eccles Hall, overlooking the Market Place, was built in 1724 and became the home of the headmaster of the Grammar School in 1878.

The village received its market charter in 1250; by the 14th century it was a flourishing centre for the local wool trade. Today the village is home to a number of craftspeople working in buildings converted from other uses. The excellence of their work is apparent, not only in the items they display, but also in the splendid well-dressing they help to enact, annually on the Saturday nearest St John the Baptist's Day (24th June).

Peak Forest

11 miles NW of Bakewell off the A623

High on the White Peak plateau, the village of Peak Forest takes its name from the fact that it once stood at the centre of the Royal Forest of the Peak. The parish **Church of King Charles the Martyr** speaks of the fierce

Morris Dancing, Tideswell

independence of the village inhabitants. It was built in 1657 by the wife of the 2nd Earl of Devonshire, during a time when there was a ban on building churches. The church that stands today on the site of the former chapel was built in 1878.

A quirk of ecclesiastical law ensured – up until early in the 19th century – that the village was outside the jurisdiction of the bishop. Thus it was not subject to the laws regarding posting the banns before marriage; hence it became known as 'the Gretna Green of the Peak'. If one or other of the couple has lived in the village for 15 days prior to the ceremony, to this day they can still be married in the church without banns being read.

At Chamber Farm, rebuilt in the 18th century, the Forest courts were held, attended by some 20 foresters whose job it was to maintain the special laws of the area.

Within walking distance of Peak Forest is the 'bottomless' pit of **Eldon Hole**. Once thought to be the Devil's own entrance to Hell, stories abound in which various people were lowered down on increasingly longer pieces of rope. They all returned, in differing states of mental anguish, but none ever reached the bottom! However, seasoned pot-holers, who view the hole as no more than a practice run, maintain that it is, in fact, 'only' 180 feet deep.

Taddington

5 miles E of Buxton off the A6

Now lying just off the main Bakewell to Buxton road, Taddington was one of the first places to be bypassed. A small village and one of the highest in England, the cottages here are simple but the church is rather grand. Like many churches in the Peak District, it was rebuilt in the 14th century with money gained from the then-booming woollen and lead industries in the area.

Taddington Hall, one of the smaller of the Peak District manor houses, dates back to the 16th century though much

Taddington

of the building seen today was constructed in the 18th century. As with all good halls, Taddington has its share of ghost stories. One in particular concerns two brothers. The pair ran a hessian factory from the Hall and one day they quarrelled. The next day one of the brothers, named Isaac, was found dead. The other brother was found guilty of the act. It is said that Isaac has been heard wandering around the passages of the Hall from time to time.

Miller's Dale

Up on Taddington Moor can be found **Five Wells** tumulus, at 1400 feet, the highest megalithic tomb in England. The harsh moorland weather has eroded the earth away to reveal two limestone slabs, the burial chambers of 12 people. Flint tools and scraps of pottery were also found in the chambers.

Miller's Dale

7 miles NE of Buxton off the B6049

The hamlet takes its name from one of several charming and compact dales that lie along the River Wye and provide excellent walking. The nearby nature reserve occupies land that was originally a limestone quarry, which was last used in 1971. This tiny settlement, situated in the narrow valley of the River Wye, began life as late as the 1860s when it was built to provide housing for the workers building the London to Manchester railway. All this has now gone but the dramatic Monsal Dale Viaduct (built in the 1860s to carry the railway line) remains and is now crossed by walkers taking the Monsal Trail. The disused railway has been converted to a track for walkers, cyclists, horse riders and less active people, including wheelchair users. Between Blackwell and Monsal Head the trail follows the deep limestone valley of the River Wye for eight and a half miles. It is unsuitable for cycling and wheelchairs at its western half, with rocky diversions around tunnels. Level access is available from Miller's Dale Station, for half a mile west or 2 miles east.

Wormhill

4 miles E of Buxton off the A6

The pretty hamlet of Wormhill was recorded in the *Domesday Book* and was a much more important settlement in the past. In Norman times it was one of the administrative centres of the Royal Forest of the Peak.

On the pretty, sloping village green in Wormhill there is an ornate memorial to James Brindley, erected in 1895. This memorial is the centrepiece for the village's well-dressings at the end of August every year. The parish church of St Margaret was largely rebuilt in 1864, though it retains its medieval tower. **Wormhill Hall**, built by the Bagshawe family in 1697, is a late 17th-century stone mansion (privately owned) which can be seen on the approach to the village from the Wye valley.

Tunstead

3 miles E of Buxton off the A6

High in the hills above the valley of the River Wye, Tunstead is a small hamlet with a very famous son in James Brindley, born here in 1716. Known as the father of the canal system, Brindley never learned to read or write but became a millwright in 1742. His skills in engineering brought him before the Duke of Bridgewater, who commissioned Brindley to build the Bridgwater Canal to carry coal between Manchester and Worsley. Brindley went on to construct many more canals throughout Britain.

King Sterndale

2 miles SE of Buxton off the A6

King Sterndale is a charming limestone hamlet high above Ashwood Dale. The cosy parish church was built in 1847 in Gothic style, to a design by Bonomi. Inside the church there is a memorial to Miss Ellen Hawkins of the neighbouring village of Cowdale, founder of the church. Other memorials include those to the Pickford family, as the one commemorating William Pickford, a judge who later became Lord Sterndale, Master of the Rolls.

South and West of Bakewell

Sheldon

3 miles W of Bakewell off the A6

Situated 1,000 feet up on the limestone plateau, black marble was also mined here, as it was at nearby Ashford in the Water, but Sheldon was not as successful as its neighbour as there was not enough water for the process. However, **Magpie Mine**, to the south of the village, produced lead for over 300 years. This important site of industrial archaeology has been preserved, from the Cornish-style chimney stack, engine house and dynamite cabin right down to the more recent corrugated iron-roofed buildings. Now owned by the Peak District Mines Historical Society, guided parties are taken round to see the techniques used by the miners.

The village itself is chiefly a single row of mainly 18th century cottages lining the main street. The **Church of St Michael and All Angels**, with some notable features, is well worth a visit. Prehistoric monuments litter the limestone plateau above the village and, from Sheldon, numerous footpaths lead into the surrounding countryside to Monyash, Flagg and Monsal Dale.

Flagg

5 miles W of Bakewell off the A515

The characteristic ridges and furrows of the medieval open fields, enclosed by stone walls in the 18th and 19th centuries, have been preserved in the farmland around Flagg. During the period of enclosure, hundreds of miles of stone walls were built, dividing the land into geometric patterns. Most of this can still be seen today, all over the Peak District, and is one of the particular features of the area. The Elizabethan manor house, **Flagg Hall**, is visible from the main road, and is well worth seeing, although it is not open to the public.

Chelmorton

7 miles W of Bakewell off the A5270

The second highest village in the county, the remains of the narrow strips of land that were allotted to each cottage in medieval times can still be seen. Outside these strips lay the common land and then the parish boundary. Beyond the boundary can be

Chelmorton

seen the regular fields that were laid out after the first enclosures of 1809. The layout of the village is unchanged probably since Saxon times. It is a single street, with farms at intervals along the street.

To the north of the village, some 1,440 feet up on **Chelmorton Low** there is a Bronze Age tumulus and also the source of an unusually named stream, Illy Willy Water. The oldest part of the village lies near the top of this hill following the course of the stream, and curiously, the village church and inn now seem to be at the end of a cul-de-sac.

Monyash

5 miles W of Bakewell off the B5055

Monyash was recorded in the *Domesday Book* as Maneis, thought to derive from 'many ash trees'. It is a picturesque village clustered around the village green. Farming and tourism are its main industries now but it was once at the centre of the Peak District's lead mining industry (from mediaeval times to the end of the 19th century) and had its own Barmote Court. Its market charter was granted in 1340 and the old market cross still stands on the village green. Due to its isolated position, Monyash had for many years to support itself and this led to a great many industries within the village. As far back as prehistoric times there was a flint-tool 'factory' here and, as well as mining, candle-making and rope-making, mere-building was a village speciality.

Today, Monyash, which is situated at the start of Lathkill Dale, is busy during the season with walkers keen to discover the surrounding countryside. The valley of the River Lathkill, **Lathkill Dale** is a road-free beauty spot with ash and elm woods that was designated a National Nature Reserve in 1972. The **River Lathkill**, like others in the limestone area of the Peak District, disappears underground for parts of its course. In this case the river rises, in winter, from a large cave above Monyash, known as Lathkill Head Cave. In summer, the

The Bulls Head

Church Street, Monyash, Bakewell,
Derbyshire DE45 1JH
Tel: 01629 812372

The outstanding **Bulls Head** is situated just opposite the village green in picturesque Monyash, some five miles west of Bakewell off the B5055. The inn has been here since the 17th century, when it began life as a farmhouse. The farmer began brewing his own beer and providing accommodation for herdsmen driving their cattle down to Bakewell market. Today owner Sharon Barber continues the inn's long history of hospitality and service, with great food, drink and accommodation. She has been here since 1991, and has made the inn a great success.

Open every session Monday to Thursday and all day Friday to Sunday, the inn stocks three real ales and a mild, along with a good range of lagers, wines, spirits, cider, stout and soft drinks. Quality food is served at lunch and dinner (and all day Sunday), with a range of tempting traditional favourites, all home-made and using the freshest local ingredients. The accommodation comprises three attractive and comfortable guest bedrooms.

river emerges further downstream at Over Haddon.

Pomeroy

7 miles W of Bakewell off the A515

Pomeroy is a charming hamlet with some lovely buildings, some dating back to medieval times. Parts of the Duke of York Inn in Pomeroy date back to the early 1400s. The chestnut tree in the car park was planted in the 1900s by the then Prince of Wales, later King Edward VIII, on an occasion when he was visiting the area with Sir Thomas Pomeroy.

Earl Sterndale

5 miles S of Buxton off the A515

At the less well-known northern end of Dove Valley, Earl Sterndale is close to the limestone peaks of Hitter Hill and High Wheeldon. Over 1,100 feet above sea level, it is surrounded by lovely farmland. A number of the farmsteads are called 'granges', a relic of the Middle Ages when the granges were where monks of the local Abbey lived. The parish **Church of St Michael**, built in the early 19th century, was the only church in Derbyshire to suffer a direct hit from a Second World War bomb. It was refurbished and restored in 1952, though it retains a Saxon font.

The village inn, the Quiet Woman, has a sign showing a headless woman, with the words 'Soft words turneth away wrath'. It is supposedly of a previous landlord's nagging wife, known as

Biggin Hall Country House Hotel

Biggin-by-Hartington, Buxton,
Derbyshire SK17 0DH
Tel: 01298 84451 Fax: 01298 84681

Found three-quarters of a mile off the main A515 (Buxton-to-Ashbourne road) in the village of Biggin-by-Hartington, **Biggin Hall Country House Hotel** is a gracious and distinctive establishment offering superior accommodation. Owner James Moffett arrived here in 1974, when the premises was a derelict farmhouse. Over the ensuing 30 years he has created a wonderful and justly renowned retreat.

Set in 40 acres, most of it pastureland with over an acre of mature gardens, this is

the place to recharge your batteries in style and comfort. Handily placed to visit all of Derbyshire's major towns, pretty villages and sights and attractions, this historic 17th century premises offers the finest in comfort and service.

There are 20 ensuite guest bedrooms dotted throughout the grounds – eight in the main hall, three in the Lodge (70 yards from the main house and with its own carpark), three in the Bothy (attached to the main house) and six in the Courtyard, a tastefully converted 18th century stone building 30 yards from the main house. All rooms are spacious and furnished with attractive antiques, while also offering every modern amenity (tv, tea-making facilities, telephone and silent fridge).

The main house offers visitors a choice of two sitting rooms (one with library) and the dining room. All guests have use of all the facilities in the main house. Guests can stay on a bed-and-breakfast or dinner, bed-and-breakfast basis. Non-residents are also welcome to dine (booking essential). Dinners feature traditional country house foods, complemented by a good wine list. Much of the food is of local origin and there's an emphasis placed on free-range wholefoods.

Children over 12 welcome. With all the delights of the region within easy reach, Biggin Hall makes an excellent touring base.

'Chattering Charteris', whose husband cut off her head.

Crowdecote

6 miles SE of Bakewell off the B5053

Crowdecote is situated in the deep limestone valley of the River Dove, just on the border with Staffordshire. The limestone reef knolls of the upper part of the valley can be clearly seen from vantage points near the village. Seen as hills, such as **Chrome Hill** and **Parkhouse Hill**, they are as close to peaks as they get in the Peak District. These knolls are actually the remnants of coral reefs - hard to believe, but perhaps not so puzzling when one remembers that much of this landscape has been formed by the action of water. The stone bridge over the River Dove, built in 1709 to replace an earlier wooden one, was a crossing point for the old pack horse route. The nearby Packhorse Inn dating back to 1723 was used by traders when this was the main road to Leek and Buxton.

Longnor

8 miles SE of Bakewell off the B5053

Over the county line into Staffordshire, yet in the heart of the Peak District, on a ridge between the River Manifold and the River Dove, Longnor, with its old gritstone houses stands between the browns of the Dark Peak country and the bright greens of the limestone White

The Lathkil Hotel

Over Haddon, Bakewell, Derbyshire DE45 1JE
Tel/Fax: 01629 812501
e-mail: info@lathkil.co.uk
website: www.lathkil.co.uk

The charming **Lathkil Hotel** enjoys a peaceful location above Lathkill Dale, in the heart of the Peak District. Ideal for a special break, here you will find good old-fashioned hospitality, delicious food and a relaxing atmosphere. Situated in the village of Over Haddon, not far from Bakewell, the hotel boasts spectacular views and is surrounded by quiet valleys and rolling fields. For tourists there is plenty to see and do, with numerous pretty villages, historic houses and the spa towns of Ashbourne and Buxton to explore, as well as the superb Lathkill Dale Trail for walkers.

Home-cooked food is available at lunchtimes and in the evening in the light and airy dining room, which has waist-to-ceiling windows to take best advantage of the superlative views. The décor is classic and simple, and the dining room is no-smoking throughout. In summer months lunch is in the form of a hot and cold buffet table, with choices such as minty lamb, venison and blackberry, brie and broccoli bake and smoked trout. An extensive à la carte menu is served in the evenings and complemented by an interesting wine list.

The bar boasts a wealth of warm wood and an open fire, and is open daily serving a choice of several real ales, including local brew Hartington, Wards plus rotating guest ales. The fine selection has been recognised by *The Good Beer Guide*, in which the Lathkil has featured for over 20 years. The hotel also offers four attractively furnished and very comfortable guest bedrooms, all doubles or twins, and complete with ensuite facilities. Little extras such as the hot drinks tray, tv, clock/radio and personal bar help to make your stay even more comfortable.

Park House Hill, Crowdecote

Peak landscape. It was once the meeting point of several packhorse routes. Then an important market town and the centre of a prosperous farming community, its **Market Hall** was built in 1873 - outside the hall there is a posting of the market charges of the time. The town's prosperity declined with the onset of the agricultural depression, and there was an accompanying fall in the population. However, this decline has in recent years been reversed. Longnor is now a conservation area and has attracted a good many craftspeople. The Market Square is one of the oldest in England, dating back to medieval times.

Main showroom for the work of local craftspeople and artisans, **Longnor Craft Centre** occupies the beautifully restored Market Hall in the centre of Longnor village. The village also has some fascinating narrow flagged passages, which seem to go nowhere but suddenly emerge into the most beautiful scenery.

Though the late 18th century **Church of St Bartholomew** is rather plain, the early Norman font of an older church is still within. The churchyard has a most interesting gravestone. The epitaph tells the tale of the life of William Billinge, born in 1679, died in 1791 - which made him 112 years old at the time of his death! As a soldier Billinge served under Rooke at Gibraltar and Marlborough at Ramilles. After being sent home wounded, he recovered to take part in defending the King in the rebellions of 1715 and 1745. The village is the location for the filming of the TV series 'Peak Practice' and fans of the series will easily spot Dr Tom's House, The Beeches Surgery, The Black Swan among other familiar sights around Longnor village.

Over Haddon

1½ miles SW of Bakewell off the B5055

A former lead mining village Over Haddon is a picturesque village at the top of the steep side of the Lathkill valley. A typical rural settlement of the limestone plateau, it was at the centre of a gold rush in the 1850s when iron pyrites ('fools' gold') was found. The village is now visited by walkers as it lies on the **Lathkill Dale Trail** which

The Old Smithy

Chapel Hill, Beeley, Derbyshire DE4 2NR
Tel: 01629 734666

A newly opened village shop and licensed café, **The Old Smithy** is a charming and welcoming place to enjoy fresh food and drink amid very pleasant surroundings.

Located in the beautiful and unspoilt village of Beeley, on the magnificent Chatsworth estate, the shop and café can be reached by turning off the main A6 (Bakewell – Matlock Road) at Rowsley and taking the B6012 signposted for Baslow and Beeley. After three-quarters of a mile, turn right into Beeley village – by taking a left turn opposite the village pub, you'll find this excellent shop and café on your right.

The brainchild of Helen Grosvenor, who ran the village pub for many years before opening here in May of 2004, as its name tells us the buildings was once the village smithy, and parts of the premises date back to the 1600s. The shop is housed in the former smithy, while an extension to the rear is where the licensed café can be found. Both the shop and café specialise in the best that local agriculture has to offer.

The shop features local produce with an emphasis on delicious 'deli' foods – cheeses, meats, jams and more – and also stocks basic day-to-day items (if it's the morning paper you want, you'll find it here).

The café seats 40 inside with room in the garden and on the patio for a further 50. The décor and furnishing are classic country style with a clean, modern touch. It provides wholesome country foods all day – everything from hearty breakfasts through cream teas and light bites to main-course specials such as Cajun steak, lamb with herb mash and gravy and pork loin in an apple cream sauce. As a member of Peak District Cuisine, wherever possible all ingredients are sourced locally. The Sunday lunch is particularly popular and well worth sampling.

The café is also licensed to serve wines and beers with meals, or guests can enjoy just a drink and the relaxed, welcoming atmosphere.

The hospitality is second to none, and all guests are sure to appreciate the superb surroundings and quality food and drink on offer.

The shop is open every day from 8 a.m. until 7 p.m. The café is open from 9 a.m. to 7 p.m. (food served 9.30 to 6.30) daily. No smoking indoors. Children welcome.

follows the River Lathkill up the valley to beyond Monyash. Along the riverbank can be found many remains, some more hidden than others, of the area's lead mining industry. There is an old engine house at **Mandale Mine** that was built in 1847 and further upstream from the mine are the stone pillars of an aqueduct, built in 1840, which carried water down to the engine house. Downstream from the village is the first National Nature Reserve established in the Peak District in 1972. Set mainly in an ash and elm wood, the reserve is home to many varieties of shrubs.

Beeley

3 miles SE of Bakewell off the B6012

This is another estate village to the great Chatsworth House which lies to the north. However, although much of the village was built for the 6th Duke of Devonshire by Paxton, there are some older buildings here including an early 17th century Hall (now a private farm) with stone mullioned and transomed windows, and Beeley Hill Top, a gabled 16th century house. The parish **Church of St Anne** is an inspirational sight, especially in the spring when the tree-lined churchyard is filled with daffodils. It has a Norman south door and a squat, square tower, but was over-zealously 'restored' by the Victorians.

To the west of Beeley a small road climbs up onto Beeley Moor and here, along a concessionary path from Hell Bank, can be found **Hob Hurst's House**. Local folklore tells that this was the home of a goblin but it is only one of 30 or so Bronze Age barrows, which lie up here amongst the heather.

Rowsley

4 miles SE of Bakewell off the A6

The older part of this small village, at the confluence of the Rivers Wye and Derwent, lies between the two rivers, while to the east is the 'railway village' around the former Midland railway station, now occupied by an engineering works. The two areas are quite distinct. The old part has gritstone cottages and farmhouses, while the newer part is clearly Victorian. The most impressive building in Rowsley is the Peacock Hotel. It was built in 1652 by John Stevenson, founder of the Lady Manners School in Bakewell, in 1636, and private secretary to Lady Manners, mother of the 8th Earl of Rutland. It is aptly named as above the entrance there is a carved stone peacock. It was at one time a dower house of Haddon Hall and the peacock is actually part of the family crest of the Manners family, whose descendants still live at nearby **Haddon Hall** (see page 51).

On the banks of the River Wye lies **Caudwell's Mill**, a unique Grade II listed historic roller flour mill. A mill has stood on this site for at least 400 years; the present mill was built in 1874, powered by water from the River Wye, and was run as a family business for over a century up until 1978. Since then the Mill has undergone extensive restoration

Rowsley Hall Farm

Rowsley, Matlock, Derbyshire DE4 2EG
Tel: 01629 732175
e-mail: rowsleyhallfarm@connectfree.co.uk
website:
www.smoothhound.co.uk/hotels/bakewell

Superb farmhouse bed and breakfast accommodation can be enjoyed at **Rowsley Hall Farm**, situated in Rowsley and a couple of hundred metres off the main A6, on the B6012. A 200-acre holding centred round a 300-year-old farmhouse, it is an idyll of rural tranquillity. There are two comfortable and welcoming ensuite guest bedrooms, available all year round. Each has its own private entrance; both are spacious and attractively decorated and furnished.

An outstanding breakfast awaits guests – leave plenty of time to enjoy the hearty cooked dishes and to choose from among the splendid array of home-made jams and breads, home-produced honey and freshly-laid eggs. A paradise for walkers, Rowsley also makes an ideal base from which to explore Chatsworth House, Bakewell, Matlock Bath and the many other sights and attractions of the region. Fishing on the local rivers can also be arranged. Children welcome. No smoking. Ample parking and good-quality restaurants and pubs nearby.

by a group of dedicated volunteers and, using machinery that was installed at the beginning of this century, the Mill is once again producing wholemeal flour. Other mill buildings on the site have been converted to house a variety of craft workshops, shops and a restaurant.

On Chatsworth Road near the terminus of the Peak Rail line, **Peak Village** is an extensive factory outlet shopping centre offering a range of ladies' and mens' fashion, sports and outdoor wear, home furnishings, jewellery, toys and books, and eateries. Also on-site is the charming **Toys of Yesteryear** exhibition and collectors shop. The impressive displays feature many rare and unique exhibits including an original Steiff model, made in the German Factory around 1970, and thought to be the only one of its kind in the UK. Thousands of toys dating from the 1920s can be seen from dolls and teddies, games and comic annuals, to tinplate, clockwork and battery models. A replica of a toy shop as it would have been in the1950s is a real delight and toys both old and new are on sale.

Matlock

Much of the southeastern Peakland area around Matlock lies outside the boundaries of the National Park, but the towns, villages and much of the surrounding countryside has plenty of the typical Peak District characteristics. Matlock and its various satellite settlements provide the focus and, after a period of decline, this essentially Victorian town is, once again, a busy and bustling place with plenty to offer the visitor as well as some fine views over the Lower Derwent Valley from its well planned vantage points.

Matlock lies right on the divide between the gritstone of the Dark Peak and the limestone of the White Peak. Though the hilltops are often windswept and bleak, the numerous dales, cut deep into the limestone, provide a lush and green haven for all manner of wild and plant life. Several of the rivers are famous for their trout, particularly the Lathkill, which was greatly favoured by the keen angler and writer Sir Izaak Walton.

Matlock is a bustling town nestling in the lower valley of the River Derwent, and is the administrative centre of Derbyshire as well as being a busy tourist centre bordering the Peak District National Park. There are actually eight Matlocks which make up the town, along with several other hamlets. Most have simply been engulfed and have lost their identity as the town grew, but **Matlock Bath**, the site of the spa, still maintains some individuality.

Matlock itself is famed as, at one time, having the steepest gradient (a 1-in-5½) tramway in the world; it was also the only tram system in the Peak District. Opened in 1893, the tramcars ran until 1927 and the Depot can still be seen at the top of Bank Street. The old

Peak Rail

Matlock Station, Matlock,
Derbyshire DE4 3NA
Tel: 01629 580381 Fax: 01629 760645
e-mail: peakrail@peakrail.co.uk
website: www.peakrail.co.uk

A great day out for families, rail enthusiasts and anyone with an interest in or appreciation for the great days of steam, **Peak Rail** runs through some of the most scenic countryside in the nation. Run by a dedicated band of volunteers since 1987, this charming railway boasts several vintage steam engines and coaches. Each stop along the line offers excellent diversions and points of interest, from the bookshop at Matlock to the teashop at Darley Dale and picnic area and Peak Village Shopping Outlet at Rowsley South, where you will also find a large collection of company and privately-owned rolling stock. At Rowsley South can also be found Parkside Station, home of the Derbyshire Dales two-foot narrow-gauge railway. By the end of 2005 the line will have been extended to run from Rowsley South Station right into Matlock Station.

Special events are held throughout the year, and include Santa and Steam Specials, the Halloween Ghost Train, Diesel Mania weekends and 'the Warring Forties', when the unique atmosphere and spirit of the 1940s is re-created by a team of re-enactors in period clothing and a collection of wartime, military and vintage vehicles, memorabilia, music and more. There are also regular real ale-and-supper evenings, transport festivals and much more.

The gracious Palatine Restaurant Car is just the place to enjoy delicious food in two lovingly restored coaches with waitress service and a fully licensed bar.

In addition to all this, Peak Rail is happy to cater for children's parties and group bookings. And for those who are avid steam fans, 'the Footplate Experience' offers the opportunity to realise every childhood ambition to drive and fire a real steam engine, with one- and two-hour courses available January to November.

Please see the Rail's excellent website for more details of everything this excellent line has to offer.

View over Matlock

telephone for details. The full journey (one way) takes just 20 minutes, and passengers can alight to enjoy the picnic area at the entrance to Rowsley South Station, or the exhibition coach at Darley Dale platform (please ring for opening times) to learn about the history of the reopening of the line. The restaurant car offers Saturday evening meals, Sunday lunches and afternoon teas. Special events are held throughout the year, and engine-driving courses can be taken - the perfect gift for the steam enthusiast! As the countryside drifts by at a lovely pace, the journey in every way allows passengers to re-live the golden age of steam.

Ticket Office and Waiting Room at Matlock station have been taken over by the Peak Rail Society and here can be found not only their shop, but also exhibitions explaining the history and aims of the society. The Peak Rail has its southernmost terminus just a few minutes walk from the mainline station.

Peak Rail (see panel opposite) is a rebuilt, refurbished and now preserved railway running between Matlock Riverside station (just a five-minute walk from the mainline station at Matlock) through the charming rural station of Darley Dale to the terminus Rowsley South. In future it is hoped that the line can be extended to Bakewell. Run entirely by volunteers, this lovely old steam train operates on different days throughout the year - please

Inside Matlock's **Church of St Giles** can be seen the faded and preserved funeral garlands or 'virgin crants' that were once common all over Derbyshire. Bell-shaped, decorated with rosettes and ribbons and usually containing a personal item, the garlands were made in memory of a deceased young girl of the parish. At her funeral the garland was carried by the dead girl's friends and, after the service, it would be suspended

The Duke William

91 Church Street, Matlock,
Derbyshire DE4 3BZ
Tel/Fax: 01629 582585
e-mail:
dukewilliam@matlock91.wanadoo.co.uk

Found just over a mile from the centre of Matlock, heading towards Starkholmes, **The Duke William** is a fine old, stone building enjoying an elevated position. Dating back to 1737, this former coaching inn lies in the oldest part of town, opposite the original village green, and there is also a lovely footpath that leads to Matlock Bath. The inn is also handy for sights and attractions such as the Heights of Abraham, Gulliver's Kingdom, Peak Rail, Cromford Mill, Lea Gardens and Chatsworth House.

This friendly establishment has Peter and Louise Groves at the helm, ably assisted by mum and dad Margaret and Alan. Peter and Louise have been here for nearly four years, having previously run a restaurant in the area.

The bar serves four real ales – Marstons Pedigree, Marstons Bitter, Old Empire and a changing guest ale – together with a good selection of lagers, cider, stout, wines, spirits and soft drinks.

Open at every session, food is served 12–2 and 6–9 in summer. Carvery 12-3 & 6-9 on Sundays, with a regular printed selection supplemented by numerous daily specials, updated daily. Everything is prepared using the freshest of ingredients and offers excellent value for money. It is worth leaving room for a pudding, with the toffee apple crumble being among the many mouth-watering options.

The cosy, traditional interior provides a separate no-smoking restaurant area, and meals can be taken in any part of the pub. Children are welcome and, in warmer weather, can make use of the outdoor play area.

A small caravan and camping site to the rear of the pub provides room for up to five of each. There are showers and toilet facilities – and meals can, of course, be enjoyed at the pub.

from the church rafters above the pew she had normally occupied.

High up on the hill behind the town is the brooding ruin of **Riber Castle**. The castle was built between 1862 and 1868 and is often linked with the McCaig folly which overlooks Oban on the west coast of Scotland. The castle's creator, John Smedley, a local hosiery manufacturer who became interested in the hydropathic qualities of Matlock, drew up the designs for the building himself. Lavishly decorated inside, Smedley constructed his own gas-producing plant to provide lighting for the Castle and it even had its own well.

Following the death of first Smedley and then his wife, the castle was sold and for a number of years it was a boys' school. During the Second World War, the school having closed, the castle was used as a food store before it was left to become a ruined shell.

A fairly new attraction to the area is Matlock Farm Park, set in 600 acres of working farm and providing a great day out for all the family. The Park is home to a wide variety of animals including llamas, donkeys and peacocks which children can feed.

To the west of Matlock, down a no-through road, can be found one of Derbyshire's few Grade I listed buildings, the secluded and well-hidden **Snitterton Hall**. Little is known of the history of this fine Elizabethan manor house, though it is believed to have been built by John Milward in 1631, around the same time that he purchased half the manor of Snitterton.

On the once busy old road between Matlock and Cromford, in an area once known as Starkholmes, The White Lion Inn was formerly called The Buddles Inn, after the habit of locals who would sit in the barn adjacent and 'buddle' - the old word for washing lead.

North of Matlock

Darley Dale

2 miles NW of Matlock off the A6

The charming name for this straggling village along the main road north from Matlock dates only from the 19th century, and was either devised by the commercially-minded railway company at work in the area or by the romantically-inclined vicar of the parish. Darley Dale makes up one of three stops on the Matlock-to-Rowsley South Peak Rail line.

One of the most unassuming heroines of this part of Derbyshire must be Lady Mary Louisa Whitworth. She was the second wife of Sir Joseph Whitworth, the famous Victorian engineer whose name is associated with the Great Exhibition of 1851 and who also invented the screw thread. Sir Joseph made a fortune manufacturing, amongst other items, machine tools, munitions and nuts and bolts. Following his death in 1887, Lady Mary undertook to bring sweeping changes to the lifestyle of the local poor and needy. She allowed the grounds of her home, Stancliffe Hall, to be used for school outings and events. In 1889, the Whitworth Cottage Hospital was opened under her auspices.

The **Whitworth Institute** was opened in 1890, bringing to the community a wide range of facilities including a swimming pool, an assembly hall, a natural history museum and a library. At a time when a woman was required to take a secondary role in society, Lady Mary was determined to credit her late husband with these changes, which so benefited Darley Dale. Lady Whitworth died in France in 1896, and is buried next to her husband at the parish Church of St Helen, in the hamlet of Churchtown. The churchyard is also home to the **Darley Yew**, one of the oldest living trees in Britain which has a girth of some 33 feet. The yew predates the Norman origins of the Church and may be older than the Saxon fragments found here earlier this century. St Helen's church dates from the 12th century and contains two fine examples of Burne-Jones stained glass windows.

Much of the stone used for building in the village came from nearby Stancliffe Quarry, which also supplied stone for the Thames Embankment and Hyde Park Corner in London and the Walker Art Gallery in Liverpool. To the north of the 15th century Darley Bridge, which carries the road to Winster over the River Derwent, are the remains of **Mill Close Mine**. This was the largest and most productive lead mine in Derbyshire until 1938, when flooding caused it to be abandoned.

Darley Dale has an extensive park which is very pretty in all seasons. Another of this small village's attractions is **Red House Stables**, a working carriage museum featuring some fine examples of traditional horse-drawn vehicles and equipment. One of the finest collections in the country, it consists of nearly 40 carriages, including one of the very few surviving Hansom cabs, a stage coach, Royal Mail coach, Park Drag and many other private and commercial vehicles. Carriage rides are available, making regular trips through the countryside to places such as Chatsworth and Haddon Hall, and the carriages and horses can be hired for special occasions.

Stanton in Peak

5 miles NW of Matlock off the B5056

This is a typical Peak District village, with numerous alleyways and courtyards off its main street. A quick glance at the village cottages and the visitor will soon notice the initials WPT that appear above most of the doorways. The initials are those of William Paul Thornhill, the owner of Stanton Hall, which stands near the church and is still home to his descendents. There are some fine 17th and 18th century cottages, one of which has some of its windows still blocked since the window tax of 1697. The village pub, The Flying Childers, is named after one of the 4th Duke of Devonshire's most successful racehorses.

The gritstone landscape of **Stanton**

Moor, which rises to some 1,096 feet and overlooks the village, is encircled by footpaths and is a popular walking area. There are also several interesting features on the moorland. The folly, **Earl Grey's Tower**, was built in 1832 to commemorate the reform of Parliament. There is also an ancient stone circle dating from the Bronze Age and with over 70 burial mounds. Known as the **Nine Ladies**, the stone circle has a solitary boulder nearby called the King's Stone. Legend has it that one Sunday nine women and a fiddler came up onto the moor to dance and, for their act of sacrilege, they were turned to stone.

The nearby **Rowtor Rocks** contain caves, which were carved out at some stage in the 17th century. Not only was the living space made from the rock but tables, chairs and alcoves were also made to create a cosy retreat for the local vicar, Rev Thomas Eyre. Prior to these home improvements, the caves were reputedly used by the Druids, who did not believe in such creature comforts.

Alport

5½ miles NW of Matlock off the B5056

This is an ancient village, much older than its delightful houses of the 17th to 19th centuries would at first suggest. Considered by many one of Derbyshire's prettiest villages, it stands at the confluence of the Bradford and Lathkill Rivers. The Lathkill cascades down through the village in a series of weirs to meet the Bradford coming down from Youlgreave. Named after the portway road which ran through the settlement, the Saxon inhabitants added the prefix 'al', which itself means old.

The surrounding countryside, a lead mining area, was owned by the Duke of Rutland and, by the end of the 18th century, the industry was running into problems. In order to prevent the mines filling up with water, the Duke had a 4½ mile sough (underground drainage canal) built to run the water off into the River Derwent. Begun in 1766, this project took 21 years to complete and, in an attempt to recover some of the construction costs, a levy was put on any ore being taken from below a certain level.

Sometime after completion of the project, in 1881, the **River Bradford** disappeared underground for several years. As with other rivers in this limestone landscape, the river had channelled a route out underground, only this time the River Bradford was taking the route of the sough to the River Derwent. After sealing the chasm through which the river had joined up with Hillcar Sough, it was restored to the above-ground landscape.

Among Alport's many fine houses, **Monk's Hall** (private) is one of the best, dating from the late 16th or early 17th century and probably, at one time, was connected to a monastic grange. Another is **Harthill Hall Farm**, a gabled 17th century yeoman's farmhouse with stone mullioned and transomed windows.

The Old Dairy & Buttermilk Cottage

Cold Well End, Youlgreave,
Derbyshire DE45 1WB
Tel/Fax: 01433 630040
Mobile: 07814 301400
e-mail: pattitwose@compuserve.com

Here in Youlgreave, some six miles northwest of Matlock off the B5056, **The Old Dairy & Buttermilk Cottage** offer superb self-catering accommodation. A former small-holding with shippons and barns that date back in parts to the very early 1700s, one cottage was the former living rooms and dairy of the farmstead, while the other was part of the former shippons (cowhouses). These classic stonebuilt buildings are picturesque and cosy, where guests can enjoy a tranquil and truly relaxing break.

The Old Dairy sleeps between four and five in two double rooms and the dining room can comfortably seat 10 people. Buttermilk Cottage sleeps five and offers off-road parking. The cottages have been refurbished over the years to a very high standard, yet retain their traditional cosiness and look, with original features including exposed beamwork, flagstone floors and more. Supremely welcoming and comfortable, both have excellent facilities and amenities, with everything needed for a pleasant, relaxing and memorable stay. Both feature a wealth of wood, attractive décor and soft furnishings, and fully-fitted kitchens.

Patti Twose has owned the properties since 2000, and offers all her guests a warm welcome and genuine hospitality.

Both cottages are available all year round. Breaks for three days or longer are available out of season; please ring for details of in-season availability. The cottages make an excellent place to use as a base while touring the sights of this historic and scenic region, including great walking in the surrounding Lathkill Dale, fishing in the River Lathkill, the market towns of Bakewell and Matlock, the nearby Peak Rail, Heights of Abraham and Wildlife Park, and the Bath Hydro, model railway, Peak District Mining Museum and Temple Mine, and aquarium at Matlock Bath.

Youlgreave

6 miles NW of Matlock off the B5056

This straggling village, known locally as Pommey, lies in Bradford Dale. Once one of the centres of the Derbyshire lead mining industry, fluorspar and calcite are still extracted from some of the old mines. The village **Church of All Saints,** one of the most beautiful churches in Derbyshire, contains some parts of the original Saxon building though its ancient font is, unfortunately, upturned and used as a sundial. Inside, the working font is Norman and still retains its stoop for holding the Holy Water. It is well worth taking the time to have a look at, as it is the only such font in England. The Church also contains a small tomb with an equally small alabaster effigy; dated 1488, it is a memorial to Thomas Cockayne, who was killed in a brawl when only in his teens. A fine alabaster panel in the north aisle, dated 1492, depicts the virgin with Robert Gylbert, his wife and seventeen children. There is a glorious Burne-Jones stained glass window, which was added in 1870, when Norman Shaw very sensitively restored the church.

Further up the village's main street is **Thimble Hall**, the smallest market hall in the Peak District and still used for selling goods today. Typical of the White Peak area of Derbyshire the Hall dates from 1656 and there are also some rather grand Georgian houses to be found in the village. Nearby the old shop built in 1887 for the local Co-operative Society is now a youth hostel. It featured in the film of DH Lawrence's *the Virgin and the gypsy*, much of which was filmed in the village. Standing opposite is the **Conduit Head**, a gritstone water tank that has the unofficial name of The Fountain. Built by the village's own water company in 1826, it supplied fresh soft water to all those who paid an annual fee of sixpence. In celebration of their new, clean water supply, the villagers held their first well-dressing in 1829. Today, Youlgreave dresses its wells for the Saturday nearest to St John the Baptist's Day (24th June). Such is the standard of the work that the villagers, all amateurs,

Well Dressing, Youlgreave

are in great demand for advice and help.

The origin of the local name for Youlgreave is not known, but some say that it got this unusual name after a pig joined the village band and was heard playing 'Pom pom pom' down the village street. However colourful this derivation, the name more likely stems from the time of the Napoleonic Wars when French prisoners were brought to the area to work.

The Rivers Lathkill and Bradford are almost unique in Britain in that they both flow entirely through limestone country and their water quality, while being able to support crayfish, is also responsible for the formation of the unusual mineral tufa. **Lathkill Dale**, which can really only be experienced by walking along the path by the banks of the quiet river, is noted for its solitude and, consequently, there is an abundance of wildlife in and around the riverbank meadows. The upper valley is a National Nature Reserve; those who are lucky enough may even spot a kingfisher or two. One of the country's purest rivers, the Lathkill is famed for the range of aquatic life that it supports as well as being a popular trout river. Renowned for many centuries, it was Izaak Walton who said of the Lathkill, back in 1676, 'the purest and most transparent stream that I ever yet saw, either at home or abroad; and breeds, 'tis said, the reddest and best Trouts in England.'

Two or three miles to the west of the village is **Arbor Low**, sometimes been referred to as the 'Stonehenge of the Peak District'. About 250 feet in diameter, the central plateau is encircled by a ditch, which lies within a high circular bank. On the plateau is a stone circle of limestone blocks, with a group of four stones in the centre cove. There are a total of 40 stones each weighing no less than 8 tonnes. Probably used as an observatory and also a festival site. It is not known whether the stones, which have been placed in pairs, ever stood upright, although there is no archaeological evidence to suggest that they did. Gaps in the outer bank, to the northwest and southeast could have been entrances and exits for religious ceremonies. Arbor Low dates to the Neolithic or Early Bronze Age period, and there is much evidence in the dales along the River Lathkill that they were inhabited in the Bronze Age. Nearby there is a large barrow known as Gib Hill, which stands at around 16 feet. When it was excavated a stone cist was discovered, containing a clay urn and burned human bones. This circular mound to the south of the stone circle, offers some protection against the weather and it is from this that Arbor Low got its name – 'sheltered heap'.

The Danes also occupied land here and their legacy is the name Lathkill, a Norse word meaning 'narrow valley with a barn'. For several centuries the valley was alive with the lead mining industry that was a mainstay of the economy of much of northern Derbyshire, and any walk along the riverbanks will reveal remains from those workings as well as from limestone quarries.

Middleton by Youlgreave

7 miles NW of Matlock off the A5012

Just outside this leafy village is **Lomberdale Hall**, once the home of Thomas Bateman, the 19th century archaeologist who was responsible for the excavation of some 500 barrows in the Peak District over a 20 year period - it is said that he managed to reveal four in one single day! Many of the artefacts he unearthed can be seen in Sheffield Museum. The village lies in the valley of the River Bradford, at the point where it becomes Middleton Dale, and is unusual among villages in this area of the Peak District in that it has a large number of trees.

Wensley

2½ miles W of Matlock off the B5057

There has not been a sudden leap into North Yorkshire - Derbyshire too has a Wensley and a Wensleydale, though the Derbyshire dale does not produce cheese. Lying just within the boundaries of the National Park, this quiet village does not feature on many tourist-favoured routes through the area, and as a result provides a peaceful and pleasant alternative to many other villages.

Wensley Dale can be easily accessed from the village and offers the opportunity for a charming walk. On the very edge of a limestone plateau, the valley is dry and its gently sloping grassed banks make a change from the dramatic limestone gorges nearby. Just down the Dale from Wensley is **Oker Hill**, the summit of which provides magnificent views over both Wensley and Darley Dale. Local legend has it that two brothers climbed the hill and each planted a tree before they separated to make their ways in the world. Only one of the two trees flourished, though it has been bent by the winds over the years. Wordsworth was so inspired by this evocative story that he wrote a poem about it.

Birchover

4 miles W of Matlock off the B5056

Birchover's main street meanders gently up from the unusual outcrops of **Rowtor Rocks** at the foot of the village, heading up towards neighbouring Stanton Moor. The name of this hillside village, which means 'birch-covered steep slope', describes it perfectly.

Birchover was once home to father-and-son amateur antiquarians J C and J P Heathcote, who systematically investigated the barrows and monuments on Stanton Moor and kept a detailed and fascinating private museum in the old village post office in the main street. The Heathcote collection is now in Sheffield's Weston Park Museum.

The strange Rocks of Rowtor, behind The Druid Inn, are said to have been used for Druidical rites. The Reverend

Thomas Eyre, who died in 1717, was fascinated by these rocks and built the strange collection of steps, rooms and seats which have been carved out of the gritstone rocks on the summit of the outcrop. It is said that the Reverend would take his friends there to admire the view across the valley below - a view, which nowadays is obscured by trees. Prehistoric cup-and-ring marks have been discovered on the rocks and several rocking stones can be moved by the application of a shoulder. One of these, weighing about 50 tons, could once be rocked easily by hand, but in 1799 fourteen young men decided to remove it for a bit of a lark. However when they put it back, they couldn't get the balance right.

Thomas Eyre lived at the Old Vicarage in the village below Rowtor Rocks, and also built the lovely little church known as the Jesus Chapel or **Rowtor Chapel**. The chapel had been demoted to the village cheese shop before Eyre's restoration, and it now features, among fragments of Norman work, unusual carvings and some wonderful decorative features, including modern stained glass by the artist Brian Clarke, who lived at the vicarage for a time during the 1970s.

The equally strange outcrops of **Robin Hood's Stride** and **Cratcliff Tor** can be found nearby. A medieval hermit's cave, complete with crucifix, can be seen at the foot of Cratcliff Tor hidden behind an ancient yew tree.

Winster

4 miles W of Matlock off the B5056

This attractive gritstone village was once a lead mining centre and market town. Today, it is a pleasant place with antique shops in the high street and some fine late 18th century houses. Less splendid than the surrounding houses, but no less interesting, are the *ginnels* - little alleyways - which run off the main street. The most impressive building here, however, must be the **Market House**, owned by the National Trust and found at the top of the main street. The Trust's first purchase in Derbyshire, the rugged, two-storey Market House dates from the 17th and early 18th century and is an excellent reminder of Winster's past importance as a market town. Built from an attractive combination of brickwork and stone, the House is open to the public and acts as an information centre and shop for the Trust.

The **Ore House** at Winster is the best preserved ore house left in the Peak District. Up to 50 years ago miners used it to lodge lead ore in safety over night. It had a chute at the back for depositing the lead ore and a vaulted roof for security. The ore house has been preserved by the Peak Park Authority.

Winster Hall, built in 1628 by Francis Moore, has, like all good manor houses, its own ghost, which haunts the grounds. The ghost is said to be that of a daughter from the Hall, who fell in love with one of the coachmen. Her parents were horrified at her choice of husband and vowed to find a more suitable partner. However, before such a match could be made the girl and her lover climbed to the top of the Hall and jumped, together, to their deaths.

The annual Shrove Tuesday Pancake Race, from the Crown Inn to the Market House is a much-anticipated event that is taken seriously in the village. Small frying pans are issued to the men, women and children, it is an open event, and the pancakes are specially made with an emphasis on durability rather than taste.

Finally, although Morris dancing is traditionally associated with the Cotswold area, two of the best known and most often played tunes, The Winster Gallop and Blue-eyed Stranger, originate from the village. Collected many years ago by Cecil Sharpe, a legend in the world of Morris dancing, they were rediscovered in the 1960s. The Winster Morris men traditionally dance through the village at the beginning of Wakes Week, in June, finishing, as all good Morris dances do, at one of the local pubs.

Elton

5 miles W of Matlock off the B5056

Situated at over 900 feet above sea level, the village lies on a ridge where limestone meets gritstone. The contrast of the vegetation, the lime-loving flowers and ash trees on one side with a scattering of oak trees on the other, is very marked. The two very different stones can also be seen in the buildings of the village, some of limestone, some of gritstone, though many are built using a combination of the two materials. To the north of the village, on Harthill Moor, is **Castle Ring**, an Iron Age hill fort behind Harthill Moor Farm. The landscape is dominated by Robin Hood's Stride, a natural gritstone crag, which was thought to have been used for ancient fertility rites. At twilight it looks like a large house, giving it its alternative name, 'Mock Beggars Hall'. It is popular with visitors and rock climbers and is now covered with modern rock carvings and graffiti. Nearby to the north is the stone circle called **Nine Stone Close** or the Grey Ladies. It is the only circle in the Peak District that still has large standing stones although the stones are not on the same scale as those at Arbor Low. There were originally nine stones, but only four now remain. A fifth stone is now a gatepost in the wall to the south of the circle.

South of Matlock

Lea

4 miles SE of Matlock off the A615

This charming village is famous for its associations with Florence Nightingale, who spent many happy summers as a girl in nearby Holloway.

The building now home to **The Jug & Glass** in Lea was once a hospital for the employees of the Nightingale family, who resided at nearby Lea Hurst; it was perhaps here that Florence Nightingale discovered her vocation for tending the sick. The edifice dates back to 1782, though is older in some parts. **Lea Gardens** offer a rare collection of rhododendrons, azaleas, alpines and conifers in a superb woodland setting. This unique collection including kalmias and other plants of interest has been introduced from all over the world to this area in the heart of Derbyshire. The gardens provide a stunning visual display to enthral the whole family. Covering an area of some four acres, the site is set on the remains of a mediaeval millstone quarry and includes a lovely rock garden with dwarf conifers, alpines, heathers and spring bulbs. A mile of walks takes visitors through a blaze of spring colour.

Tansley

1 mile SE of Matlock off the A615

This tiny and picturesque village has an 18th century mill, Tansleywood Mill and some good 18th century houses including Knoll House with an impressive carved doorway. It is well worth a visit by keen gardeners for its four garden centres and two horticultural nurseries.

Holloway

4½ miles SE of Matlock off the A6

This tiny village has one famous daughter, Florence Nightingale, who lived here at **Lea Hurst**, a 17th century gabled farmhouse. Named after the Italian city where she was born in 1820, Florence was the second child of Edward William Shore, who later changed his name to Nightingale. Edward Nightingale began to alter and enlarge the house in 1825 and he also sold some land to Richard Arkwright so that he could build Willersley Castle, overlooking the River Derwent.

Florence's father left Lea Hurst to her in his will and, after her courageous work in the dreadful conditions of the Crimean War, she retired to the house and spent the next 50 years writing, specifically on the subject of hospital organisation. Florence died in London in 1910 and the house remained in the family until 1940. Still in private hands, Lea Hurst is occasionally opened to the public.

Matlock Bath

1 mile S of Matlock off the A6

It is not known whether the Romans discovered the hot springs here, but by the late 17th century the waters were being used for medicinal purposes and the Old Bath Hotel was built. Like many other spa towns up and down the country, it was not until the Regency period that Matlock Bath reached its peak. As well as offering cures for many of the ills of the day, Matlock Bath and the surrounding area had much to offer the visitor and, by 1818, it was being described as a favourite summer resort. The spa town was compared to Switzerland by Byron and it has also been much admired by the Scottish philosopher, Dr Thomas Chalmers, and Ruskin, who stayed at the New Bath Hotel in 1829. Many famous people have visited the town, including the young Victoria before she succeeded to the throne.

The coming of the railways, in 1849, brought Matlock Bath within easy reach, at small cost, to many more people and it became a popular destination for day excursions. Rather than being a town for the gentility, it became a place for the genteel. Today, it is still essentially a holiday resort and manages to posesses an air of Victorian charm left over from the days when the puritanical Victorians descended on the town looking for a 'cure'.

One of the great attractions of the town is **The Aquarium** (see panel below), which occupies what was once the old Matlock Bath Hydro that was established in 1833. The original splendour of the Bath Hydro can still be seen, in the fine stone staircase and also in the thermal large pool which now is without its roof. The pool, maintained at a constant temperature of 68 degrees Fahrenheit, was where the rheumatic patients would come to immerse themselves in the waters and relieve their symptoms. Today the pool is home to a large collection of Large Mirror, Common and Koi carp, while the upstairs consulting rooms now house tanks full of native, tropical and marine fish.

Matlock Bath Aquarium

110 North Parade, Matlock Bath,
Derbyshire DE4 3NS
Tel: 01629 583624 Fax: 01629 760793

All the attractions are set in a lovely Victorian building which was formerly the Matlock Bath Hydro, dating back to 1883. Reminders of its former splendour can be seen in the fine stone staircase, the drinking fountain and huge iron girders spanning the thermal pool.

The pool is fed by a spring from the hillside gushing 600,000 gallons a day, at a constant temperature of 20°C. This is where patients would immerse themselves in the pool or take the waters to relieve rheumatic ailments and improve digestive disorders.

Today, the health giving properties of the water are enjoyed by the famous collection of Large Mirror, Common and Koi Carp, weighing over 30 lbs. Visitors are welcome to feed the fish with food obtainable from the Aquarium.

The former Victorian consulting rooms are now home to the Aquarium containing a selection of British and Tropical freshwater species - Piranhas to Terrapins as well as many interesting fish from different regions of the world including the beautiful Malawi Cichlids.

Almost forgotten now, even in Matlock Bath where several Wells were once visited by thousands of Victorian trippers is the Petrifying Well. Here you can come and see the 'petrifying' process taking place in our working well as the famous Matlock Bath thermal water is sprayed onto objects gradually turning them to stone.

Matlock Bath

Down by the riverbank and housed in the old Pavilion can be found the **Peak District Mining Museum and Temple Mine**, the only one of its kind in the world. Opened in 1978 and run by the Peak District Mines Historical Society, the Museum tells the story of lead mining in the surrounding area from as far back as Roman times to the 20th century. As well as the more usual displays of artefacts and implements used by the miners over the years, one of the Museum's most popular features are the climbing shafts and tunnels which allow the whole family to get a real feel for the life of a working lead miner. The Museum also houses a huge engine, dating from 1819, which was recovered from a mine near Winster. A unique survivor in Britain, the engine used water instead of steam to provide it with pressure. Adjacent to the Museum can be found the restored workings of Temple Mine.

Being a relatively new town, Matlock Bath has no ancient place of worship, but the Church of the Holy Trinity is a fine early Victorian building which was added to in 1873 to accommodate the growing congregation. Of greater architectural merit is, however, the **Chapel of St John the Baptist**, found on the road between Matlock and Matlock Bath. Built in 1897, it was designed to be a chapel-of-ease for those finding it difficult to attend St Giles' in Matlock, but it also became a place of worship for those who preferred a High Church service.

Though on the edge of the splendid countryside of the Peak District National Park, Matlock Bath is surrounded by equally beautiful scenery. Found in the Victorian Railway Station buildings is the **Whistlestop Countryside Centre**, which aims to inform and educate the public on the wildlife of the county as well as manage wildlife conservation. Set up by the Derbyshire Wildlife Trust and run by volunteers, the Centre has an interesting and informative exhibition and a gift shop, and the staff are qualified to lead a range of environmental activities.

For spectacular views of Matlock Bath, nothing beats a walk on **High Tor Grounds**. There are 60 acres of nature trails to wander around, while some 400 feet below, the River Derwent appears like a silver thread through the gorge. A popular viewing point for Victorian visitors to the town, today rock climbers practise their skills climbing the precipitous crags of the Tor. For those a little less energetic, a relatively steady walk to the top is amply rewarded by the magnificent views over the town and surrounding area.

On the opposite side of the valley are the beautiful wooded slopes of Masson Hill, the southern face of which has become known as the **Heights of Abraham** (see panel on page 94); this particular name was chosen after the inhabitants of Matlock had shown great enthusiasm for General Wolfe's victory in Quebec, this part of the Derwent valley being seen to resemble the gorge of the St Lawrence River and the original Heights of Abraham lying a mile north of Quebec. Today it is a well-known viewing point, reached on foot or, more easily, by cable car. The Heights of Abraham have a long history. For many years the slope was mined for lead but, in 1780, it was first developed as a Pleasure Garden and since then trees and shrubs have been planted to make it a pleasing attraction for those visiting the town to take the waters. In 1812, the **Great Rutland Show Cavern**, on the slope, was opened to the public, a new experience for tourists of the time, and it was visited by many including the Grand Duke Michael of Russia and Princess Victoria. Following this success, in 1844, the **Great Masson Cavern** was opened and construction of the **Victoria Prospect Tower** was begun. Built by redundant lead miners, the Tower became a new landmark for the area and today still provides a bird's eye view over Derbyshire. The Heights of Abraham are today as popular as ever and provide all the amenities of a good country park.

To the south of the town centre is a model village with a difference; **Gulliver's Kingdom** theme park makes a great day out for all the family. Set on the side of a wooded hill, each terrace is individually themed with styles including Fantasy Land, the Old Wild West and the Royal Mine ride. There are plenty of fun rides, a monorail, water slides and other diversions, as well as a café and restaurant.

Life in a Lens is a museum of popular photography set in a beautiful renovated Victorian house. Displays include cameras of all ages, toy and novelty

Heights of Abraham

Matlock Bath, Derbyshire DE4 3PD
Tel 01629 582365 Fax 01629 580279
e-mail: enquiries@h-of-a.co.uk
website: www.heights-of-abraham.co.uk

Featuring steep rocky gorges, vast cavems, fast running rivers, wide panoramic views and a cable car, it is easy to understand why the Victorian's called Matlock Bath "Little Switzerland"; however, the **Heights of Abraham Country Park and Caverns** overlooks the famous spa town, and provides a unique aspect to a day out or holiday in the Derbyshire Dales and Peak District.

The journey to the summit of the country park is easily made by taking the cable car adjacent to Matlock Bath railway station and car park. The cable car ticket includes all the attractions in the grounds, as well as the two spectacular underground caverns. Tours throughout the day allow you to experience the exciting underground world within the hillside, with the "miner's tale' in the Great Rutland Cavern Nestus Mine, and the multivision presentation of the "story in the rock" at the Masson Cavern Pavilion.

The sixty acre country park also features woodland walks, the Owl Maze, the Explorers Challenge, play and picnic areas, Victoria Prospect Tower, plus the High Falls Rocks & Fossils Shop featuring Ichthyosaur remains. When you have worked up an appetite, why not relax with a drink on the terrace and take in the views, or enjoy a snack in the Coffee Shop or a meal in the Woodlanders Restaurant. So next time you are planning a trip to the mountains, remember The Heights of Abraham at Matlock Bath "Little Switzerland" is nearer than you think.

cameras, carte-de visite, postcards and much more.

Matlock Bath's Illumination and Venetian Nights are held annually from the end of August to the end of October.

Cromford

2 miles S of Matlock off the A5012

Cromford is a model village known the world over, which was developed by Richard Arkwright into one of the first industrial towns. In addition to housing, he also provided his workers with a market place and a village Lock-Up. Born in Lancashire in 1732, Arkwright was the inventor of the waterframe, a machine for spinning cotton that was powered by water. He built his first mill at Cromford in 1771, the project taking a further 20 years to complete. It was the world's first successful water-powered cotton spinning mill. The area he had chosen proved to be perfect: the River Derwent, described by Daniel Defoe as 'a fury of a river', provided an ample power supply; there was an unorganised but very willing workforce, as the lead mining industry was experiencing a decline, and probably most importantly, Cromford was away from the prying eyes of Arkwright's competitors. In 1792, Arkwright commissioned the building of the village church, where he now lies. The Mill proved to be a great success and became the model for others both in Britain and abroad, earning Arkwright the accolade 'Father of the Factory System'. His pioneering work and contributions to the great Industrial Age resulted in a knighthood in 1786, and one year later he became High Sheriff of Derbyshire. **Cromford Mill** and the associated buildings are now an International World Heritage site. Tours of the mill and Cromford village are available throughout the year. Continuing refurbishment and conservation by The Arkwright Society, who bought the site in 1979, ensures that future visitors will be able to follow the fascinating history behind this pioneering establishment. It is sponsored by Derbyshire County Council and the Derbyshire Dales District Council. Within the complex of the mill site there are a range of craft workshops and also the Mill Restaurant with its excellent home-cooked refreshment including a wide selection of wholefood dishes.

Cromford has a rather odd 15th century bridge, which has rounded arches on one side and pointed arches on the other. It was from this bridge, in 1697, so local folklore has it, that a horse and rider took a flying leap from the parapet, plunged into the river 20 feet below and lived to tell the tale. The **Cromford Venture Centre** is an ideal base for study visits, holidays, training and self-development courses. It offers self-catering accommodation for parties of up to 24 young people and four staff. It is run by the Arkwright Sociey in association with the Prince's Trust.

For lovers of waterways, there is an opportunity at **Cromford Canal** to wander along the five-mile stretch of towpath to Ambergate. At the **Cromford Wharf Steam Museum** the exhibits include the 1902 Robey horizontal engine donated by Friden Brickworks from nearby Hartington. The Museum is open by arrangement for private steamings and working demonstrations. The old **Leawood Pumping Station**, which transferred water from the River Derwent to the Cromford Canal, has been fully restored. Inside, the engine house is a preserved Cornish-type beam engine which is occasionally steamed up. Close by the Pump House is the **Wigwell Aqueduct**, which carries the Canal high over the River Derwent.

The **High Peak Trail**, which

Leawood Pumping Station, Cromford Canal

stretches some 17 miles up to Dowlow near Buxton, starts at Cromford and follows the trackbed of the Cromford and High Peak Railway. First opened in 1880, the railway was built to connect the Cromford Canal with the Peak Forest Canal and is somewhat reminiscent of a canal as it has long level sections interspersed with sharp inclines (instead of locks) and many of the stations are known as wharfs. After walking the trail it is not surprising to learn that its chief engineer was really a canal builder! The railway was finally closed in 1967; the old stations are now car parks and picnic areas; there is an information office in the former Hartington station signal box. Surfaced with clinker rather than limestone, the trail is suitable for walkers, cyclists and horses.

Bonsall

2 miles SW of Matlock off the A5012

In a steep-sided dale beneath Masson Hill, Bonsall was once a famous lead mining centre and many of the fields and meadows around are still littered with the remains of the miners' work. This typical Peak District village has some fine 17th century limestone cottages clustered around its ball-topped 17th century cross. This is encircled by 13 gritstone steps in the steeply sloping market square. It is also one of the Derbyshire villages which continues the tradition of well-dressing, usually on the last Saturday in July.

Beside the market square cross stands The King's Head inn, dating from the late 17th century and said to be haunted. Another pub in the village reflects the traditional occupations of its residents, as it is called the Barley Mow. Another was called the Pig of Lead but is now a private residence. Above the village centre stands the battlemented parish church of **St James**, with its distinguished pinnacled tower and spire. Built mostly in the 1200s, it has a wonderful clerestory lighting the nave. The Baptist Chapel dates from 1824. From one end of the main street, the road climbs up some 400 feet to the Upper Town which lies just below the rim of the limestone plateau. In order to cope with the steep hill, the village church is split-level.

Bonsall Brook, the power source for many of the textile mills in the village, also supplied power to the original Viyella mill, built in the 1790s by Philip Gell of Hopton Hall. Soon after building the mill, Gell constructed a road from his lead mines in Grangemill to the smelting house at Cromford. Called **Via Gellia** (and in the 19th century known locally as Via Jelly) it was the name of this road, which ran close to the mill, that was adapted to 'Viyella' by the owners of the former Hollin Mill when they invented a new brand of hosiery.

Middleton by Wirksworth

4 miles SW of Matlock off the A5012

Just to the north of the village, which is also known as Middleton, lies the **Good Luck Mine**, which is now a lead mining museum. Usually open the first Sunday in the month, this old mine, found in the Via Gellia Valley, is typically narrow and, in places, the roof is low. Not a place for the claustrophobic, it does, however, give an excellent impression of a lead mine. The village also has another mine, where a particularly rare form of limestone is quarried. Hopton Wood Marble from here has been used in Westminster Abbey, York Minster and the Houses of Parliament.

Lying close to the Cromford and High Peak Railway, there was a particularly steep incline near the village, so steep in fact, that, as in other places, a steam engine was required to haul the wagon and carriages up the slope. **Middleton Top Winding Engine**, to the west of the village, can be easily picked out as the engine house has a distinctive tall chimney.

Wirksworth

4 miles S of Matlock off the B5023

Nestling in the lush green foothills of the Peak District where north meets south, Wirksworth is home to a distinctive **Heritage Centre** (see panel on page 98), housed in a former silk mill, which takes visitors through time from the Romans in Wirksworth to the present day. Quarrying, lead mining and local customs such as clypping the church (a ceremony in which the parish church is encircled by the congregation holding hands around it) and well-dressing are explored with interactive and fascinating exhibits. One of the town's most interesting sights is the jumble of cottages linked by a maze of tiny lanes on the hillside between The Dale and Greenhill, in particular the area known locally as 'The Puzzle Gardens'. Babington House dates back to Jacobean Wirksworth. Another former lead merchant's house, **Hopkinsons House**, was restored in 1980 as part of a number of restoration schemes initiated by the Civic Trust's 'Wirksworth Project'. The ancient **Parish Church of St Mary's** is a fine building standing in a tranquil close and

Wirksworth Heritage Centre

Crown Yard, Wirksworth,
Derbyshire DE4 4ET
Tel: 01629 825225
e-mail: heritage@gilkin.demon.co.uk
website: www.gilkin.demon.co.uk

A visit to the **Wirksworth Heritage Centre** will take you on a journey of discovery from the Romans in Wirksworth to the present day. Housed in a former silk mill, the mysteries of the town's ancient lead mining industry are unveiled and you can pit your wits against the computer and rescue the injured lead miner or enter the Dream Cave and imagine how it felt to discover the remains of the prehistoric Woolly Rhino! Discover the local customs of clypping the Church and well dressing. The towns links with quarrying are also well represented here with a re-creation of a quarrymans house in which he describes life in the early 1900s. Learn about the regeneration of this historic market town, with its George Eliot connections and enjoy some wonderful views of Wirksworth from the windows. The Crown Yard Kitchen, a licensed restaurant, offers a full range of meals and drinks.

bounded by Elizabethan 'Gell Almshouses' and the former (Georgian) grammar school. The church holds one of the oldest stone carvings in the country: known as the Wirksworth Stone, it is a coffin lid dating from the 8th century.

Wirksworth's well-dressing takes place during the last few days of May/first week of June.

The **National Stone Centre** tells 'the story of stone', with a wealth of exhibits, activities such as gem-panning and fossil-casting, and outdoor trails tailored to introduce topics such as the geology, ecology and history of the dramatic Peak District landscape. Nearby, the **Steeple Grange Light Railway Society** runs along a short line over the High Peak Trail between Steeplehouse Station and Dark Lane Quarry at weekends between May and September. The former quarry is now overgrown with shrubs, trees and a profusion of wildflowers and birds. Power is provided by a battery-electric locomotive; passengers are carried in a manrider salvaged from Bevercotes Colliery in Nottinghamshire. Meanwhile, dedicated volunteers for the **Ecclesbourne Light Valley Railway Association** maintain and run a line of track and rolling stock from Wirksworth to Duffield.

At **North End Mills**, visitors are able to witness hosiery being made as it has been for over half a century; a special viewing area offers an insight into some of the items on sale in the Factory Shop.

Carsington Water just outside Wirksworth is one of Britain's newest reservoirs. This 741-acre expanse of water is a beauty spot that has attracted well over a million visitors a year since it was opened by Queen Elizabeth in

1992. It can be reached on foot from Wirksworth along a series of footpaths and aims to be disabled friendly with wheelchairs available and access to as many attractions as possible. Sailing, windsurfing, fishing and canoeing can be enjoyed here, as well as just quiet strolls or bike rides. The Visitor Centre on the west bank offers visitors the opportunity to learn about Severn Trent Water and all aspects of water supply. An impressive exhibit in the courtyard is the Kugel Stone, a massive ball of granite weighing over 1 tonne, which revolves on a thin film of water under pressure. It can be moved with a touch of the hand! Some half a million trees and shrubs have been planted and are managed to attract wildlife and to enhance the landscape. There are two bird hides and a wildlife centre to help visitors understand the variety of wildlife and observe the birdlife that visits the reservoir. The reservoir is stocked for fishing either from the bank or boats available for hire. There is a large adventure playground and numerous open spaces for families to relax.

PLACES TO STAY, EAT AND DRINK

The Coach & Horses, Ashbourne, Derbyshire	45	Pub, Food & Accommodation	p104
Gallery Café, Ashbourne, Derbyshire	46	Café	p106
The Shire Horse, Wyaston, Derbyshire	47	Pub with Food	p107
The Shoulder of Mutton, Osmaston, Derbyshire	48	Pub with Food	p108
The Red Lion, Kniveton, Derbyshire	49	Pub with Food	p110
The Bluebell Inn, Tissington, Derbyshire	50	Pub with Restaurant	p114
Bent Farm, Tissington, Derbyshire	51	B&B	p115
Bassett Wood Farm, Tissington, Derbyshire	52	B&B and Tea Rooms	p116
The Peveril of the Peak, Thorpe, Derbyshire	53	Hotel	p120
Leehouse Farm, Waterhouses, Derbyshire	54	B&B	p123
The Watts Russell Arms, Alstonefield, Derbyshire	55	Pub with Food	p124
The Red Lion Inn, Waterhouses, Derbyshire	56	Pub with Food	p125
The Royal Oak Hotel, Mayfield, Derbyshire	57	Pub, Food & Accommodation	p130
Home Farm Cottages, Wootton, Derbyshire	58	Self Catering	p131

Denotes entries in other chapters

3 Dovedale and the Staffordshire Moorlands

This area of Derbyshire, which includes a southern section of the Peak District, is probably best known for the beautiful Dovedale. The large car park near Thorpe which gives general access to the Dale is often crowded, but there is plenty of room for everyone and the wonderful valley, just a few hundred yards from the car park, is well worth experiencing. It is also the place to have a go at crossing a river on stepping stones, something that has delighted children for many, many years, though there is a bridge just downstream, which ensures that the crossing can be made with dry feet, particularly when the water level is high.

The River Dove is also a mecca for keen fishermen. A favourite spot for Izaak Walton, who wrote his famous book, *The Compleat Angler*, that was first published in 1653, and his influence is impossible to escape. An old farmhouse, at the head of the Dale, was converted, many years ago, into the well-known and much-loved Izaak Walton Hotel.

Dovedale is not the only dale worth exploring. The River Manifold offers some equally wonderful scenery and, in

PLACES TO STAY, EAT AND DRINK

● Denotes entries in other chapters

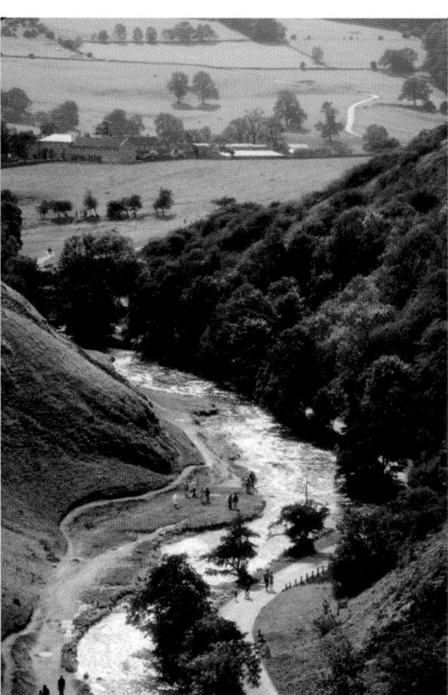

Dovedale

spring was of utmost importance. If this dried up, the lives of the whole community were at risk. There are plenty of theories as to why well-dressing began or was revived at Tissington. One centres on the purity of the Tissington wells during the Black Death, which swept through the country in the mid-1300s. During this time some 77 of the 100 clergy in Derbyshire died and the surviving villagers simply returned to the pagan custom of well-dressing. Another plausible theory dates back only as far as the great drought of 1615, when the Tissington wells kept flowing though water everywhere was in very short supply. Whichever theory is true, one thing is certain, that in the last 50 years or so many villages who had not dressed a well for centuries, if ever, are now joining in the colourful

particular, there is Ilam. A beautifully preserved estate village, with a well established youth hostel, this is also a popular starting point from which to explore the Manifold Valley.

The ancient custom of well-dressing is almost exclusively confined to the limestone areas of the county. The porous rock, through which rainfall seeped leaving the surface completely dry just a few hours after heavy rainfall, meant that, for the people of these close knit communities, the well or

Thors Cave, Manifold Valley

tradition.

On the southern edge of the Peak District, the Staffordshire Moorlands certainly rival their neighbour in terms of scenic attraction. The undulating pastures of the moorlands, along with the fresh air and ancient weather-worn crags, make this the ideal place to walk, cycle or trek. It is also an area full of character, with charming scattered villages, historic market towns and a wealth of history, and many of the farms and buildings date back hundreds of years. The Industrial Revolution also left its mark on the landscape, though the two great reservoirs of Rudyard and Tittesworth, built to provide a water supply to the growing industry and population of the Midlands, now offer peaceful havens for a wide variety of plants, animals and birds as well as recreational facilities such as fishing and boating.

View over Ashbourne

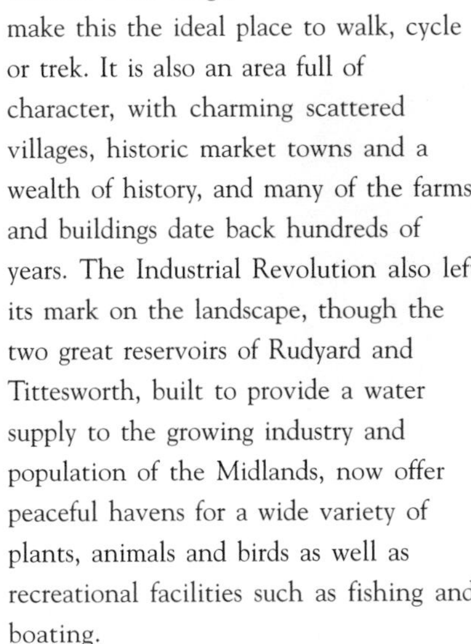

Ashbourne

Ashbourne featured in the *Domesday Book* as 'Essiburn', derived from the local stream with its many ash trees. It was originally a small settlement lying on the northern bank of Henmore Brook, which already had a church. It was a 13th century lord of the manor who laid out the new town to the east around its unusual shaped market place. Many of the town's traders, in order to continue to enjoy the benefits without paying the town's tolls, built themselves houses on the south side of the Brook. The area became known as Compton and it was slowly absorbed into the town. When writing *Adam Bede*, George Eliot based 'Oakbourne' in 'Stonyshire' on the town.

Often called The Gateway to the North, Ashbourne lies on the boundary of the old red sandstone of southern Derbyshire and the limestone which surrounds Dovedale and the White Peak. It is one of Derbyshire's finest old towns, with a wealth of wonderful Georgian architecture. It is a pleasure to visit, with plenty of shop-filled streets to potter up and down. The triangular cobbled **Market Square**, in the heart of Ashbourne, was part of the new development begun in the 13th century that shifted the town to the east, away from the Church. Weekly markets have

THE COACH & HORSES

27 Dig Street, Ashbourne,
Derbyshire DE6 1GF
Tel: 01335 345491
e-mail: georgedelphe@aol.com

The Coach & Horses is a welcoming and impressive inn in the heart of Ashbourne.

The leaseholders, George and Delphe, have many years' experience and bring a wealth of enthusiasm and professionalism to the task – providing top-quality food, drink and accommodation for all their guests.

The interior is a tasteful mix of traditional and modern, with a wealth of wood panelling, exposed beam work and a large games room with pool table. Outside there's a large beer garden – perfect for enjoying a relaxing pint or meal on fine days.

Open all day, every day for ale, the regulars are Bass and Marstons Pedigree, together with the occasional guest ale and a good range of lagers, bitters, cider, stout, wines, spirits and soft drinks.

In the summer months food is available between midday and tea-time, when guests can choose off the menu or specials board from a selection of hot and cold dishes. The food is hearty and traditional, expertly prepared by Delphe using the freshest local ingredients available. At weekends entertainment takes the form of karaoke, a disco or live music; at Sunday lunchtime there's a meat draw.

The inn also boasts two attractive and comfortable ensuite guest bedrooms. The décor is tasteful and both rooms are kept in tip-top condition. One has a double and two single beds; the other has three single beds – thus the rooms can accommodate everyone from single visitors to families. The tariff include Delphe's outstanding breakfast (breakfast times are flexible).

The inn occupies an ideal position in the centre of Ashbourne, handy for touring the Peak District, Derbyshire Dales, Staffordshire moorlands and the many sights, attractions, stately homes and pursuits such as walking and cycling available in the area.

The Gingerbread Shop, Ashbourne

been held in the square since 1296, and now take place every Saturday. It was from this market place, that used to be lined with ale houses, that Bonnie Prince Charlie proclaimed his father to be King James III, at the height of the Jacobite Rebellion of 1745. Though the old bull ring no longer exists, the town boasts many fine examples of 18th century architecture as well as some much older buildings, notably the **Gingerbread Shop** which is timber framed and probably dates from the 15th century. Traditional Ashbourne gingerbread is said to be made from a recipe that was acquired from French prisoners of war who were kept in the town during the Napoleonic Wars.

Also worthy of a second glance is the **Green Man and Black's Head Royal Hotel**. The inn sign stretches over the St John's Street and was put up when the Blackamoor Inn joined with the Green Man in 1825. Though the Blackamoor is no more, the sign remains and it claims to be the longest hotel name in the country. Of Georgian origin, the amalgamated Hotel has played host to James Boswell, Dr Johnson and the young Princess Victoria. Ashbourne was, in fact, one of Dr Johnson's favourite places; he came to the town on several occasions between 1737 and 1784. He also visited the hotel so often that he had his own chair with his name on it! The chair can still be seen at the Green Man.

A stroll down Church Street, described by Pevsner as one of the finest streets in Derbyshire, takes the walker past many interesting Georgian houses - including the Grey House, which stands next to the **Grammar School**. Founded by Sir Thomas Cockayne on behalf of Elizabeth I in 1585, the school was visited on its 400th anniversary by the present Queen. Almost opposite the Grey House is **The Mansion**, the late 17th century home of the Reverend Dr John Taylor, oldest friend of Dr Johnson. In 1764, a domed, octagonal drawing room was added to the house, and a new brick façade built facing the street. Next to The Mansion are two of the many almshouses established in Ashbourne during the 17th and 18th centuries.

Gallery Café

50 St John Street, Ashbourne,
Derbyshire DE6 1GH
Tel: 01335 347425
e-mail: sjsg@aol.com
website: www.sjsg.co.uk

In the heart of historic Ashbourne you will find two wonderful establishments under one roof : On the ground floor is The St John Street Gallery which showcases contemporary fine arts and crafts – paintings, sculpture, glass, ceramics, jewellery and much more. Upstairs, you will find the **Gallery Café**, which is open Tuesday to Saturday (10am – 5pm). Here you will be served with a range of delicious home-cooked meals and snacks, including a good selection of vegetarian dishes.

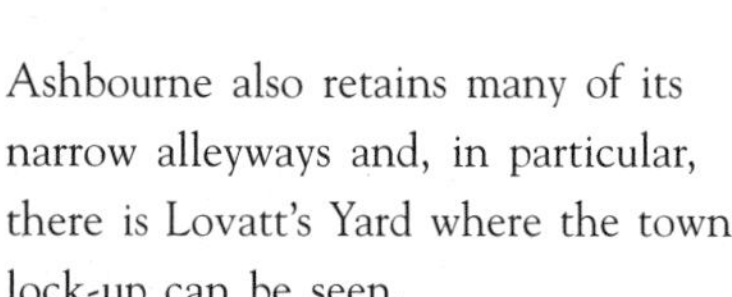

Ashbourne also retains many of its narrow alleyways and, in particular, there is Lovatt's Yard where the town lock-up can be seen.

In **St Oswald's Parish Church** Ashbourne has one of the most impressive and elegant churches in the country, described by George Eliot as 'the finest mere parish church in England'. James Boswell said that the church was 'one of the largest and most luminous that I have seen in any town of the same size'. St Oswald's stands on the site of a minster church mentioned in the *Domesday Book*, though most of what stands today dates from rebuilding work in the 13th century. There is a dedication brass in the south transept dated 1241. The south doorway, with its dog-toothed decoration and ribbed moulding, reflects the church's classic Early English style. St Oswald's has chapels to its transepts, adding to the spacious feeling that is more reminiscent of a small cathedral than a parish church.

The alabaster tombs and monuments to the Bradbourne and Cockane families in the north transept chapel are justly famous. Perhaps the best-known monument is that to Penelope Boothby, who died in 1791 at the tender age of five. Thomas Banks' white Carrara marble figure of the sleeping child is so life like that she still appears to be only sleeping. The moving epitaph reads: 'She was in form and intellect most exquisite; The unfortunate parents ventured their all on this frail bark, and the wreck was total.' It is said that Penelope's parents separated at the child's grave and never spoke to each other again. The tower and gracious 212-feet spire of the church were erected between 1330 and 1350, at the crossing of the nave and transepts.

Ashbourne is home, too, to the famous Shrovetide football game played on Shrove Tuesday and Ash Wednesday. The two teams, the 'Up'ards' (those born

The Shire Horse

Edlaston, Wyaston, Ashbourne,
Derbyshire DE6 2DQ
Tel/Fax: 01335 342714

The Shire Horse is an excellent village inn. Brothers Simon and David and their wives Julie and Fiona took over in September of 2003 – Simon has been a chef for over 20 years – and together they have made this inn a special place to visit. Picture-postcard inside and out, the setting is unbeatable and the cuisine out of this world.

Originally called The New Inn, parts of the premises date back to the 18th century. The village smithy once stood next door.

Food is not served on Mondays but the inn is open for fine food and drink at every other session. The three ales served are Bass, Marstons Pedigree and a changing guest ale. Meals are served at lunch Tuesday to Saturday (12 – 2) and dinner Monday to Saturday (7 – 9); on Sundays the hours are 12 – 2.00 and 7 – 8.30 Easter-September. Booking is advised at all times and is essential for Sunday lunch at this justly popular place. Char-grilled steaks are just one of Simon's specialities amid a comprehensive menu and specials list featuring everything from wild boar to sea bass.

north of the Henmore Brook) and the 'Down'ards' (those born south of it) begin their match at 2 p.m. behind the Green Man Hotel. The game continues until well into the evening. The two goals are situated three miles apart, along the Brook, on the site of the old mills at Clifton and Sturston. It is rare for more than one goal to be scored in this slow-moving game.

South and East of Ashbourne

Yeldersley

3 miles SE of Ashbourne off the A52

Yeldersley has long been the home of gentlemen farmers and those who love the countryside. This picturesque village offers many scenic delights. **Yeldersley Hall** is a spacious country house, which was built in 1760.

Osmaston

2½ miles SE of Ashbourne off the A52

Osmaston is a sleepy, beautiful village just five minutes' drive from Ashbourne. Neither crowded nor bustling, it offers the visitor a real haven of tranquility. It is the archtypical English village, with thatched cottages, village green, village pond, pub and church! It was originally an estate village built in the 19th century to house the workers at the

The Shoulder of Mutton

Osmaston, Ashbourne, Derbyshire DE6 1LW
Tel/Fax: 01335 342371
e-mail:
shoulderofmutton.osmaston@barbox.net

Found in the centre of the village, **The Shoulder of Mutton** is a charming inn personally run by Paul and Tina since 1993. The pub occupies a unique position in the hearts and affections of locals and visitors alike. All but five properties in the whole of Osmaston village are owned by the Walker Okeover Estate (important local country landowners). A date stone from 1805 is the only extant proof of the pub's origins, all other records having accidentally been destroyed by fire, but the pub is known to date back much further than this. Recent refurbishment includes an extension to the lounge towards the lovely garden, to increase its spaciousness and relaxed ambience. The atmosphere at this traditional and cosy inn is always warm and welcoming.

Open all day in summer, food is available from midday until 2 and from 7 to 9 p.m. daily. Snacks and cream teas are served at other times. Meals can be taken in either the comfortable lounge, bar or outside in the very picturesque beer garden. Guests choose from the specials board from a range of delicious meals and snacks, including Whitby breaded scampi, home-made steak-and-kidney pie, lasagne, cheese and broccoli bake and home-made beef curry. The Sunday roasts are particularly popular. The choice of ales include Bass and Marstons Pedigree as well as keg beers and milds, lagers, cider, wines, spirits and soft drinks.

The pub also offers outside bars and caters for any required function.

Paul and Tina also run the Village Post Office based at the pub. The Office is open Monday/Tuesday/ Thursday 9am-Midday and Friday 2pm-5pm.

Butterly Iron Works. The manor house, Osmaston Manor, was built in 1849 for Francis Wright, the owner of the ironworks, and was demolished in 1964. The estate at Osmaston today is the location for the annual Osmaston Horse Trials and the Ashbourne Shire Horse Show.

Bradley

3 miles E of Ashbourne off the A517

A regular visitor to the Georgian Bradley Hall (private) was Dr Johnson, who would visit the Meynell family here when he was staying in Ashbourne with his friend, Dr John Taylor. The Meynells had come to Bradley in 1655 and bought the hall from Sir Andrew Kniveton, who had been financially ruined by the Civil War.

Opposite the hall stands the **Church of All Saints**, which is interesting in having a bell turret but no tower on its 14th century nave and chancel. The original wooden bell tower was struck by lightning. There are several memorials to the Meynell family in the church. The base and part of the shaft of a Saxon cross stand in the churchyard. The archway crossing the formerly gated road between cottages at Moorend is known locally as 'The Hole in the Wall'. The former village pub had the distinction, common in Derbyshire, of two official names, The Jinglers and the Fox and Hounds. Nearby **Bradley Wood** was given to the people of Ashbourne in 1935 by Captain Fitzherbert Wright.

Kirk Ireton

6 miles NE of Ashbourne off the A517

Kirk Ireton is a picturesque village, much of it built from locally quarried gritstone. In the hills near Carsington Reservoir it sits at 700 feet above sea level. Much of the village is 17th century and one of the oldest buildings is the Barley Mow Inn. When decimalization was introduced in 1971, the 87-year-old landlady refused to accept the new money. The Barley Mow was one of the last places in the country to go decimal.

Kniveton

3 miles NE of Ashbourne off the B5035

This tiny village of grey stone houses, surrounding the small church lies close to Carsington Reservoir, sheltered in a dip in the hills. Its little church of St Michael has a 13th century tower, a Norman doorway, a 13th century font, small lancet windows, battlements and a short spire. The medieval glass in the chancel depicts the arms of the family of Kniveton. Sir Andrew Kniveton became so impoverished through his loyalty to Charles the First that he had to sell most of the family estates. A huge sycamore tree and an ancient yew stand in the churchyard. The yew has grooves in its bark, said to have been made by archers sharpening their arrows.

Just north of the village is the Bronze Age burial mound at Wigber Low which

The Red Lion

Main Street, Kniveton, Ashbourne,
Derbyshire DE6 1JH
Tel: 01335 345554

The Red Lion in Kniveton is a quite outstanding, picture-postcard inn located on the B5035 (Wirksworth-to-Ashbourne Road). Dating back to the early 1700s, this traditional coaching inn is an impressive place offering great food, well-kept ale and superb hospitality.

Jay and Sue have been leaseholders here since 2003, and have a great success on their hands thanks to their hard work and commitment to offering first-rate service and a warm welcome to all their guests.

The interior is very attractive, with a handsome stonebuilt bar, open fires, exposed beamwork and traditional (no-smoking) dining room.

There are two real ales to sample – Bass and Black Sheep – together with a good variety of draught keg ales, lagers, cider, stout, wines, spirits and soft drinks.

Tasty food is served at lunch and dinner every day; guests choose from the menus or specials board from a good range of delicious dishes in hearty portions. Booking is advised on Friday, Saturday and Sunday at this justly popular inn.

has revealed some important remains from the village's past.

Hognaston

4 miles NE of Ashbourne off the B5035

The picturesque village of Hognaston stands on a hillside overlooked by Hognaston Winn, which rises to 1,000 feet. It has been in existence for at least 1000 years and there is evidence of medieval field structures, where long demolished houses once stood. It used to be a busy place in coaching days when the London to Manchester coaches passed through the village. St Bartholomew's Church, dating back to the 12th century, has some extraordinary Norman carvings over the doorway and an early Norman font. Two of the bells date back to the 13th century. The clock and three of the other bells were a gift from John Smith and Sons, the famous Derby clock-makers as a memorial to John Smith who lived in the village. The village lies close to **Carsington Water**, Britain's newest reservoir, owned by Severn Trent Water. Opened by the Queen in 1992, the reservoir has already blended well with the local countryside. Unlike many of the Peak District reservoirs, which draw their water from the acid moorland, Carsington is different and the lake and surrounding area is able to support a whole host of wildlife. One controversial resident is the American ruddy duck. Once unknown outside wildlife reserves, the duck escaped and, in little over 50 years, the breed has become widespread throughout Europe.

Set in eight acres of picturesque grounds overlooking Carsington Water is the famous **Knockerdown Inn**. The property dates back to the 17th century, and opened as a beerhouse in 1838, when it was known officially as The Greyhound but was given the affectionate name 'The Nock'. The famous stagecoach 'The Devonshire' used to call here en route from Wirksworth to Ashbourne.

Hopton

8 miles NE of Ashbourne off the B5035

This village, now by- passed by the main road, is dominated by the Carsington Water Reservoir. The land rises to the north of Hopton and here can be found the **Hopton Incline**, once the steepest railway incline in the British Isles. Lying on the **High Peak Railway** line, carriages were hauled up using fixed engines on their journey from Cromford to Whaley Bridge. It is now part of the High Peak Trail.

Until 1989 **Hopton Hall** was the home of the Gell family and in particular, the home of Philip Gell the owner of the Viyella mill at Cromford. Though the actual date of the original building is unknown, the Gell family have been known to have lived in the area since 1208 and they have held the manor of Hopton since the 15th century. The Gell family made their fortune in the nearby limestone quarries and they also were responsible for the construction of the Via Gellia, a road which runs along a valley to the west of Cromford.

Bradbourne

4 miles NE of Ashbourne off the A5056

This is an ancient village, standing high on a ridge between the valleys of Bradbourne Brook and Havenhill Dale. Even at the time of the recording of the *Domesday Book* its name, Bradeburne (meaning broad stream) was well established. For more than 300 years the monks at Dunstable Priory grazed their sheep on the land round Bradbourne, and also supplied vicars to the parish Church of All Saints. Essentially Norman, but with some fragments of Saxon work - especially on the north side of the nave where typical long-and-short work is visible - the church is surrounded by its hilltop churchyard which contains not only the remains of a Saxon cross, dated approx 800AD, but also a scene of the crucifixion. Originally the shaft would have been topped with a cross. The cross would be set up to mark a place, where people gathered to worship. This one was found in use as a squeeze stile into a nearby field before being identified and placed in the churchyard. Also found in the churchyard is the grave of Nat Gould. Nat worked on his uncle's farm opposite the Church and by the time of his death in 1919 he had written 130 horse racing novels.

The church's large, unbuttressed west tower is Norman and has an elegantly decorated south door. Most of the rest of this appealing little church dates from the 14th century, but there are some fine modern furnishings which owe much to William Morris' Arts and Crafts movement. Some of the wall paintings date from the 17th and 18th centuries. While in the village it is also worth taking a look at the fine grey stone Elizabethen manor house Bradbourne Hall (private), with its three gables and beautiful terraced gardens. The Old Parsonage, which has a rather peculiar appearance as it was built in three completely different styles and materials, is also worthy of note.

Brassington

7 miles NE of Ashbourne off the B5056

This grey stone village, 800 feet above sea level and known to the locals as 'Brass'n', has its past firmly entrenched in the lead mining and quarrying traditions of this part of Derbyshire. The hollows and bumps in the green meadows tell of 200 years of underground industry in pursuit of lead, and now lead-tolerant flowers such as mountain pansy, sandwort and orchids flourish here.

Protected from the wind by the limestone plateau that soars some 1,000 feet above sea level, the village sits by strange shaped rocks, the result of weather erosion, with names like **Rainster Rocks** and **Harborough Rocks**. Stone Age man found snug dwellings amongst these formations and there is evidence that animals like the sabre-toothed tiger, brown bear, wolf and hyena also found comfort here in the caves. As late as the 18th century families were still living in the caves. Once standing on the main London to Manchester road, this was once a prosperous village and many of the 17th and 18th century cottages survive from those days. Today's post office used to be the tollhouse on the Loughborough to Brassington road, which became a turnpike in 1738; the Gate Inn stood next to the turnpike gate. Brassington's oldest 'resident' is a relief carving depicting a man with one hand over his heart, which can be seen inside the Norman tower of the parish church of **St James**. It may date back to Saxon times, but most of the rest of the church is Norman, heavily restored by the Victorians. Nearby is the Wesleyan Reform Chapel, one of the so-called 'Smedley Chapels' built by local millowner, Mr Smedley, in 1852. Smedley was a keen Revivalist and his two other chapels in the village are now the village hall and a private house respectively.

Ballidon

5 miles N of Ashbourne off the A515

Ballidon is an almost deserted village,

which, some 800 years ago, was a thriving community. All that can be seen today are four rather grand 17th century farms and the Norman Chapel of All Saints (much restored) standing isolated in a field surrounded by old crofts and tofts.

Overshadowed by its gigantic limestone quarry, the legacy of this tiny hamlet's days as a robust medieval village remain in the numerous earthworks, lynchets and evidence of ridge-and-furrow cultivation in its fields.

Aldwark

9 miles NE of Ashbourne off the B5035

Close to the High Peak Trail, just inside the Peak Park boundary, Aldwark is one of the most unspoilt villages in Derbyshire. A quiet and tranquil backwater the highest recorded population was 97 inhabitants in 1831, although there is evidence of earlier occupation. A chambered tomb was discovered at Green Low, just to the north of the village, which contained pottery, flints and animal bones dating from 2000 BC.

Fenny Bentley

2 miles N of Ashbourne off the A515

Fenny Bentley is the first village of the Peak for visitors coming from the South, with its steep hill up into the Peak District and the old railway bridge where the Tissington Trail passes through the village. The Tissington Trail is a 13-mile trail for walkers or cyclists from the old Ashbourne Station to The High Peak Trail at Parsley Hay.

Inside **St Edmund's Church** can be found the tomb of Thomas Beresford, the local lord of the manor who fought, alongside eight of his 16 sons, at Agincourt. The effigies of Beresford and his wife are surrounded by those of their 21 children - each covered by a shroud as, by the time the tombs were built nobody could remember what they had looked like! During the Civil War, much of the Church, and its rectory, were destroyed. On returning to his parish after the restoration of Charles II in 1661, the rector resolved to rebuild the rectory, which was all but rubble, and restore the Church to its former glory. Both of these he managed. The 15th century square tower of the fortified manor house, now incorporated into Cherry Orchard Farm, which belonged to the Beresford family and was once the home of Charles Cotton, is a local landmark that can be seen from the main road.

Tissington

4 miles N of Ashbourne off the A515

Sitting at the foothills of the Pennines, Tissington is, perhaps, most famous for its ancient festival of well-dressing, a ceremony which dates back to 1350, or earlier. Today this takes place in the middle of May and draws many crowds who come to see the spectacular folk art created by the local people. The

The Bluebell Inn & Restaurant

Buxton Road, Tissington, Ashbourne, Derbyshire DE6 1NH
Tel: 01335 350317 Fax: 01335 350103
e-mail: enquiries@bluebelltissington.co.uk
website: www.bluebelltissington.co.uk

Standing alongside the main A515 (Ashbourne-to-Buxton road) at Tissington, **The Bluebell Inn & Restaurant** is a quality establishment well known for its excellent food and ales.

Once part of the Tissington Estate, dating back some 400 years and more, this former farmhouse and associated farm buildings were converted into a pub in 1940 by the 3rd Baronet of Tissington, Sir Henry FitzHerbert.

Tenant Ruth Sampson has been here since 1994, and brings her experience and expertise to bear on running, with her husband Phil, this superior inn and restaurant.

The interior is handsome and traditional, with a wealth of polished wood, exposed beamwork and other original features.

Dishes carrying with the Peak District Cuisine logo indicate those made from food produced in the area. Most dishes are made fresh to order. Just a small sample from the extensive menu includes such tempting main courses as local Mayfield rainbow trout, salmon and dill fishcakes, Hartington chicken, giant Yorkshire pudding filled with 'boozy' beef casserole, Bakewell sausage and fried eggs, lamb shank, mixed grill, vegetarian pie and wild mushroom lasagne. The menus are designed to include people with special dietary needs, and to encourage children to eat more healthily. Delicious snacks like Bakewell burgers, open sandwiches, toasties and more, as well as delicious afternoon teas with a choice of a range of cakes and scones, are also available.

All the real ales available are supplied by the Hardy and Hansons Brewery, while there's also a good selection of lagers, wines, spirits and soft drinks – something to quench every thirst and accompany the excellent food.

Open midday until 11 p.m. Monday to Saturday, and midday until 10.30 p.m. on Sundays

During the lifetime of this edition, a self-catering cottage will be made available – please ring for details.

Cyclists on the Tissington Trail

significance of the event in Tissington may have been to commemorate those who survived the ravages of the Black Death when it raged throughout the villages of Derbyshire in the mid-1300s. During this time some 77 of the 100 clergy in Derbyshire died; the surviving villagers simply returned to the pagan custom of well-dressing. Another plausible theory dates back only as far as the great drought of 1615, when the Tissington wells kept flowing though water everywhere was in very short supply. Whichever theory is true, one thing is certain: in the last 50 years or so many villages that had not dressed a well for centuries, if ever, began to take part in this colourful tradition.

A total of six wells are dressed at Tissington, the Hall, the Town, the Yew Tree, the Hands, the Coffin and the Children's Wells; each depicts a separate scene, usually one from the Bible. Visitors should follow the signs in the village or ask at the Old Coach House.

Very much on the tourist route, particularly in the early summer, Tissington has plenty of tea rooms and ice cream shops to satisfy the hot and thirsty visitor. The village, though often overlooked in favour of the colourful well-dressings, has some interesting buildings. The **Church of St Mary**, situated on a rise overlooking

Tissington, has an unusual tub-shaped font, which dates back to the time of the original Norman Church. The pulpit too is unusual; converted from a double-decker type, it once had a set of steps leading out from the priest's stall below.

Home of the FitzHerbert family for 500 years, **Tissington Hall** is a distinguished and impressive stately home which was built by Francis FitzHerbert in 1609. The estate consists of 2,400 acres comprising 13 farms, 40 cottages and assorted lettings. The Hall boasts a wealth of original pieces, artwork, furnishings and architectural features tracing the times and tastes of the FitzHerbert family (now headed by Sir Richard FitzHerbert) over the centuries. The oak-panelled Main Hall has the original stone-flagged floor and is dominated by a stunning Gothic fireplace installed in 1757. Here visitors will also find a pair of late 18th century Chippendale bookcases, a rosewood piano and other fine pieces. The Dining Room, originally the old kitchen, is also panelled in oak and has an original Waring & Gillow table with a matching set of 13 chairs. The frieze work was added in the early 1900s. Paintings of country scenes and family portraits adorn the walls. The Library is a stunning repository of over 3,000 books, and is adorned with a superb frieze depicting a woodland scene. Other fine pieces include the bracket clock made by Jasper Taylor of Holborn in about 1907. Among the other wonderful rooms to

explore are the East and West Drawing Rooms. Tissington Hall and Gardens are open to the public on 28 afternoons throughout the summer. Please call the Estate Office for details. In addition, the gardens are open on several days for charity including the National Gardens Scheme. Private groups and societies are welcome by written appointment throughout the year. The refurbished Old Coach House on the estate now houses comfortable and attractive tea rooms, opened in September 1997, it overlooks the handsome village church.

Following the old Ashbourne to Parsley Hay railway line, the **Tissington Trail** is a popular walk which can be combined with other old railway trails in the area or country lanes to make an enjoyable circular country walk. The Tissington Trail passes through some lovely countryside and, with a reasonable surface, it is also popular with cyclists. Along the route can also be found many of the old railway line buildings and junction boxes and, in particular, the old Hartington station, which is now a picnic site with an information centre in the old signal box.

Parwich

5 miles N of Ashbourne off the A515

This typical Peak District village is delightful, with stone houses and an 1870s church around the village green. Conspicuous amongst the stonebuilt houses is **Parwich Hall**, constructed of brick and finished in 1747. The wonderful gardens at the Hall were created at the turn of the 20th century and it remains today a family home, though, over the years it has changed hands on several occasions.

Parwich Moor, above the village, is home to many mysterious Bronze Age circles, which vary in size. Though their function is unknown, it is unlikely that they were used as burial chambers. Close to Parwich is Roystone Grange, an important archaeological site where, to the north of the farmhouse, the remains of a Roman farmhouse have been excavated and, to the south, are an old engine house and the remains of the old medieval monastic grange. Both Roystone Grange and Parwich lie on the interesting and informative **Roystone Grange Archaeological Trail,** which starts at Minniglow car park. Some 11 miles long, the circular trail follows, in part, the old railway line that was built to connect the Cromford and the Peak Forest Canals in the 1820s before taking in some of the Tissington Trail.

Alsop-en-le-Dale

5 miles N of Ashbourne off the A515

The old station on the Ashbourne-Buxton line, which once served this tiny hamlet is today a car park on the Tissington Trail. The tranquil hamlet itself is on a narrow lane east of the main road towards Parwich, just a mile from Dovedale. Alsop-en-le-Dale's parish church of St Michael is Norman, though it was rebuilt substantially during

Victorian times. The nave retains Norman features, with impressive double zigzag mouldings in the arches, but the west tower is only imitation Norman, and dates from 1883. One unusual feature, which dominates this small church is its extraordinary 19th century square mock-Gothic pulpit.

Opposite the church is the graceful and slender building known as **Alsop Hall**, constructed in the early 1600s. Though privately owned, it is worth seeing even for its exterior, as it is built in a handsome pre-classical style with stone-mullioned windows.

Alsop makes a good base for exploring the White Peak. It is also convenient for Dovedale. The renowned **Viator's Bridge** at Milldale is only a mile away to the west, as immortalised in Izaak Walton's *The Compleat Angler* in a scene in which the character Viator complains to another about the size of the tiny, two-arched packhorse bridge, deeming it 'not two fingers broad'.

Newhaven

11 miles N of Ashbourne off the A5012

The High Peak Trail crosses Newhaven to link up with the Tissington Trail. This charming village is also along the White Peak tourist route, though it retains a tranquil air.

Arbor Low

13 miles N of Ashbourne off the A515

This remote **Stone Circle** is often referred to as the 'Stonehenge of the Peaks', and it is still an impressive sight. There are several stone circles in the Peak District but none offer the same atmosphere as Arbor Low, nor the same splendid views. Built around 4,000 years ago by the early Bronze Age people, there are a total of 40 stones, each weighing no fewer than 8 tonnes. Probably used as an observatory and also a festival site, it it likely that the stones, which have been placed in pairs, never actually stood upright.

Stone Circle, Arbor Low

Mappleton

2 miles NW of Ashbourne off the A515

Mappleton is a village that has existed in some form or other since before 1086, when it is recorded in the *Domesday Book*. It is a secluded and charming village of the Dove Valley, with attractive views and a wealth of exciting natural beauty. The 18th century village church of St Mary's is unusual in that it has a dome rather than a tower or a steeple. There has been a church here since at least the reign of Edward I.

Mappleton's main claim to fame is its annual New Year's Day charity bridge jump, when 10 teams of 3 people paddle down half a mile of the river Dove and then jump off a bridge. The Dove is not easily navigable, the bridge is 30 feet high and after the jump there is a 500-yard sprint to the pub. It is a grand spectator sport and hundreds of people come to watch!

Thorpe

3 miles NW of Ashbourne off the A515

Thorpe was mentioned in the *Domesday Book* and is one of the few villages in the Peak whose name has Norse origins, for the Danish settlers did not generally penetrate far into this area. It lies at the confluence of the Rivers Manifold and Dove, and is dominated by the conical hill of **Thorpe Cloud**, which guards the entrance to **Dovedale**. Cloud is a corruption of the Old English word 'clud', meaning hill. The summit is a short but stiff climb from any direction, but whichever way you go the climb is rewarded by a panoramic view over Dovedale all the way to Alstonefield as well as Ilam and the lower Manifold valley. Although the Dale becomes overcrowded at times, there is always plenty of open space to explore on the hill as well as excellent walking. For much of its 45-mile course from Axe Edge to its confluence with the River Trent, the **River Dove** is a walker's river as it is mostly inaccessible by car. The steep sides to its valley, the fast-flowing water and the magnificent white rock formations all give Dovedale a special charm. Dovedale, however, is only a short section of the valley; above Viator Bridge it becomes **Mill Dale** and further upstream again are **Wolfscote Dale** and **Beresford Dale**. The temptation to provide every possible amenity for visitors, at the expense of the scenery, has been avoided and the village of Thorpe, clustered around the church, remains an unspoilt and unsophisticated limestone village. The beautiful little church with a Norman tower, was built about 1100, with some Saxon work here and there. The nave was added in the 14th century, possibly replacing a Saxon construction, and a vestry in the 19th century. It has walls of limestone rubble which give the curious impression that the building is leaning outwards. If on horseback it is possible to read the curious sundial at the Church, but otherwise it is too high up! There is a fine tomb of the Millward family (1632) by the altar.

Close by the River Dove, not far from the village, is the 17th century farmhouse that has been sympathetically transformed into the Izaak Walton

The Peveril of the Peak

Thorpe, Dovedale, Ashbourne,
Derbyshire DE6 2AW
Tel: 01335 350396 Fax: 01335 350507
e-mail: frontdesk@peverilofthepeak.co.uk
website: www.peverilofthepeak.co.uk

Set in 11 acres of grounds, **The Peveril of the Peak** is a superlative hotel in the heart of Dovedale yet just 3 miles from Ashbourne and close to many popular sights and attractions such as Alton Towers, Matlock Bath, Carsington Water and Chatsworth House.

Taking its name from an historical novel by Sir Walter Scott, this three-star hotel, which dates back to the 1830s, offers 45 handsome and very comfortable rooms, delicious meals and attentive yet unobtrusive service. The staff are friendly and welcoming, and the atmosphere always relaxing.

Here amid the spectacular scenery of the Peak District National Park, guests enjoy the very best-quality accommodation. Twenty-three of the rooms are located on the ground floor, and families are welcome. Guests can stay on a room-only, bed-and-breakfast or dinner, bed-and-breakfast basis.

This licensed hotel is open to non-guests for drinks and food. The bar is stocked with real ales and a full range of wines, spirits, lager and soft drinks. The no-smoking restaurant features a comprehensive selection of tempting dishes, its first-rate chefs using the freshest ingredients to prepare an assortment of traditional favourites and innovative creations featuring roast beef, lamb, pork, chicken, turkey, fish, seafood and vegetarian choices. The restaurant is open daily to residents and non-residents from 12 – 2 and 7 – 9.30. Booking advised at all times.

Originally the local vicarage, this fine country hotel is a wonderful retreat, perfect for a weekend away or as a setting for family celebrations. Within the grounds there are tennis courts, mature gardens and car parking space for 80 vehicles. There's also good walking along the River Dove. Peace and tranquillity are the bywords here, and every guest is sure to receive the finest service and very best hospitality during a stay here.

The Stepping Stones, Dovedale

Hotel. The delights of trout fishing along this stretch of the river have been much written about, and most famously in *The Compleat Angler*, by Sir Izaak Walton. His fishing house, which he shared with his friend Charles Cotton, is preserved and can be seen in Beresford Dale. At this point along the river there is also a public car park, complete with other amenities useful to the walker and sightseer. A stroll up Dovedale from this point, as far as Milldale, will show the beauty of this stretch of valley to its fullest. The walking, along the river bank, is relatively easy (in many places wheelchairs will have no problem) but after a period of rain it can get quite muddy.

The Victorians delighted in visiting Dovedale, it was praised by such writers as Byron and Tennyson and soon became as popular as Switzerland. However, their enthusiasm for the Dale also had a down side and, as well as providing donkey rides up the Dale, in the late 19th century sycamore trees were planted along the sides of the Dale. Not native to this area, they overshadow the native ash and obscure many of the rock formations that make this such a special place. The National Trust are keeping the trees in check and encouraging the ash to grow. On higher, more windswept ground, the story would have been different as sycamore trees are ideal for providing a natural wind break.

The **Stepping Stones**, a delight for children, are the first point of interest, though for those who do not want to cross the river at this point there is a foot bridge closer to the carpark just below Thorpe Cloud. Further up the

Dale is the limestone crag known as **Dovedale Castle** and, on the opposite bank, the higher hill known as Lover's Leap after a failed lover's suicide. Other interesting natural features with romantic names found along the way include the Twelve Apostles and the Tissington Spires.

Ilam

4 miles NW of Ashbourne off the A52

The village was inhabited in Saxon times and the church still displays some Saxon stonework as well as the tomb of the Saxon saint, Bertram, who lived as a hermit in this area. Now a model village of great charm, Ilam was originally an important settlement belonging to Burton Abbey. Following the Reformation in the 16th century, the estate was broken up and Ilam came into the hands of the Port family. In the early 1800s the family sold the property to Jesse Watts Russell, a wealthy industrialist. He moved the village from its position near Ilam Hall and rebuilt it in its current location in 'Alpine style'. This explains both the unusual style of the buildings and the surprising distance between them and the village church. As well as building a fine mansion, **Ilam Hall**, for himself, Russell also spent a great deal of money refurbishing the village. Obviously devoted to his wife, he had the Hall rebuilt in a romantic Gothic style and, in the centre of the village, he had the Eleanor Cross erected in her memory. No longer a family home, Ilam Hall is now a Youth Hostel.

The ancient parish **Church of the Holy Cross**, with its saddleback tower, was largely rebuilt in 1855, and again the family are not forgotten as there is an enormous Watts Russell mausoleum dominating the north side. Opposite, on the south side, there is a little chapel which was rebuilt in 1618 and contains the shrine of a much-loved Staffordshire saint and local Saxon prince, Bertelin. The chapel became the object of many pilgrimages in medieval times. Another important Saxon item inside the church is the font in the nave while outside in the churchyard there are several Saxon cross shafts. As with many other churches in Derbyshire, it was the custom for garlands to be hung in the Church on the death of a young girl in the parish. The sad, faded 'virgin crants', referred to by Shakespeare at the death of Ophelia, can still be seen.

Many places in the Peak District have provided the inspiration for writers over the years and Ilam is no exception. The peace and quiet found here helped William Congreve create his bawdy play *The Old Bachelor*, while Dr Johnson wrote *Rasselas* while staying at the Hall. In the valley of the River Manifold, a much-used starting point for walks along this beautiful stretch of river, the Manifold disappears underground north of the village in summer, to reappear below Ilam Hall. The village is also the place where the Rivers Manifold and

Dove merge. Though Dovedale is, and probably deservedly so, the most scenic of the Peak District valleys, the Manifold Valley is very similar and while being marginally less beautiful it is often much less crowded. The two rivers rise close together, on Axe Edge, and for much of their course follow a parallel path, so it is fitting that they should also come together.

Waterhouses

6 miles NW of Ashbourne off the A523

Between here and Hulme End, the Leek and Manifold Valley Light Railway, a picturesque narrow-gauge line, used to follow the valleys of the Manifold and the Hamps, crisscrossing the latter on little bridges. Sadly, trains no longer run but its track bed has been made into the **Hamps-Manifold Track**, a marvellous walk which is ideal for small children and people in wheelchairs, since its surface is level and tarred throughout its eight miles. The Track can be reached from car parks at Hulme End, Waterhouses, Weags Bridge near Grindon, and Wetton.

The **River Hamps** is similar to the River Manifold and, indeed, other rivers which pass over limestone plateaux, in that it too disappears underground for some of its course. In the case of the Hamps, it disappears at Waterhouses and reappears again near Ilam before it merges with the River Manifold.

Waterfall

7 miles NW of Ashbourne off the A523

The tiny village of Waterfall is a small Staffordshire village, set on the moors, named after the way that the River Hemp disappears underground through crevices in the ground. It was once the starting point of the Manifold Valley Light Railway, a narrow gauge railway from the main Leek-Ashbourne railway line, via Wetton to Hume End. The line has since been removed and now the track is the Manifold Trail, a well used tourist trail for walkers and cyclists.

The Watts Russell Arms

Hopedale, Alstonefield, Ashbourne,
Derbyshire DE6 2GD
Tel: 01335 310126 Fax: 01335 310439
e-mail: corcellio@hotmail.com

Located on the border of Derbyshire and Staffordshire, **The Watts Russell Arms** is an impressive inn set in scenic Dovedale. The premises date back to 1780, and was at one time known as The New Inn. It took its current name from two local families, joined by marriage, who took it over and christened it with both their surnames.

Now owned by Chris and Bruce, who have been here since December of 2003, it's their first venture together into this type of business, though they have been in licensing and catering for some six years.

The interior boasts a wealth of exposed beams and a handsome brickbuilt fireplace. Outdoors there's a lovely and lush beer garden.

Closed Sunday evenings and all day Monday (except Bank Holidays), there are two real ales served here – Black Sheep and Timothy Taylor Landlord – together with the occasional guest ale.

Food is served at lunch (12–2) and dinner (7–9). Bruce does the cooking, creating a range of tempting and freshly prepared dishes. The menu is distinct from the usual pub fare. Bruce is originally from New York though he has lived in the UK for more than 40 years, and among his specialities are his New York-style salt beef dishes (with beef cured on the premises), beef and ale casserole and black pudding dishes. Equally good are other dishes from the menu and specials board at lunch, evening and Sundays, such as wheat pancake wraps filled with dressed crab, kabanos (smoked Continental sausage), peak pesto or Stilton dip, lasagne Americaine (covered with a creamy crab and brandy sauce), chicken livers, pan-fried salmon, vegetarian or beef Sunday lunch and more. The puddings include a range of Dovedale Dairy Farm ice creams.

No smoking area. Children welcome.

The Red Lion Inn

Townend Lane, Waterfall, Waterhouses,
Staffordshire ST10 3HZ
Tel: 01538 308279
e-mail: redlionwaterfall@btinternet.com
website: http://uk.geocities.com/
redlionwaterfall@btinternet.com

The Red Lion Inn enjoys an enviable location within the picturesque village of Waterfall on the edge of the Peak District National Park. Dating back to the late 19th century, the inn is constructed of local stone and is built into a small hill, which has led to the creation of an unusual terraced beer garden. Just a small place, it is very beautiful inside and boasts bags of traditional character. There are two cosy bars and a dining area.

Owners Brian and Kathleen Hunt have been here for three years, and have established a fine reputation for quality and service. Food is served evenings daily (7 – 8.30 p.m.) and weekends from midday to 2 p.m. Kathleen creates a delicious range of home-cooked dishes using the finest and freshest locally-sourced ingredients. Booking required for Sunday lunch. This Free House stocks two real ales as well as lagers, stout, scrumpy, wines, spirits and soft drinks.

The village church of **St James and St Bartholomew** is originally Norman but was largely rebuilt in the 19th century. However, the Norman Chancel has been retained.

Hopedale

7 miles NW of Ashbourne off the A515

Hopedale is a charming hamlet just south of Alstonefield. It was the site of one of the first co-operative cheese producing factories in the country, with cheese being produced from 1874. They made a Derby cheese, but eventually greater demand and improved methods of distribution led to the closure of this small co-operative.

Grindon

7 miles NW of Ashbourne off the B5053

This unique moorland hill village stands over 1,000 feet above sea level and overlooks the beautiful Manifold Valley. Recorded in the *Domesday Book* as Grendon, meaning green hill, 'an ancient manor in the 20th year of the reign of William the Conqueror', Grindon is reputed to have been visited by Bonnie Prince Charlie on his way to Derby. It was once a staging post on the packhorse route from Ecton Hill and the most productive copper mine in the country, where many of the local people would have worked.

The splendid isolation in which this village, like others nearby, stands is confirmed by a look around the churchyard. The names on the epitaphs and graves reflect the close knit nature of the communities. The Salt family, for instance, are to be seen everywhere, followed closely by the Stubbs, Cantrells, Hambletons and, to a lesser extent, the Mycocks. The church, with its soaring spire, dates only from the 19th century, but there has been a church here since at least the 11th century. Outside the church entrance there is a 'Rindle' stone. This records that: 'The Lord of the Manor of Grindon established his right to this rindle at Stafford Assizes on March 17th 1872'. A rindle is a brook which runs only in wet weather. In the church can also be found a memorial to six RAF men who were killed in 1947 when their Halifax aircraft crash-landed during a blizzard on Grindon Moor when trying to parachute in food packages to the surrounding villages, which had been totally cut off by the excessive snowfall.

Wetton

7 miles NW of Ashbourne off the B5053

Wetton Mill has been sympathetically converted by the National Trust into a café, a very welcome sight for those walking the **Manifold Valley Trail**. There is also a car park here for the less energetic and a picnic area for those who would rather cater for themselves. Much of the hillside either side of the track also belongs to the National Trust and is a splendid place for walks.

Below the Mill can be found the ominous-sounding **Thor's Cave**, situated some 250 feet above the River Manifold. Though the Cave is not deep, the entrance is huge, some 60 feet, and the stiff climb up is well worth the effort for the spectacular views, all framed by the great natural stone arch. The acoustics too are interesting, and conversations can easily be carried out with people far below. In the village churchyard is the grave of Samuel Carrington, who, along with Thomas Bateman of Youlgreave, found evidence that Thor's Cave was occupied in Iron Age times. The openings at the bottom of the crag on which the Cave sits are known as **Radcliffe Stables** and are said to have been used by a Jacobite as a hiding place after Bonnie Prince Charlie had retreated from Derby.

Carrington also excavated the fields close to Wetton, where he was schoolmaster in the mid 1800s, and found an abandoned village, though neither he nor his friend Bateman could put an age to the settlement.

Alstonefield

7 miles NW of Ashbourne off the A515

This ancient village, situated between the Manifold and the Dove valleys, lies at the crossroads of several old packhorse routes and even had its own market charter granted in 1308. The market ceased in 1500 but the annual cattle sales continued right up until the beginning of the 20th century.

Its geographical location has helped to maintain the charm of this unspoilt village. There has been no invasion by the canal or railway builders (it lies at 900 feet above sea level) and it is still two miles from the nearest classified road. One hundred and fifty years ago Alstonefield was at the centre of a huge parish which covered all the land between the two rivers. There has been a church here since, at least, AD 892 but the earliest known parts of the present Church are the Norman doorway and chancel arch of 1100. There is also plenty of 17th century woodwork and a double-decker pulpit dated 1637. Izaak Walton's friend, Charles Cotton, and his family lived at nearby Beresford Hall, now unfortunately no more, but their elaborate greenish pew is still in the church.

The village also retains its ancient **Tithe Barn**, found behind the late 16th century rectory. The internal exposed wattle and daub wall and the spiral stone staircase may, however, have been part of an earlier building.

Cottage at Alstonefield

Ecton

9½ miles NW of Ashbourne off the B5054

The tiny hamlet of Ecton, close to Hulme End, was once the site of great activity. The copper mines here were owned by the Duke of Devonshire and it is generally accepted that the profits from the ore extraction paid for his building of The Crescent at Buxton. One of the mines, Deep Ecton, to the north of **Ecton Hill**, was, at nearly 1,400 feet, one of the deepest in Europe. Work had ceased in the mines by 1900 but, so impervious was the surrounding limestone that the workings took several years to flood though now they are under water.

Warslow

9 miles NW of Ashbourne off the B5054

Situated opposite Wetton on the other side of the River Manifold, the village is one of the main access points to this dramatic section of the Manifold Valley. Lying below the gritstone moorlands this was an estate village for the eccentric Crewe family, who lived at Calke Abbey in south Derbyshire.

Hulme End

9 miles NW of Ashbourne off the B5054

This is the ideal place from which to explore the **Manifold Valley**. From here to Ilam, the River Manifold runs southwards through a deep, twisting limestone cleft, between steep and wooded banks. For much of its dramatic course the Manifold disappears underground in dry weather, through swallow holes, which is typical of a river in a limestone area.

The village also lays at the terminus of the **Leek and Manifold Valley Light Railway**, which opened in 1904. Already aware of the tourism possibilities of the Peak District by the beginning of the 20th century, the other reason for constructing the railway was to transport coal and other raw materials to the surrounding settlements. A narrow-gauge railway, which left the standard gauge at Waterhouses, progressed through this seemingly inhospitable land of deep valleys by following the banks of the River Hamps - a tributary of the River Manifold. The line, however, was unable to pay its way, particularly after the creamery at Ecton, just a mile south of Hulme End, closed in 1933 and the following year the railway ceased operation. The tracks were taken up and, if it had not been turned into a semi-long distance footpath, the route of the railway might have been lost forever.

Considering that the buildings at Hulme End station were constructed using materials that were not designed to withstand the test of time, chiefly corrugated iron and wood, it is surprising to find that two of the three survive. Though the station, along with the railway, closed in 1934, the sheds are still in use today.

Hartington

10 miles NW of Ashbourne off the B5054

This charming limestone village was granted a market charter in 1203 and it is likely that its spacious market place was once the village green. Now a Youth Hostel (the oldest in the Peak District, opening in 1934), **Hartington Hall**, built in the 17th century and enlarged in the 19th century, is typical of many Peak District manor houses and a fine example of a Derbyshire yeoman's house and farm. The village is also the home to the only cheese factory remaining in Derbyshire. From the dairy, not far from the village mere, Stilton, veined, plain or flavoured, is still made and can be

Well Dressing, Hartington

bought at the dairy shop.

The village is very much on the tourist route and, though it is popular, Hartington has retained much of its village appeal. As well as the famous cheese shop, there are two old coaching inns left over from the days when this was an important market centre, which still serve refreshments to visitors. One of these goes by the rather unusual name of The Charles Cotton; named after the friend of Izaak Walton. Situated in the valley of the River Dove, Hartington is an excellent place from which to explore both the Dove and the Manifold valleys. To the south lies **Beresford Dale**, the upper valley of the River Dove and easily as pretty as its more famous neighbour Dovedale. It was immortalised by Izaak Walton and Charles Cotton when *The Compleat Angler* was published in 1653. Telling of their fishing experiences on this famous trout river, it is not surprising that the pair chose this Dale as their favourite site. Together they built a fishing temple on the banks of the River Dove in Beresford Dale bearing the inscription Piscatoribus Sacrum. The temple still stands on private land. Cotton was born and lived at Beresford Hall until financial difficulties forced him to sell it in 1681.

Mayfield

2½ miles SW of Ashbourne off the A523

Mayfield is a large village on the edge of Ashbourne, divided into Upper Mayfield

Beresford Dale

The Royal Oak Hotel

Hanging Bridge, Mayfield, Ashbourne,
Derbyshire DE6 2BN
Tel: 01335 300090

Standing adjacent to the A52 about a mile out of Ashbourne at Hanging Bridge, Mayfield, **The Royal Oak Hotel** is a friendly and very attractive place dating back to the late 1700s.

This fine Free House offers two real ales – Bass and a changing guest ale – complemented by a good range of lagers, cider, stout, wines, spirits and soft drinks. Great food is available every day at lunchtime (12 – 2) and Monday to Saturday evenings (7 – 8.30). Booking required at weekends. The menu and specials board boast a selection of home-cooked dishes. Owner Jan Snelling does all the cooking, and among his specialities is home-made steak-and-ale pie. Jan is ably assisted by his daughter-in-law Christelle, and they and their staff offer all their guests a warm welcome and genuine hospitality.

This superb hotel also has six comfortable and lovely ensuite guest bedrooms – two doubles, two twins and two family rooms. The tariff includes a hearty breakfast.

Children welcome.

and Middle Mayfield. Mayfield is just over the border from Derbyshire and lies in Staffordshire.

Mayfield was originally a Saxon village, dating back over a thousand years and listed in the *Domesday Book* as Mavreveldt. The first Norman church was probably built about 1125 during the reign of Henry I, and the present parish church of **St John the Baptist**, illustrates the progressive styles of architecture since that date, with a 14th century chancel and a 16th century tower. In the churchyard there is an original Saxon cross. The ballad writer, Thomas Moore lived at Moore Cottage, formerly Stancliffe Farm. His young daughter Olivia is buried in the local churchyard, her slate tombstone reading 'Olivia Byron Moore, died March 18, 1815'. Moore was friendly with Lord Byron, who visited him here.

On 7 December 1745 Bonnie Prince Charlie and his army passed through Mayfield on their retreat from Derby, terrorising the local populace. They shot the innkeeper at Hanging Bridge as well as a Mr Humphrey Brown, who refused to hand over his horse to them. Many of the terrified villagers locked themselves in the church. The soldiers fired shots through the door and the bullet holes can still be seen in the woodwork of the west door. Legend has it that many of the rebels were caught and hung from gibbets on the old packhorse bridge, whose 500-year-old grey stone arches can still be seen, although the bridge has been rebuilt.

There is however a road out of the village, leading to the main Leek highway marked on the Ordnance Survey map as "Gallowstree Lane", suggesting that those to be hung went their way via the bridge and Gallowstree Lane to Gallowstree Hill.

Today it is a pleasant walk rewarded by a lovely view down the Dove Valley.

The Mayfield Mill site has the fairly rare distinction of a history of almost 200 years of textile production. The first mention of any sort of mill occurs in a property valuation of 1291: most of Mayfield then belonged to the Priory of Tutbury and it included a corn mill. By

Café Davide

23 Getliffes Yard, Leek,
Staffordshire ST13 6HU
Tel: 01538 372255 Fax: 01538 373344
e-mail: mike@cafedavide.co.uk
website: www.cafedavide.co.uk

Situated just off Leek's main street, **Café Davide** is a stylish and very impressive restaurant and brasserie with a unique charm and style.

Getliffe's Yard had fallen for a time into dereliction, but now most of the former workmen's houses have been transformed into craft shops and other small businesses, and Café Davide is one of the newest of these. In the short time since it opened it has become a popular place to dine or just socialise, while enjoying the tasteful, modern surroundings and convivial atmosphere. The exterior is notable for its cobbled paving and charm, while the sign over the door boasts an image of a detail of the head of the famous Michelangelo statue that gives the bistro its name.

The restaurant area is all polished wood and tightly-woven pale carpeting, with attractive mauve paintwork and comfortable and attractive dark brown leather dining chairs. In another area, plush red leather sofas make for an intimate and relaxing alcove in which to enjoy a drink or meal. The bar area is similarly sleek and modern.

Open Tuesday to Sunday from10 a.m. to 11 p.m. (food served until 9 p.m.), the menu boasts a range of tempting delights to suit the time of day. During the earlier hours of the day there's an excellent choice of coffees, teas and snacks; at lunch guests have a choice of tapas and other light meals, and from 7 p.m. dinner is served. The professional chefs create a range of tempting dishes such as Moroccan lamb, lemongrass chicken breast, pork loin in a peanut-and-chilli marinade, and more. There is seating for 50 inside and an additional 28 in the handsome covered courtyard, with large palms, slate tables and lovely wicker seating set out amongst the pavestones.

The wine list is very good, and there are also draught kegs and other thirst-quenchers available. Booking required for Friday and Saturday evenings.

1793 there had been various owners of the site which has developed to include two corn mills, two fulling mills and a leather mill. Textiles first appeared in 1795 when the cotton mill was completed. Unfortunately in 1806 the interior of the building, together with most of the machinery, was destroyed in a fire. When the mill was eventually rebuilt it was with a cast iron framework and brick vaulted ceilings, as can still be seen in the oldest of the buildings, to prevent a repetition of the fire.

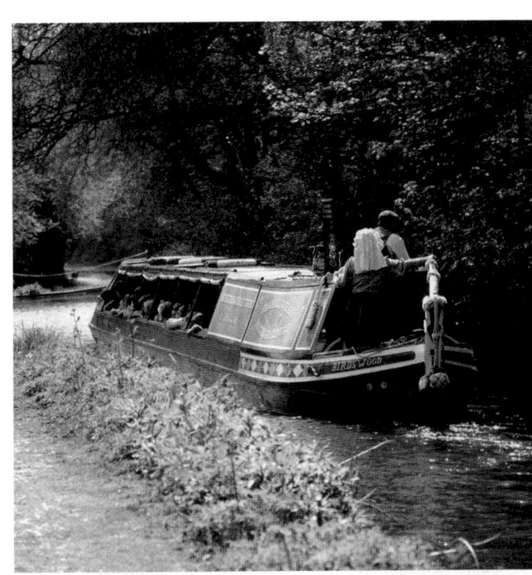

Barge on the Canal, Cauldon

The spinning of cotton continued in Mayfield with various degrees of economic success until 1934 when it was sold to William Tatton and Company who used the mill to process silk. Since then it has seen changes of ownership and production but the mill remains.

Swinscoe

4 miles W of Ashbourne off the A523

The peaceful hamlet of Swinscoe straddles the Derbyshire/Staffordshire border, not far from the River Manifold.

Cauldon

8 miles SE of Leek off the A52

This was the site of the quarry from which wagons travelled, down a railway track, to Froghall Wharf.

Leek

15 miles NW of Ashbourne on the A523

Known as the 'Queen of the Moorlands', this is an attractive textile centre on the banks of the River Churnet. It was here that French Huguenots settled, after fleeing from religious oppression, and established the silk industry that thrived due to the abundance of soft water coming off the nearby moorland. Until the 19th century, this was a domestic industry with the workshops on the top storeys of the houses; many examples of these 'top shops' have survived to this day. Leek also became an important dyeing town, particularly after the death of Prince Albert, when 'Raven Black' was popularised by Queen Victoria, who remained in mourning for her beloved

The Abbey Inn

Abbey Green Road, Leek,
Staffordshire ST13 8SA
Tel: 01538 382865 Fax: 01538 398604
e-mail: jo@abbeyinn.co.uk
website: www.abbeyinn.co.uk

Situated on the outskirts of Leek, backing onto the Peak District National Park, **The Abbey Inn** is a delightful 17th century inn. This family-run establishment extends a warm welcome to all, offering fine real ales, good food and comfortable accommodation. It enjoys a far-reaching reputation for its superb food with a wide-ranging selection of classic English dishes catering to all tastes and appetites and available at every session. Bed and breakfast or self-catering accommodation is available in an adjoining annexe.

The exterior is handsome and welcoming – a large and impressive traditional brickbuilt premises with a raised area outside with comfortable seating. Inside,the ambience is always cosy and relaxed.

Owned and run by the Sargeant family since 1988, this fine inn offers rotating guest ales (between two and three per week) together with a full range of lagers, cider, stout, wines, spirits and soft drinks.

Closed Tuesdays, throughout the rest of the week the inn serves food at lunch (11 – 2) and dinner (6.30 – 9) weekdays and Saturdays, and for Sunday roast lunch (12 – 2). The food is hearty and delicious, and makes good use of the finest and freshest local ingredients available. Tempting dishes from the evening menu include plaice, scampi, spinach and ricotta cannelloni, porcini mushroom ravioli, beef curry, steak-and-mushroom pudding, mixed grills and more.

The accommodation is nothing short of superb, with outstanding facilities, tasteful décor and comfortable furnishings. One room is suitable for self-catering if preferred, although breakfast is available at the inn. It boasts a king-sized bed. The other two rooms are doubles, though one is spacious enough to be considered a suite. All rooms are on ground-floor level.

husband for many years.

William Morris, founder of the Arts and Crafts movement, lived and worked in Leek for many months between 1875 and 1878. Much of his time here was spent investigating new techniques of dyeing but he also revived the use of traditional dyes. His influence cannot only be seen in the art here but also in the architecture. The **Nicholson Institute** holds exhibitions on the wonderful and intricate work of the famous Leek School of Embroidery that was founded by Lady Wardle in the 1870s. A replica of the Bayeux Tapestry, now on display in the Museum of Reading was first displayed here in 1886. Elizabeth Wardle, along with thirty-five members of the Leek Embroidery Society

Lampost and Clock Tower, Leek

Den Engel Belgian Bar and Restaurant

11-13 Stanley Street, Leek,Staffordshire
ST13 5HG
Tel: 01538 373751
e-mail: denengel@netcentral.com
website: www.denengel.co.uk

Beer is to Belgians what whisky is to Scots, and **Den Engel Belgian Bar and Restaurant** is a credit to the grand tradition of beer-brewing (and drinking!) in the land of the Flemish and Walloons. One of about a dozen such bars in the UK it has been judged one of the best outside Belgium by Tim Webb noted writer on Belgian beer and bars. Handsome and stylish inside and out, with a classic simplicity to the décor, owner Geoff Turner has over 15 years' experience of Belgian beer and makes regular trips to keep up to date with the latest brands.

The choice of brews includes 11 draught beers including Jupiler, Blanche de Bruxelles, De Koninck, Westmalle Trappist, Chimay Tripel and Liefmans Kriek, no fewer than 110 bottles lining the shelves, together with special export Guinness, Kwak, Orval and much more. The new restaurant due to open during the life time of this edition, will feature many traditional beer-based dishes, created back in the days when water was not considered safe to cook with. Den Engel is open Monday & Tuesday 5 – 11 pm, Wednesday to Saturday 11 – 11pm and Sundays 12 – 10.30pm.

The Hollybush Inn

Denford Road, Denford, Leek,
Staffordshire ST13 7JT
Tel: 01538 371819

What a lovely place **The Hollybush Inn** is! It sits with the Caldon Canal to the front and the Leek branch of the canal to the rear, and is a favourite stopping-point for people cruising the waters and exploring the tow paths. Dating back to the 17th century, it was actually a corn mill before it became a pub, and today's visitors will find a picturesque whitewashed building with small-paned windows and an inn sign that incorporates a clock. The inside is equally delightful and everything an English inn should be: the floors are part quarry tiles, there are old oak beams, open fires, copper and brass ornaments and comfortable seating. The restaurant area is roomy and well appointed, seating up to 50 people, though you can also eat in the conservatory or elsewhere in the hostelry if you wish.

The Hollybush Inn has been in the hands of the Prime family since 1979, and run by Steve and Linda since January 2000, assisted by Steve's cousin Angela who acts as manager and is also one of the chefs. The family extend a warm, friendly welcome to all, and the result is a very popular country pub with lots of regular customers. Open all day, every day, the bar offers a good range of drinks including Courage Best, Directors, Burton, Bass 4X Mild, Worthington Creamflow, Carling, Kronenbourg, Black Sheep, London Pride, Youngs Specials, Tiger, Strongbow and Guinness. The superb food is also available seven days a week, all day throughout the year, with last orders taken at 9 p.m. Such is the popularity at weekends that booking ahead is recommended. There is a printed menu from which to choose, and all the dishes are prepared in the inn's own kitchens from fresh ingredients that are sourced locally where possible. Try the speciality of the house, home-made beef and ale pie, or a dish that is infamous throughout the area, the Hollybush grill. To accompany your meal there is a selection of wines.

You'd think that Steve would have very little time to spare from running this popular pub, but he is an active member of the Norton Tug of War team, which uses the pub as its headquarters. This is no amateur team, though: they have recently become European Champions for 2003 in the 560-kg class, and have won a number of World titles, too. Their impressive collection of trophies is on display within the inn.

The Butter Market, Leek

and other embroiderers from the surrounding area completed the tapestry in just over a year. Each embroiderer stitched her name beneath her completed panel.

Leek is by no means a recent town that grew up in the shadow of the Industrial Revolution. An ancient borough, granted its charter in 1214, Leek was a thriving market centre rivalling Macclesfield and Congleton. **The Butter Cross**, which now stands in the **Market Place**, was originally erected near the junction of Sheep Market and Stanley Street by the Joliffe family in 1671. Every road coming into the town seems to converge on the old cobbled Market Place and the road to the west leads down to the Parish Church. Dedicated to Edward the Confessor (the full name is **St Edward's**

The Railway Inn

Froghall, Staffordshire Moorlands, ST10 2HA
Tel: 01538 754782 Fax: 01538 267002
e-mail:
the-railway-inn@froghall.fsbusiness.co.uk
website: www.the-railway-inn.com

Standing in the village of Froghall on the A52, opposite Kingsley and Froghall Railway Station, where the privately-owned Churnet Valley Preserved Railway runs, **The Railway Inn** is a quality inn serving great food and drink. It is also close to Alton Towers, and makes a convenient and welcoming place to stay before or after a visit to the park.

Built as an inn in the late 19th century, the handsome interior boasts some interesting railway memorabilia, while outside there's a lovely beer garden with picnic tables and a wealth of greenery. The dining area is simple and elegant, with muted colours and a relaxing ambience.

Leaseholders Paul and Claire have been here since March 2003, and have a knack for making all their guests feel welcome and comfortable.

There are two regular real ales – Marstons Pedigree and Hobgoblin – together with an occasional guest ale in summer and a range of lagers, cider, stout, wines, spirits and soft drinks.

Claire is a superb chef, creating a range of delicious dishes at lunch and dinner. The comprehensive menu includes specialities such as beef and Guinness pie, homemade lasagne and a good selection of fresh fish dishes. All dishes are freshly prepared to order. Booking required Friday and Saturday evenings and Sunday lunchtime.

Open (summer) Tuesday evenings and all day Wednesday to Sunday and Bank Holidays; (winter) all day Wednesday to Sunday and Bank Holidays.

This fine inn also boasts five handsome and welcoming ensuite guest bedrooms, including one room on the ground floor. Two have four-poster beds, and the ground-floor family room sleeps up to six. The tariff includes a hearty and delicious breakfast – just the thing to set guests up for a day's sightseeing or walking in the region, which offers much in the way of sights and attractions.

and All Saints' Church), the original Church was burnt down in 1297 and rebuilt some 20 years later though the building is now largely 17th century. The timber roof of the nave is well worth a second look and is the Church's pride and joy. It is boasted that each of the cross beams was hewn from a separate oak tree and, in the west part of the nave, an enormous 18th century gallery rises up, tier on tier, giving the impression of a theatre's dress circle!

Although much has been altered inside the Church, most notably in 1865 when GE Street rebuilt the chancel, reredos, sanctuary, pulpit and stalls, there still remains a rather unusual wooden chair. Traditionally this is believed to have been a ducking stool for scolds, which was used in the nearby River Churnet. Outside, in the churchyard, can be found a rather curious inscription on a gravestone: 'James Robinson interred February the 28th 1788 Aged 438'! To the north side of the Church is an area still known locally as 'Petty France', which holds the graves of many Napoleonic prisoners of war who lived nearby.

Another building worthy of a second glance is the imposing **Nicholson Institute**, mentioned earlier, with its copper dome. Completed in 1884 and funded by the local industrialist Joshua Nicholson, the Institute offered the people of Leek an opportunity to learn and also expand their cultural horizons. Many of the great Victorian literary

The Cricketers Arms

The Square, Oakamoor,
Staffordshire Moorlands ST10 3AB
Tel: 01538 702548
e-mail: patchmeadow2@aol.com

The Cricketers Arms is a fine old English pub proudly upholding the grand tradition of quality and service. Found in the pretty village of Oakamoor on the B5417, a short drive from Alton Towers, local man Steve Barber became tenant here in 2003. The inn dates back to the early 18th century. Part of the Caldon Canal once ran adjacent to the inn, but now this part of the canal has been filled in and the surrounding region is dominated by the Hawksmoor Nature Reserve and bird sanctuary.

The interior is warm and welcoming, while outside there's a large and handsome beer garden.

During the lifetime of this edition (spring 2005) the inn will be open every lunchtime, though at present it is open evenings only throughout the week and all day at weekends. There are four real ales to enjoy – Tetley, Bass, Marstons Pedigree and Abbot Ale – together with a good range of lagers, cider, stout, wines, spirits and soft drinks. The kitchen is presently undergoing a comprehensive refurbishment, so that by spring of 2005 there will be meals available at lunch and dinner.

Abbot's Haye

Cherry Lane, Cheadle,
Staffordshire ST10 4QS
Tel: 01538 750645 Mob: 07970724271
e-mail: abbots.haye@btopenworld.com

Set in the heart of the Staffordshire moorlands, **Abbot's Haye** is an excellent country guest house dating back to Tudor times. Set in six acres, two of which are gardens, the house is close to Alton Towers, the Potteries and the many other sights and attractions of the region. The accommodation comprises five spacious and welcoming ensuite guest bedrooms (four family rooms and a double), at a tariff that includes a hearty breakfast. Evening meals also available by arrangement. The house can be found just a short distance from Cheadle along the B5417. Owners Pamela and Robert Piers-Leake offer unbeatable hospitality and a genuinely warm welcome to all their guests, an achievement attested to by their many return visitors. Open all year round, this superb country house makes an ideal place for a relaxing break or as a base from which to explore the area.

giants, including George Bernard Shaw and Mark Twain, came here to admire the building. The town's **War Memorial**, built in Portland stone and with a clock tower, has a dedication to the youngest Nicholson son, who was killed in the First World War. Leek was the home of James Brindley, the 18th-century engineer who built much of the early canal network. A water-powered corn mill built by him in 1752 in Mill Street has been restored and now houses the **Brindley Water Museum** (known as Brindley Mill), which is devoted to his life and work. Visitors can see corn being ground and see displays of millwrighting skills. Leek has a traditional outdoor market every Wednesday, a craft and antiques market on Saturday and an indoor 'butter market' on Wednesday, Friday and Saturday.

The Roaches

The Old Red Lion

Froghall Road, Ipstones,
Staffordshire Moorlands ST10 2NA
Tel: 01538 266345

Set in the picturesque village of Ipstones, found off the main A53 and on the B5053, **The Old Red Lion** is a quality inn dating back to 1754. A Free House owned and personally run by Linda and Mike since 1995, the interior boasts original features, from the exposed stonework and beamwork to the open fires, that enhance the inn's warm and relaxed ambience. Inside and out, this is a handsome and welcoming place.

Open every evening weekdays and all day Saturday and Sunday, there are three real ales to choose from – Directors and two rotating guest ales – together with a good range of lagers, cider, stout, wines, spirits and soft drinks.

Excellent food is served every evening from 7 – 9 p.m. and Saturday and Sunday lunchtimes from midday until 3 p.m. Booking required for Sunday lunchtime. Linda does much of the cooking, and guests choose off the menu or specials board from a range of delicious dishes.

There are three charming, spacious and comfortable ensuite guest bedrooms, including two family rooms.

The Ramblers Retreat

Dimmingsdale, Alton, Staffordshire ST10 4BX
Tel: 01538 702730 Fax: 01538 703133

The Ramblers Retreat in Dimmingsdale, in the heart of the Churnet Valley, has a long and distinguished history. In the very early 1800s the Earl of Shrewsbury transformed the entire village to his own purposes, turning it from a minor centre of iron- and lead-smelting into his own private country paradise.

Part of this transformation included the creation of Dimmingsdale Lodge, now the Ramblers. After being used as a private residence, the premises had fallen into dereliction until, in 1978, Gary and Margaret Keeling bought it and, two years later after extensive refurbishment, made it their home. Many ramblers passing by would stop and chat to the Keelings in their garden, and after a year they decided to open up their living room as a place for ramblers to enjoy a cup of tea and a scone – and so this charming retreat was born, where the ambience is always warm and welcoming.

Offering a range of high-quality, traditional dishes, almost all the dishes on the menu are home-made on the premises and make use of the best local produce wherever possible. Dishes such as steak, ale and mushroom pie, salmon fillet, cheese, bacon and broccoli quiche, Staffordshire roast of the day and oatcake pizzas, complemented by a good choice of light bites, side orders and mouth-watering puddings, are sure to tempt every palate.

Guests can enjoy their meal in the cosy lounge, airy conservatory or outside in the beautiful gardens. There's a very good wine list and selection of alcohol and soft drinks. Surrounded by ancient woodland that cloaks the valley on both sides, the Ramblers is close to many established moorland walks. Open every day except Christmas Day, from 10 a.m. to 6 p.m. in summer (April to September) and 10 a.m. to 5 p.m. October to March, booking is required for lunch and tea in summer.

Ramshaw Rocks

The **River Churnet**, though little known outside Staffordshire, has a wealth of scenery and industrial archaeology. It is easily accessible to walkers and its valley deserves better recognition. The river rises to the west of Leek in rugged gritstone country, but for most of its length it flows through softer red sandstone countryside in a valley that was carved out during the Ice Age. Though there are few footpaths directly adjacent to the riverbank, most of the valley can be walked close to the river using a combination of canal towpaths and former railway tracks.

Four miles to the north of Leek on the A53 rise the dark, jagged gritstone outcrops of **The Roaches, Ramshaw Rocks** and **Hen Cloud**. Roaches is a

Sheila's Restaurant and Tearooms

Intake Farm, Rushton, Macclesfield,
Cheshire SK11 0RB
Tel: 01260 226284

Sheila's Restaurant and Tearooms is a truly outstanding place found at Intake Farm, about a mile off the A523 Macclesfield-to-Leek road at Rushton. To reach Sheila's you turn off the A523 in Rushton and follow that road uphill – the premises will be on your right side about a mile up. It's a scenic location which makes a perfect backdrop to a memorable meal.

Owned and personally run by Sheila Turnock since 1988, this superb establishment is housed within a magnificent and spacious farmhouse, parts of which date back over 400 years.

Set in landscaped gardens Sheila's is the perfect stop for all occasions. Whether it be a refreshing cup of tea or something more substantial, they pride themselves on serving freshly prepared homemade food of the highest standard.

Their tea menu includes homemade soup, various generously filled sandwiches and toasties, Italian Ciabattas with chilli and cheese, homemade cakes and scones with jam and cream. A popular choice is their Cream Tea which consists of mixed sandwiches, a scone with jam and cream, homemade cakes and as much tea as you can drink.

On Sunday's they serve a traditional three course roast (due to it's popularity it is advisable to book). They offer a choice of several homemade starters, a choice of two home cooked roasts of the day served with seasonal vegetables. This is followed by a selection of their much talked about homemade sweets served with fresh cream that is bought from a local farm and to finish there is freshly brewed coffee and mints. Hungry yet? Then don't miss your next opportunity to visit this wonderful establishment. Tea room opening times are Easter to October, Wednesday, Thursday & Friday 12.00 - 4.30pm, Saturday, Sunday & Bank holidays 12.00 - 6.00pm. October to Easter, Saturday & Sunday 12.00 - 4.30pm. This popular place is also happy to book for larger parties.

Ancient Cave Dwellings, Kinver Edge

corruption of the French word 'roches' or rocks and was reputedly given by Napoleonic prisoners: 'cloud' is a local word used for high hills. Just below The Roaches there is another delightful stretch of water, **Tittesworth Reservoir**, which is extremely popular with trout fishermen. It has some super trails, a visitor centre with an interactive exhibition, a restaurant and a gift shop.

Rudyard

2 miles NW of Leek off the A523

In fond memory of the place where they first met in 1863, Mr and Mrs Kipling named their famous son, born in 1865, after this village. The nearby two mile long Rudyard Lake was built in 1831 by John Rennie to feed the Caldon Canal. With steeply wooded banks the lake is now a leisure centre where there are facilities for picnicking, walking, fishing and sailing. The west shore of the Reservoir is also a section of the Staffordshire Way, the long distance footpath which runs from Mow Cop to **Kinver Edge**, near Stourbridge. This is a sandstone ridge covered in woodland and heath, and with several famous rock houses which were inhabited until the 1950s.

Back in Victorian days, Rudyard was a popular lakeside resort, which developed after the construction of the North Staffordshire Railway in 1845. The Rudyard Lake Steam Railway uses miniature narrow gauge steam trains to give a three-mile return trip along the side of Rudyard Lake. Its popularity became so great that, on one particular day in 1877, over 20,000 people came here to see Captain Webb, the first man to swim the English Channel, swim in the Reservoir.

Rushton Spencer

5 miles NW of Leek on the A523

This pleasant, moorland village nestles under the distinctive hill the Cloud and is the ideal starting point for a walk to the summit. It is also well known for its lonely church, the '**Chapel in the Wilderness**', originally built of wood in the 14th century, which served both Rushton Spencer and neighbouring Rushton James. It has been almost rebuilt in stone.

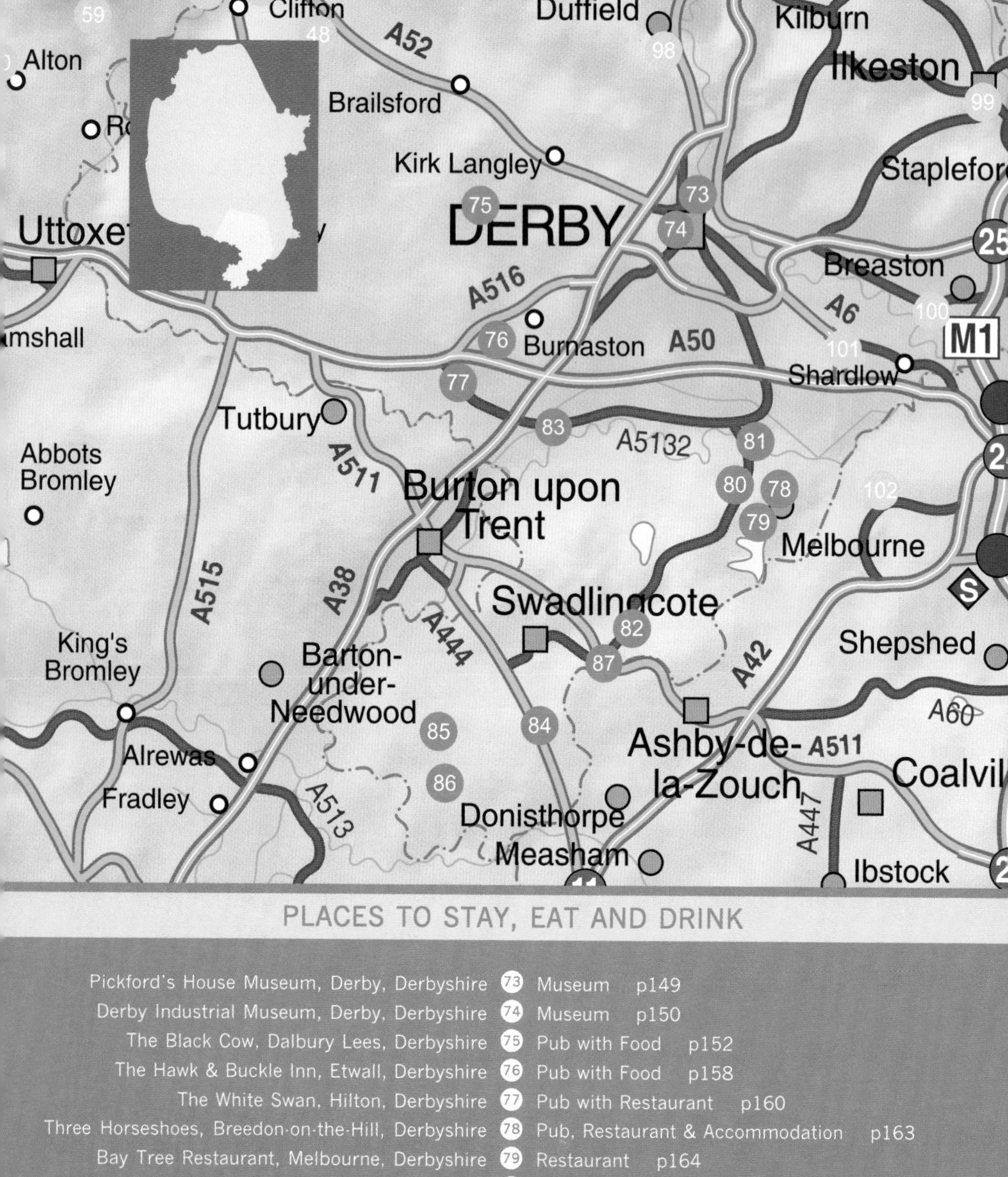

PLACES TO STAY, EAT AND DRINK

Place	No.	Type	Page
Pickford's House Museum, Derby, Derbyshire	73	Museum	p149
Derby Industrial Museum, Derby, Derbyshire	74	Museum	p150
The Black Cow, Dalbury Lees, Derbyshire	75	Pub with Food	p152
The Hawk & Buckle Inn, Etwall, Derbyshire	76	Pub with Food	p158
The White Swan, Hilton, Derbyshire	77	Pub with Restaurant	p160
Three Horseshoes, Breedon-on-the-Hill, Derbyshire	78	Pub, Restaurant & Accommodation	p163
Bay Tree Restaurant, Melbourne, Derbyshire	79	Restaurant	p164
The Bulls Head at Wilson, Wilson, Derbyshire	80	Pub with Food	p165
Ivy House Farm, Stanton-by-Bridge, Derbyshire	81	Guest House	p166
The Bulls Head, Hartshorne, Derbyshire	82	Pub, Food & Accommodation	p167
The Green Dragon, Willington, Derbyshire	83	Pub with Food	p168
Mount Pleasant Inn, Castle Gresley, Derbyshire	84	Pub with Food	p170
The Plough Inn, Rosliston, Derbyshire	85	Pub with Food	p170
The Queens Head, Coton-in-the-Elms, Derbyshire	86	Pub, Food & Accommodation	p171
New Inn, Woodville, Derbyshire	87	Pub with Food	p172

● Denotes entries in other chapters

4 The Trent Valley

In the valley of the River Trent, which runs through the southern part of the county of Derbyshire, can be found many splendid stately homes, including Kedleston Hall and the eccentric Calke Abbey. The scenery affords ample opportunities to enjoy pleasant walks. This chapter also includes the western side of the region known as Erewash.

Derbyshire was at the forefront of modern thinking at the beginning of the Industrial Revolution. The chief inheritor of this legacy was Derby, and this city is still a busy industrial centre and home to the Industrial Museum. There are plenty of other places to visit in Derby, which is not, as is often supposed, the county town (that honour goes to Matlock).

Truly an area of hidden places, among the many explored in this chapter that are well worth a visit are the picturesque villages of Church Gresley and Castle Gresley, the welcoming centres of Melbourne and Hartshorne, quiet Repton on the River Trent and the 'border' town of Swadlincote and the surrounding area.

Town Centre, Derby

Derby

Essentially a commercial and industrial city, Derby's position, historically and geographically, has ensured that it has remained one of the most important and interesting cities in the area and, consequently, there is much for the visitor to see, whether from an architectural or historical point of view. There are, however, two things that most people, whether they have been to the city before or not, know of Derby: Rolls-Royce engines and Royal Crown Derby porcelain. When in 1906 Sir Henry Royce and the Hon C S Rolls joined forces and built the first Rolls-Royce (a Silver Ghost) at Derby, they built much more than just a motor car. Considered by many to be the best cars in the world, it is often said that the noisiest moving part in any Rolls-Royce is the dashboard clock!

The home of **Royal Crown Derby**, any visit to the city would not be complete without a trip to the factory and its museum and shop. The guided tours offer an intriguing insight into the high level of skill required to create the delicate flower petals, hand gild the plates and to hand paint the Derby Dwarves. The latest addition to the entrance to the factory is the illuminated ceramic window created by local artist Angela Verdon along with staff at Royal Crown Derby. Japanese influences were combined with the translucent quality of Royal crown Derby china to achieve this very innovative design, using simple images of the natural world . The museum houses the most comprehensive collection of Derby Porcelain to be seen anywhere in the world, including 18th century figurines, many interpretations of the Japanese designs for which the company is famous, the delicate 'Eggshell' China by French Art Director Desire Leroy, and examples of the Crown Derby ware commissioned for the restaurants of the *Titanic*.

The city's **Cathedral of All Saints** possesses a fine 16th century tower, the second highest perpendicular tower in England and the oldest ring of ten bells in the world. The airy building was actually built in the 1720s by James Gibbs. Inside is a beautiful wrought-iron screen by Robert Bakewell and, among the splendid monuments, lies the tomb of Bess of Hardwick Hall. Originally Derby's Parish Church, it was given cathedral status in 1927. In the late 1960s the building was extended eastwards and the retrochoir, baldacchino and sacristy were added along with the screen. Only five minutes walk from the Cathedral, the beautifully restored medieval **St Mary's Chapel on the Bridge** is one of only six surviving bridge chapels still in use, and well worth a visit.

One of Derby's most interesting museums is **Pickford's House** (see panel opposite), situated on the city's finest Georgian street at number 41. This Grade I listed building was erected in 1770 by the architect Joseph Pickford as a combined family home and place of work. Pickford House differs from the majority of grand stately homes in that it does not have a wealth of priceless furniture or works of art. Instead, visitors are able to gain a true insight into everyday middle-class life during the 1830s. Pickford House is the epitome of a late-Georgian professional man's residence. There is an exciting programme of temporary exhibitions as well as other displays which deal with the history of the Friargate area and the importance of Joseph Pickford as a Midlands architect. The displays include a late 18th century dining room, breakfast rooms and an early 19th century kitchen and scullery. One special feature of Pickford House is the excellent collection of costumes, some dating back to the mid-1700s. A period 18th century garden is also laid out at the rear of the house.

Just a short walk from Pickford House is the **Industrial Museum**. (see panel on page 150) What better place to house a museum devoted to the preservation of Derby's industrial heritage than the beautiful old **Silk Mill**, a building which stands on one of the most interesting sites in the country and which preceded Richard Arkwright's first cotton mill by over 50 years. The Silk Mill was badly damaged by fire in 1910 and had to be substantially rebuilt, however it still gives an impression of Lombe's original mill and tower. The whole of the ground

Pickford's House Museum

41 Friargate, Derby DE1 1DA
Tel: 01332 255363

Pickford's House Museum is a Grade I listed building of 1770 built by Joseph Pickford, an important Midlands architect, as his home and workplace. Pickford worked on a number of architectural products throughout the Midlands including a prestigious factory and hall at Etruria for the potter Josiah Wedgwood.

Visitors today can see the comfort of the family rooms contrasting with the living and working conditions of the servants. The house is reconstructed as it might have looked when members of the Pickford family lived here.

Displays include a dining room, drawing room and servants' bedroom of about 1800, and a morning room, laundry and kitchen of about 1825.

The museum also houses a fine collection of historic costume and textiles and displays part of the nationally-important Frank Bradley collection of toy theatres. There is a lively programme of temporary exhibitions and events throughout the year.

floor galleries are devoted to the Rolls-Royce aero engine collection and illustrate the importance played by the aeronautical industry in the city's history.

Since 1915 Derby has been involved with the manufacture of engines, and this section of the Museum displays model aircraft and sectioned engines demonstrating how aircraft fly. A specially designed annexe houses a complete RB211 Turbo-fan engine. On the first floor of the building there is an introduction to other Derbyshire industries with displays of lead and coal mining, iron founding, limestone quarrying, ceramics and brick making. There is also a railway engineering gallery complete with a signal box and displays on the growth of the railway works in Derby since the 1840s. Since the coming of the railways in 1839, the railway industry has also played a large part in the life of the City. Along with Rolls Royce, British Rail Engineering Ltd (BREL) is one of the largest employers in Derby and its development is well documented within the Museum and allows visitors to broaden their knowledge.

The **City Museum and Art Gallery** is also well worth visiting. Opened in 1879, it is the oldest of Derby's museums and the displays include natural history, archaeology and social history exhibits. Derbyshire wildlife and geology feature in an exciting series of natural settings and hands-on exhibits. One section of the museum is devoted to a Military Gallery and relates to Derby's local historical regiments. The walk-in First World War trench scene attempts to capture the experience of a night at the front. The Bonnie Prince Charlie room commemorates Derby's role in the 1745 uprising.

A ground floor gallery houses the city's superb collection of fine porcelain, manufactured in Derby from the mid-18th century. The porcelain collection is displayed in a new, Lottery

Derby Industrial Museum

Full Street, Derby DE1 3AR
Tel: 01332 255308

Derby Industrial Museum specialises in the history of the railway engineering background of the city, as well as having a gallery looking at sources of power for industry. Other displays include the local mining, textile and iron industries. The musuem is also home to the Rolls-Royce aircraft engine collection, and this covers the earliest engine, the 'Eagle' of the first World War, through to today's jets.

The largest single exhibit is a RB211 turbofan engine used to power many present day airliners. There is a constantly changing programme of temporary exhibitions.

RB211 Rolls Royce Jet Engine

Derby Cathedral

funded, gallery, complete with a colourful database of the collection. The museum is also home to a collection of portraits, landscapes, scientific and industrial scenes by the local painter Joseph Wright, ARA. On the second floor of the Museum are temporary exhibition galleries. These change every three or four weeks and cover not only the museum's own collection but also travelling exhibitions representing an exciting range of arts and crafts both modern and traditional in a variety of styles and techniques.

The **Derby Heritage Centre** has local history displays, tea room and souvenir shop housed in one of the city's oldest buildings. Opened in 1992 by local Historian, Richard Felix, visitors can book to go on various ghost walks around the city of Derby and now also Tutbury Castle. The city centre ghost walk takes in Derby city centre, including the site of Derby's first jail where witches, heretics and traitors were imprisoned, the scene of the brutal murder of a policeman and a subterranean trip into the barrel-vaulted tunnels beneath the Guildhall Theatre.

Along the theme of crime and punishment, **The Derby Gaol** is situated in the depths of the original dungeons of the Derbyshire County Gaol, dating back to 1756. The Derby Gaol offers a reminder of the city's grisly past. It includes the condemned cells and was the site of the last hanging, drawing and quartering in the country, after England's last revolution, the Pentrich Rebellion.

Pride Park Stadium, the home of Derby County Football Club, was officially opened in 1997, by Her Majesty the Queen. Visitors can take a 'behind the scenes' look at 'the Rams' new sporting arena. A guided tour includes visits to the director's box, corporate areas, crowd control centre and even the police cells. But the high point for any football fan has to be emerging from the players' tunnel on to the pitch.

The ancient custom of well-dressing, more commonly associated with the villages and towns of northern Derbyshire and the Peak District, has found expression here in Derby (in Chester Green, at Mansfield Street Chapel) since 1982, on the Saturday before the late Spring Bank Holiday (Whitsun).

Around Derby

Darley Abbey

2 miles N of Derby off the A6

Darley Abbey is a tranquil village of delightfully restored mill cottages, built in rows or around squares. The Augustinian **Abbey of St Mary** was founded by Robert Ferrers, second Earl of Derby, around 1140 and grew to become the most powerful abbey in Derbyshire and possibly in the whole of the Midlands. In 1538 the Abbey was surrendered as part of the Dissolution of the Monasteries. Sadly, few monasteries could have been so completely obliterated, so much so that what is now known as The Abbey public house is the only building remaining. The layout is of a simple medieval hall house and is thought to have been used as the Abbey's guest house for travellers and pilgrims during the 13th century. During renovation, 12th century pottery was unearthed.

Darley Park, on the river Derwent, was landscaped by William Evans and has attractive flower beds, shrubberies and lawns. It once had a hall, built in 1727 but now demolished, that for 120 years was the home of the Evans family who built the cotton mill by the river in 1783.

The mill area is quite a large complex. The oldest parts, east mill, middle mill and west mill, are 5-storeyed and brick built. There is also a finishing house which has 3 storeys and sash windows, and an octagonal toll house in the mill yard. The Evans family built the red brick houses, still evident in the village, for the mill workers. They were typical paternalistic employers providing subsidised rents, coal, blankets in cold weather and even arranging burials and memorials for their workers.

Breadsall

3 miles N of Derby off the A6

Breadsall began life as a small hamlet clustered around its Norman church. It is now known primarily as a residential suburb of Derby, with new estates that have sprung up around the original centre. The parish church of **All Saints** possesses one of the most elegant steeples in the country, dating from the early 1300s. The south doorway is Norman and the tower and chancel date back to the 1200s. The church was burnt down by suffragettes in 1914 and carefully restored over the next two years. Inside there is a touching pieta from the late 1300s. This beautiful alabaster depiction of the Virgin Mary with the crucified Christ lying across her knees was found under the floor of the church after another fire, and was restored to its present position by W D Caroe.

Opposite the west end of the church can be found **The Old Hall**, which has been part of village life for over 600 years. It was originally the manor house when the village was divided into the wards of Overhall and Netherhall. In later years it has been employed as a school, farmhouse, hunting box, public house, shop, joiner's shop and post office. It currently serves as a parish hall and is used by various village organisations.

As its name suggests, **Breadsall Priory** stands on the site of an Augustinian Priory founded in the 13th century. The only part of the original building extant is an arch in the basement. Most of what stands today dates back to the Jacobean period, with many early 19th century additions and embellishments. Breadsall Priory was home to Erasmus Darwin in his later years. A poet, physician and philosopher, he is better known as grandfather of Charles Darwin. Born in 1731, he died in Breadsall in 1802, and there is a memorial to him in All Saints Church. The Priory is now a private hotel with golf course.

Mackworth

2 miles NW of Derby off the A52

Standing alone in a field near the village of Mackworth is a charming 14th century church. Although its position is unusual it is well worth taking a look inside to see the wealth of ancient and modern alabaster carving that it holds. This is not the only seemingly abandoned building in the village, as there is also a late 15th century gatehouse. This belonged to a castle built by the Mackworth family in 1495.

Kedleston Hall

Kirk Langley

4 miles N of Derby on the A52

Kirk Langley village has some fine 18th century stone houses, a mid-17th century gabled red brick rectory, an old village school and a church. The Church of **St Michael** is early 14th century, built on the site of an older Saxon church. There are monuments to the Meynell and Pole families, including a memorial to Hugo Frances Meynell, 'who was deprived of his life in a collision of carriages' in Clay Cross tunnel. The only pub is the Bluebell at Langley Common.

Kedleston

4 miles NW of Derby off the A52

Kedleston Hall has been the family seat of the Curzon family since the 12th century and, until it was taken over by the National Trust, it had the longest continuous male line in Derbyshire and one of the longest in the country. Nothing remains of the original medieval structure and little is known about it other than details recorded in a survey of 1657 which state that one of the doorways was over 500 years old and that there was also a large hall and a buttery. The present elegant mansion was built between 1759 and 1765 by Robert Adam and it remains one of the finest examples of his work. The façade represents an impressive Roman temple with six tall columns supporting a portico, and a double-armed stone stairway leading to the entrance. Inside, the elegant and extravagant Marble Hall is a massive open space, dominated by 20 pink alabaster Corinthian columns around a white marble inlaid floor with an intricate plasterwork ceiling above. As well as the design for the house and the 3-arched bridge across the lake, it is likely that Robert Adam had a hand in designing the park in the Serpentine Style. The three-mile Long Walk was created in 1776. Edwin Lutyens designed the sunken rose garden.

Since taking over the property, the National Trust has embarked on a major restoration programme and many of the stately home's rooms have been beautifully furnished with contemporary pieces; modern photographs of the family can be seen mingled with priceless paintings and other treasures such as Blue John vases. Along with the house itself and the park with its lakes, there are the boat house and fishing pavilion to explore.

One member of the family, George Nathaniel Curzon, was the Viceroy of India from 1899 to 1905. When he returned to England he brought back numerous works of art, carvings and ivories that can be seen on display in the **Indian Museum**. Though he was out in India for some time, George would not have missed his family home, as Government House in Calcutta is a copy of Kedleston Hall. Once back in England, George did not have much time to enjoy his lands: he became a member of Lloyd George's inner War Cabinet, which met over 500 times during the First World War.

Nearby **All Saints Church**, the only part of the village that was allowed to remain when the rest was moved in 1765 to make way for the landscaped park around the Hall, dates from the 12th century. It is of an unusual design for Derbyshire in that it is cruciform in shape and the tower is placed in the centre. Inside are Curzon monuments dating from 1275 to the present day; the only brass in the church is to Richard Curzon, who died in 1496. The church has an unusual east-facing sundial. Because of its orientation, the dial only catches the sun between the hours of 6 and 11am. The hour lines are parallel with each other, with half hour lines in between. The gnomon is in the form of a letter "T", the top bar of which casts a shadow across the dial. The inscription above the dial is "WEE SHALL", which cryptically links to sundial (soon die all) to make a sombre message. This is reinforced by the carvings on top of the dial, showing a skull between two hour glasses.

Brailsford

8 miles NW of Derby off the A52

Brailsford is mentioned in the *Domesday Book* as having a priest and 'half a church'. The owner then was the Saxon Elfin, who appears to have managed to retain his lordship after the Conquest. The carved Saxon cross in the churchyard of **All Saints** parish church dates from Elfin's time. The church itself is an interesting building with much Norman work and an ashlar-faced diagonally buttressed tower. At nearby Mugginton can be found 'Halter Devil Chapel', now part of a farm and built, so legend has it, by a reformed drinker who once tried to halter a cow in the mistaken belief that it was his horse. In his stupor the farmer, Francis Browen, thought he had haltered the Devil and is said to have built the chapel in 1723 in repentance.

Ednaston

7 miles NW of Derby off the A52

This is an ancient manor which was recorded, in the Domesday Survey of 1086, as being in the ownership of Henry de Ferrers of Duffield Castle. The present manor house, **Ednaston Manor** on Brailsford Brook was built by Sir Edwin Lutyens at the turn of the 20th century. Unfortunately it is not open to the public.

Long Lane

6 miles NW of Derby off the A52

Long Lane village is truly a hidden place, not found on most maps. It is south off the A52, and can be reached by heading for the village of Lees and then following the sign for Long Lane. It is set on the old Roman road bearing the same name and is not much more than a cluster of cottages, a school, a church and a pub. **The Three Horseshoes** in Long Lane dates back to 1750, when it was a grain store, where ale was brewed for the adjacent blacksmith's. Unusually, the property is owned by the village itself.

Longford

8 miles W of Derby off the A515

Truly a hidden place, Longford lies very much off the beaten track, but it is well worth finding as the village has the distinction of being the home of the first cheese factory in England. Opened on the 4th May in 1870, its first manager bore the memorable name Cornelius Schermerhorn. Derbyshire, with its excellent rail and canal links, made the county an ideal centre for the mass production of cheeses for foreign markets.

Longford Hall is a late medieval house, renovated by Pickford in 1762 and restored after a bad fire in 1942. It was the family seat of the Coke family, after the Longfords. The Longfords settled here in the 12th century and the church, which is close to the hall, was built then. The church of **St Chads,** surrounded by magnificent lime trees, still retains many Norman parts, though the tower was added in the 15th century. There are some fine monuments to both the Cokes and their predecessors the Longfords in the church.

Norbury

14 miles W of Derby off the B5033

Norbury lies on the river Dove and was recorded in the *Domesday Book* as Norberre or Nordberie, the 'norther' defence on the Dove. The mainly 14th and 15th century village church of St Mary and St Barlok is definitely worth a visit, as it houses the alabaster tombs of the 15th century FitzHerberts, one of the oldest families in Derbyshire. It is probable that the family contributed much towards the church building over the years. Those familiar with the works of George Eliot will feel much at home in this part of the county. The characters Adam and Seth from her famous novel *Adam Bede* were based on her father, Robert Evans, and his brother, and many scenes from the book are set in this village. Members of Eliot's family are buried in the churchyard.

Norbury Manor and Hall, next to the church, is a Grade I listed building. The original medieval Manor House is still attached to the later Hall. It was the seat of the Fitzherbert family from medieval times. Now owned by the National trust, it is open to the public by appointment only.

Doveridge

15 miles W of Derby off the A50

As its name suggests, this village is situated on the banks of the River Dove and, although there is a fair amount of modern housing, Doveridge still retains a rural atmosphere. The village boasts a distinguished 13th century church and, in the churchyard, an old yew tree that is reputed to be one of the largest in Derbyshire.

Boylestone

10 miles W of Derby off the A515

This isolated village amid gently rolling countryside south of Ashbourne is noted in history for an incident during the Civil War. Two hundred Royalist troops spent the night in the church of St John the Baptist on their way to Wingfield Manor. Rather foolishly they set no watch, and in the morning found themselves surrounded by Cromwell's men. The Royalists surrendered, were disarmed, and quietly filed out of the church.

The church tower is from the Victorian era and has an unusual pyramidal roof. Inside, the chancel is just as the Cavaliers would have seen it, as it dates back to the 1300s, as does a delicately moulded low recess in the chancel.

Church Broughton

10 miles W of Derby off the A50

Church Broughton is a quiet village, which was, until the early part of the 20th century, part of the Duke of Devonshire's Derbyshire estates. It is now mainly a commuter village for nearby towns. The parish church of **St Michael** dates back to the early 14th century. It has a large west tower with Victorian pinnacles and big gargoyles and is topped with a small spire. It also contains a long 14th century chancel.

Sutton-on-the-Hill

8 miles W of Derby off the A516

Despite its name this is a sheltered spot, with the church standing above the village on the hill. The church of **St Michael** has a 14th century tower with a spire that was rebuilt in 1841. A few other parts are 14th century, but mostly the church was rebuilt in 1863. It contains an unusual monument to Judith Sleigh, who died in 1634. It is a standing coffin carved in black stone

The Hawk & Buckle Inn

Main Street, Etwall, Derbyshire DE65 6LP
Tel: 01283 733471
e-mail: enquiries@hawkandbuckle.com
website: www.hawkandbuckle.com

Situated in Etwall, once along one of the main routes into Derby but now a tranquil and relaxed village, The **Hawk & Buckle Inn** is a large and handsome inn dating back to the early 1800s. Voted Marstons Cask Ale Pub of the Year in 2003, the inn is open every day from midday and serves no fewer than five real ales: Marstons Pedigree, Marstons Old Empire, Mansfield and two rotating guest ales. Together with this are lagers, spirits, cider, stout, wines and soft drinks served in the spacious bar, which is decorated and furnished in traditional style, in keeping with the exposed beamwork, brickbuilt fireplace and other original features.

The inn is at the centre of village life, and sponsors the local football team, hosts the Diving Club, Sail Training Association and many of the Well-dressing Committee meetings. Licensees Clive and Cheryl have been at the helm here since 1998. When they took over it was their first venture into the licensing trade, but they have made a great success of it. The inn is justly popular with locals and visitors alike for its hospitality, well-kept ales and great food. Among the traditional favourites served are mixed grill, steaks, liver and bacon, and all-day brunch. Cheryl is the chef, and her specials include Coronation chicken, salmon pie, lamb tagine, vegetarian lasagne and Chinese sweet-and-sour pork. There's also a full complement of light lunches and snacks with tempting sandwiches and baguettes, baked potatoes, children's meals and more. Only the freshest local ingredients are used to create dishes that are truly memorable. Food is available Monday to Saturday at lunch (12 – 2.30) and dinner (5.30 – 8.30). Bookings are required for Saturday evening. Children welcome.

The inn also proudly hosts beer festivals twice a year, in April and October, when for one weekend, from Friday to Sunday, there are 12 cask ales to sample.

with handles. Cricket fans will take special pleasure in visiting Sutton on the Hill, as it was the family home of G M and R H R Buckston, both of whom captained the Derbyshire cricket team.

Sudbury

12 miles W of Derby off the A50

This is the estate village to **Sudbury Hall**, the late 17th century mansion and home of a branch of the Vernon family who lived at Haddon Hall. The house is intriguing, the garden restful. Gifted to the National Trust in 1967, the Hall is an unexpected mixture of architectural styles. A splendid example of a house of Charles II's time, inside Sudbury Hall contains elaborate plasterwork and murals throughout, wood carvings by Grinling Gibbons, and some fine examples of mythological paintings by Laguerre. The beautiful staircase of the Main Hall featured in the BBC's *Pride and Predudice*. Of particular interest is the **Museum of Childhood,** which is situated in the servants' wing and provides a fascinating insight into the lives of children down the ages. Fascinating displays range from a wealthy family's nursery and an Edwardian schoolroom to a 'chimney climb' and coal tunnel for the adventurous. The formal gardens and meadows lead to the tree-fringed lake. Wildlife abounds, including kestrels, grey herons, grass snakes, dragonflies, newts, frogs, toads, little and tawny owls and woodpeckers. Special events are held throughout the year.

Next to the hall is the church of **All Saints**, which was recorded in the *Domesday Book* but has been extensively restored in later years. The east window was donated by Queen Victoria and Prince Albert.

Etwall

5 miles SW of Derby off the A516

This charming place has a fine range of Georgian buildings including some 17th century almshouses built by Sir John Port, the founder of nearby Repton College. The original site of **Etwall Hall**, where Sir John lived, is now the home of a large comprehensive school, which bears his name. For a village that derived its name from 'Eata's Well', it seems strange that Etwall only took up the custom of well-dressing recently and by chance. To mark the centenary of the village primary school, the teachers dressed a token well while the Women's Institute, with the help of people from two villages within the Peak District, dressed the only true well in Etwall, Town Well. This was in 1970 and the event, in mid May, was so successful that it is now an annual occasion and a total of eight wells are decorated.

As there is no long-standing tradition of well-dressing in the village the themes for the dressings are not the more usual Biblical subjects but have covered a wide range of stories and ideas including racial unity and the life and times of Sir John Port. Etwall is also the most southerly village to take part in the custom of well-dressing and its position,

The White Swan

Eggington Road, Hilton, Derbyshire DE65 5FJ
Tel: 01283 732305 Fax: 01283 735531
e-mail: dct51@aol.com
website: www.thewhiteswan.co.uk

Dating back to the early 1700s and once known as The Brown Bear, **The White Swan** has been extended and refurbished in recent years to enhance the inn's comfort and quality without losing any of its traditional appeal. The atmosphere at this fine inn is always warm and welcoming.

Open every day from midday, the inn serves two real ales – Bass and Marstons Pedigree – with plans to feature a rotating guest ale soon. The wine list is impressive.

Excellent food is served Monday to Saturday 12 – 3 and 6 – 9.30, Sundays 12 – 7. Booking is required for Friday and Saturday. The restaurant is tastefully decorated in warm woods that complement the exposed beamwork in the ceiling above. It seats 50 and is no-smoking. Guests choose from the menu and specials board (which changes daily) from a good range of dishes made with the best local ingredients, freshly prepared to order. A sample from the main-course menu includes steaks, green-lipped mussels, char-grilled courgette filled with ratatouille and goat's cheese on a bed of linguine, and slow-braised shank of lamb. Among the chef's specialities are his mouth-watering desserts, so be sure to leave room! Food themed evenings are planned for the future – please ring or visit the inn's website for details. Children are welcome, and there's a lovely beer garden with plenty of space, an attractive paved patio area commanding a lovely view of the scenic countryside all around, and a large off-road carpark.

Licensees Dawn and David have over 25 years' experience in the trade, and it shows: the quality of service and hospitality are second to none. Both local people, they have a wealth of knowledge about the region which they are happy to share with visitors.

To find this superb hidden gem, follow the Willington Village sign from the centre of Hilton. The inn is on your right before the railway crossing.

well below the harsh uplands of Derbyshire's Peak District, has ensured that there is always a good supply of flowers even though the dressing takes place late in spring.

The Port Hospital Almshouses, fronted by wrought iron gates, made by Robert Bakewell of Derby, were rebuilt in 1681 and recently restored again. Until the 1960s, Almsmen and women wore special hats or bonnets and a dark blue cloak with a silver clasp.

Hilton

8 miles SW of Derby off the A5132

Wakelyn Old Hall is an unusual half-timbered house that can be found in this small village. Dating from the 16th century, when the Wakelyn family left in 1621, the building became The Bull's Head Inn. It was also, reputedly, one of the places that Mary, Queen of Scots stopped at on her way to Tutbury Castle. The Old Talbot Inn dates back to the 15th century. The old gravel works are now a bird sanctuary and a nature reserve.

Swadlincote

Here at the extreme edge of Derbyshire, well south of the River Trent, Swadlincote shares many characteristics with Staffordshire. Among the town's thriving industries, based on the clay and coal on which it stands, are large potteries founded in 1795 as well as brickworks. Historically more a collection of villages though officially an urban district, it retains a rural feel that is charming and worth exploring.

North of Swadlincote

Hartshorne

1 mile NE of Swadlincote off the A514

One of this lovely village's most renowned sons was George Stanhope, who grew up to be a famous preacher, a bold critic and a brave writer during the reign of Queen Anne.

Hartshorne's village church was rebuilt in 1835, though it retains its 15th century tower and 14th century font. A fine altar tomb shows the alabaster figures of Sir Humphry Dethick of 1599 and his wife. The Dethicks paid long and loyal service to the Royal family of their day - one of the Dethicks went to Cleves to find a fourth wife for Henry VIII, while his son Sir William is said to have laid a pall of rich velvet on the coffin of Mary, Queen of Scots.

Calke

5 miles NE of Swadlincote off the B587

In 1985 the National Trust bought **Calke Abbey**, a large Baroque-style mansion built in 1701 on the site of an Augustinian priory founded in 1133. However, it was not until 1989 that the Trust were able to open the house to the public, for this was no ordinary house at all. Dubbed 'the house that time forgot' since the death of the owner, Sir Vauncy Harpur-Crewe in 1924 nothing had been altered in the mansion! In fact, the seclusion of the house and also the rather bizarre lifestyle of its inhabitants had left many rooms and objects untouched for over 100 years. There was even a spectacular 18th century Chinese silk state bed that had never been unpacked.

Calke Abbey

Today, the Trust has repaired the house and returned all 13,000 items to their original positions so that the Abbey now looks just as it did when it was bought in 1981. The attention to detail has been so great that none of the rooms have been redecorated. Visitors can enjoy the silver display and trace the route of 18th century servants along the brewhouse tunnel to the house cellars. Calke Abbey stands in its own large park with gardens, a chapel and stables that are also open to the public. There are three walled gardens with their glasshouses, a restored orangery, vegetable garden, pheasant aviaries and the summer flower display within the unusual 'auricular' theatre. Calke is home to lots of wildlife including fallow deer, weasels, stoats, barn, little and tawny owls, woodpeckers, common toads, butterflies and beetles.

Interior of Calke Abbey

Just over the Leicestershire border, the peaceful **Staunton Harold Church** is a few minutes from Calke Abbey. Built in an open act of defiance to Oliver Cromwell by Sir Robert Shirley, the church stands next to Harold Staunton Hall (private). Inside there are original 17th century cushions, painted ceilings and fine panelling.

Melbourne

6 miles NE of Swadlincote off the B587

This small town, which lent its name to the rather better-known city in Australia, is a successful market garden centre. A famous son of Melbourne, who started his working life in one of the market gardens, was Thomas Cook, who was born here in

The Three Horseshoes Inn

Breedon-on-the-Hill, Derbyshire DE73 8AN
Tel: 01332 695129

Breedon-on-the-Hill is a tranquil village found off the A453 and B587 midway between Ashby-de-la-Zouch and J23 of the M1. Here can be found the excellent **Three Horseshoes Inn**, located across the road from the village's old 'Lock-up' – an ancient and tiny stonebuilt, turreted structure where the village ne'er-do-wells would serve detention.

Owners Ian and Jennie have earned their far-reaching reputation for superb food at The Nags Head Inn, Castle Donington, and have now moved to this Grade II listed inn together with their brigade of chefs and front of house staff. Their intention is to refurbish and highlight the best of the inn's 230-year history and create a warm and welcoming ambience to ensure guests every comfort, which will include superb en-suite accommodation .

The bar offers a choice of real ales together with an excellent range of wines and malt whiskies.Open for lunch and dinner, food is prepared daily using only the freshest of ingredients and local produce wherever possible. Food is served in the bar or non-smoking dining room where booking is advisable.

1808. He went on to pioneer personally-conducted tours and gave his name to the famous worldwide travel company.

Full of Georgian charm, Melbourne has many fine buildings which include one of the finest Norman churches in the country, the church of **St Michael and St Mary**. This seems rather a grand church for this modest place and indeed, it is no ordinary parish church. In the 12th century, when the Bishopric of Carlisle was formed, there needed to be a place of safety for the clergy when Carlisle was being raided by the Scots. So this church was built at Melbourne and, while Carlisle was subjected to raids and violence, the Bishop retired to Melbourne and continued to carry out his duties. The church was built between 1133 and 1229 and, in 1299, the then Bishop built a palace on land that is now home to Melbourne Hall.

The birthplace of the 19th century statesman Lord Melbourne, and also the home of Lady Caroline Lamb, **Melbourne Hall** is another fine building in this area of Derbyshire. A modest building, the Hall is surrounded by beautiful gardens, the most notable feature of which is a beautiful wrought-iron birdcage pergola built in the early 1700s by Robert Bakewell, a local blacksmith from Derby. Bakewell lived in Melbourne for a time at the house of a widow named Fisher and her daughters. However when one daughter became pregnant, he moved hurriedly to Derby. Unfortunately the house is only

Bay Tree Restaurant

4 Potter Street, Melbourne,
Derbyshire DE73 1DW
Tel: 01332 863358 Fax: 01332 865545
website: www.baytreerestaurant.co.uk

Just eight miles south of Derby is the small Georgian market town of Melbourne. An attractive place to visit, there are a number of tourist attractions and pleasant places to walk within the town as well as in the surrounding countryside.

The parish church has been described as a miniature cathedral, and the privately-owned Melbourne Hall is open to the public throughout the month of August, and its gardens from April to September.

The excellent **Bay Tree Restaurant** can be found in the heart of the town, close to the church and the main shops. Generally considered the best restaurant in the area, it is housed in a building typical of the town, dating back to 1790 and retaining many original features.

This superior restaurant features in all the discerning food guides, and bookings are required (especially for Sundays) months in advance. The secret of its success lies with the co-owners, Vicki Talbott and chef Rex Howell, who opened the place back in 1988 and have built up an enviable reputation for quality and service.

Winner of many well-deserved awards, the menu changes regularly but always boasts the best of New World cuisine. Guests can choose from such tempting main courses as rack of English lamb, mignons of prime English beef, calf's liver with crispy pancetta, smoked haddock and salmon fish cakes, French duckling, free-range corn-fed chicken, a range of pasta dishes and lighter meals, and much more. There is also a good selection of 'nibbles' and the restaurant's justly-renowned champagne breakfast. All dishes are expertly prepared and presented, and make the best use of seasonally available produce, combining exquisitely fresh ingredients to create a memorable dining experience. The Bay Tree is open for luncheon Tuesday to Saturday 10.30 a.m. until 3 p.m., Sundays midday to 4 p.m., and for dinner Tuesday to Saturday from 6.30 p.m. The restaurant is closed Mondays except for private parties and on Bank Holidays.

The Bulls Head at Wilson

Wilson, Melbourne, Derby,
Derbyshire DE73 1AE
Tel: 01332 862644 Fax: 01332 863239
e-mail: jad@thebullsheadatwilson.com
website: www.thebullsheadatwilson.com

Jad Otaki, owner of the superb **Bulls Head at Wilson**, bought the inn in 1998 after establishing a restaurant at nearby Castle Donnington. An acclaimed chef with a team of three, Jad has created a justly popular place where guests come from miles around to sample the delights of the menu. Served Monday to Saturday at lunch (12 – 2) and dinner (7 – 9), Sundays midday to 3 p.m., the menu boasts an excellent choice of expertly prepared and presented dishes using the freshest ingredients. A sample from the distinguished à la carte menu includes roast rack of lamb, prime Aberdeen Angus beef, Barbary duck, fillet of cod and casserole of artichoke hearts with red beans, mushrooms and onions in a red wine sauce. Booking is essential at this superior inn.

The wine list is excellent, while other thirst-quenchers include three real ales (Timothy Taylor Landlord, Marston's Pedigree and 1744 Worthingtons) and a good selection of lagers, cider, stout, spirits and soft drinks.

open to the public in August, but the splendid and famous formal gardens are open throughout the summer season and are well worth a visit.

Swarkestone

9 miles NE of Swadlincote off the A5132

Excavations in the village of Swarkestone, at Lowes Farm, led to the discovery that the district was occupied in the Bronze Age and also in Saxon times. This small village has also been, quite literally, a turning point in history. The **Swarkestone Bridge**, with its seven arches and three-quarter-mile long causeway, crosses the River Trent. In 1745, during the second Jacobite Rebellion, the advance guard of Bonnie Prince Charlie reached the Bridge and, had they managed to cross the River at this point, they would have faced no other natural barriers on their 120-mile march to London. As it transpired, the army retreated and fled north, Bonnie Prince Charlie managed to escape and the Jacobite Rebellion was no more.

Legend has it that the original bridge at Swarkestone was built by two daughters of the Harpur family in the early 13th century. The girls were celebrating their joint betrothals when their fiancés were summoned to a barons' meeting across the river. While they were away torrential rain fell, flooding the river, and the two young men drowned as they attempted to ford the raging torrent on their return. The

Ivy House Farm Guesthouse

Stanton-by-Bridge, Derby,
Derbyshire DE73 1HT
Tel: 01332 863152
e-mail: mary@guesthouse.fsbusiness.co.uk
website: www.ivy-house-farm.com

Just a few miles south of Derby off the A514, **Ivy House Farm Guesthouse** is a charming and welcoming place set on a working arable farm amid scenes of rural delight: the River Trent and Swarkestone Bridge are less than a mile away, and the guesthouse is also handy for visiting sights and attractions such as Calke Abbey, Alton Towers and Twycross Zoo. The six guest bedrooms are spacious and handsome; facilities for guests include a hot tub.

girls built the bridge as a memorial to their lovers. Both girls later died impoverished and unmarried.

Barrow-on-Trent

8 miles NE of Swadlincote off the A514

Barrow-on-Trent, as its name tells us, stands between the River Trent and the Trent and Mersey Canal in this rich agricultural part of south Derbyshire.

The row of parish cottages, built by parish levy in the 18th century, is an interesting feature of this attractive village. First rented for 30 shillings (£1.50) a year, the parish council still keeps them in a good state of repair.

The village **Church of St Wilfrid** is first mentioned in the *Domesday Book*, but the present building, which is approached down a pretty lane which also leads towards the river, dates mainly from the 13th century. The north arcade with its original columns is a notable feature. The plain glass windows lend the church a light and airy atmosphere. The base of the square tower and the north aisle date from the 1300s; there is also a Georgian east window.

The village chapel, unsurprisingly in Chapel Lane, was erected on arches so that it could reach the level of the road. This was not to everyone's liking: the marks of shots fired on the building can still be seen in the inscription stone set in the front of the building.

Milton

5 miles N of Swadlincote off the A514

Milton is a small village, once owned by the Burdett family, who built the nearby church of St Saviour.

Bretby

2 miles N of Swadlincote off the A50

Now a leafy rural backwater, Bretby was first mentioned in Domesday as an agricultural settlement around a green. There was once a castle in this quiet village until it was demolished and the stones used to build a mansion house. In the 18th century, that too was

The Bulls Head

1 Woodville Road, Hartshorne,
Derbyshire DE11 7ET
Tel: 01283 215299 Fax: 01283 221380

The Bulls Head is an impressive and welcoming inn located in the small and delightful village of Hartshorne. New tenants Becky and Doug arrived in 2003. Doug has been in the licensing trade for 14 years, and brings his experience to bear on offering all guests great food and drink, and real hospitality. This lovely and elegant premises dates back in parts to Elizabethan times, with Georgian additions.

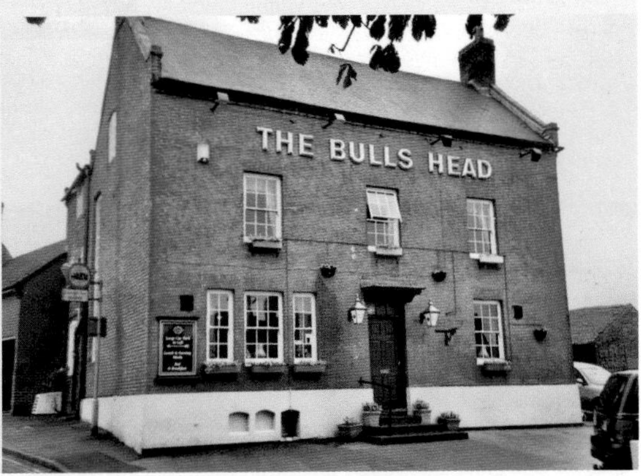

Open every session, the inn boasts two real ales from the Burtonwood Brewery range. Delicious food is served daily at lunch (12 – 2.30) and dinner (6.30 – 9.30). Both Becky and Doug cook, creating a menu and daily specials such as steaks, grilled trout, home-made lasagne, Stilton gammon and other hearty favourites.

Booking is required for Friday and Saturday evenings and Sunday lunchtime.

This fine inn also has five ensuite guest bedrooms available all year round. There's a good mixture of different-sized rooms, all tastefully decorated and supremely comfortable.

Children welcome.

demolished and **Bretby Hall**, as seen today, was built in 1813 by Sir Jeffrey Wyatville, the designer of the 19th century extension at Chatsworth House.

Repton

5 miles N of Swadlincote off the B5008

This village, by the tranquil waters of the River Trent, is steeped in history. The first mention of Repton came in the 7th century when it was established as the capital of the Saxon kingdom of Mercia. A monastery, housing both monks and nuns, was founded here sometime after AD 653 but the building was sacked by the Danes in AD 874. A battleaxe, now on display in the school museum, was excavated a little distance from the church. It had apparently lain undisturbed for well over 1,000 years.

The parish **Church of St Wystan** is famous for its Anglo-Saxon chancel and crypt, but it also contains many of the major styles of medieval architecture. When the chancel and part of the nave were enlarged in 1854, the original Anglo-Saxon columns were moved to the 14th century porch. The crypt claims to be one of the oldest intact Anglo-Saxon buildings in England. The burial place of the Kings of Mercia, including St Wystan in AD 850, the crypt was rediscovered by chance in 1779 by a workman who was digging a hole for a grave in the chancel floor.

The ancient **Cross**, still at the central

The Green Dragon

Willington, Derby, Derbyshire DE65 6BP
Tel: 01283 702327
e-mail: jon@thegreendragon.freeserve.co.uk

Set in the village of Willington on the A5132 within easy access of both the main A50 and A38, **The Green Dragon** is a handsome and traditional inn that dates back to the early 18th century. The village is well known for its railway links (the Derby-to-Birmingham line is across the road from the inn) and its canal (part of the Trent and Mersey Canal, which runs to the rear of the property). It began life as The Navigation; the name was changed in the mid-1700s. A blacksmith's, wheelwright's and boat-repair shop once stood adjacent.

Open all day, every day, guests can sample up to three real ales, with Marstons Pedigree the regular. All their ales are kept in tip-top condition.

The inn is a happy marriage of traditional features and up-to-date facilities. The interior is attractive and very comfortable, with polished wood floors in the dining area and part of the bar, beamed ceilings and open fireplaces.

Jon Shaw became leaseholder here in 2002. This is his first venture into the licensing trade, and has earned rave reviews from locals and visitors alike. He is ably assisted by chefs Tom and Sean and head bar-person Nicola – all offer a high standard of service and hospitality. The inn is popular with walkers, boaters and anyone tempted by great food, drink and the inn's welcoming ambience.

Above all, the food at this fine inn is outstanding. Served daily at lunch (12 – 2.30) and dinner (5.30 – 8.30), booking is essential at weekends. Guests choose off the menu and ever-changing specials board from a wide range of dishes, all expertly prepared and presented. Portions are hearty. Tuesday and Thursday evenings are steak nights, with a choice of two sirloins or two rump steaks plus glass of wine or pint of ale each for a really reasonable price. Wednesday is Pie and Pint Night, with a choice of pies for all guests.

crossroads in the village, has been the focal point of life here for centuries and it has also stood at the heart of the Wednesday market. Right up until the late 19th century a Statutes Fair, for the hiring of farm labourers and domestics, was also held here at Michaelmas.

Parts of an Augustinian priory, founded in 1170, are incorporated in the buildings of **Repton College**, itself founded in 1557. Sir John Port had specifically intended the College to be a grammar school for the local poor children of Etwall, Repton and Burnaston. These intentions have somewhat deviated over the passing years and now Repton stands as one of the foremost public schools in the country. Interestingly, two of its headmasters, Dr Temple and Dr Fisher, went on to become Archbishops of Canterbury, while Dr Ramsey was a pupil at the school under Dr Fisher's guiding light. Film buffs will recognise the 14th century gatehouse and causeway, as they featured in both film versions of the popular story *Goodbye, Mr Chips*.

Just to the west of the village is **Foremark Hall**, built by Robert Adam in 1762 for the Burdett family. It is now a preparatory school for Repton College.

South of Swadlincote

Church Gresley

2 miles SW of Swadlincote off the A444

This former mining village has a distinguished history dating back to the time of the Augustinian monks who settled here in the 12th century and founded a priory. The village's name, like that of nearby Castle Gresley, recalls the great Gresley family, said to have been the only Derbyshire family to have retained their lands from the time of the *Domesday Book* up until the 20th century.

The village church retains some links with the past. The priory and chancel buildings were pulled down during the Tudor age, and the church remained in a sad state of disrepair up until the early 19th century. A new chancel was built in 1872. Remains of the priory have been found, including fragments of painted glass, stone coffins and medieval tiles. What remains of the old church are the sturdy 15th century tower and two 14th century arches that lead to the church's north aisle.

An impressive alabaster monument depicts **Sir Thomas Gresley**, surrounded by arms showing the marriages of his ancestors dating back to the time of William the Conqueror. The church's treasure, though, are the 10 large and wonderfully carved stalls.

Castle Gresley

3 miles SW of Swadlincote off the A444

Unfortunately nothing is left of the castle built by the Gresley family which gives this attractive village its name - apart from the grassy mound on which it stood, still known as **Castle Knob**.

Mount Pleasant Inn

109 Mount Pleasant Road, Castle Gresley, Swadlincote, Derbyshire DE11 9JJ
Tel/Fax: 01283 551541

An impressive building that dates back to the early 1800s, **Mount Pleasant Inn** is an attractive and welcoming place run by Bob and Linda, who have been here as tenants since 2001. Ably assisted by cook Kathryne, they offer great food, drink and hospitality to all their guests. Closed Monday lunchtime except Bank Holidays, this fine traditional pub is open every session Tuesday to Thursday and Sunday, and all day Fridays and Saturdays.

The two real ales served are Marstons Pedigree and a rotating guest ale, together with a selection of lagers, cider, stout, wines, spirits and soft drinks.

Food is served at lunchtime (12 –3) Tuesday to Friday. Guests choose off the printed menu or specials board from a select menu that has something for everyone's taste. Children welcome.

This convivial and friendly pub has live entertainment once a month, usually on a Friday evening from 9 p.m., and hosts a bingo session with cash prizes every Saturday night from 9.

The Plough Inn

68 Main Street, Rosliston, Swadlincote, Derbyshire DE12 8JL
Tel: 01283 761354

Found just south of Burton-upon-Trent, the pretty village of Rosliston boasts the excellent **Plough Inn**. The premises date back some 400 years, and the interior has many traditional features.

Leaseholder Tim Hyde has been a professional chef for a number of years; he and his wife Vanessa took over in July of 2004 and have made a big impression. Popular with locals and visitors alike, the inn is open all day at weekends and at every session (except Monday lunchtime) through the week. The two real ales are Marstons Pedigree and a changing guest ale, complemented by a range of lagers, cider, stout, wines, spirits and soft drinks.

Food is served Tuesday to Sunday (and Bank Holidays) at lunch (12–2) and dinner (6–9). Guests choose off the menus for light bites or full meals. Filled cobs are also available all day. Specialities include chicken and prawns in a lemon and parsley butter and Tim's excellent steaks. Sunday lunch is a hearty three-course meal – booking advised.

Linton

2 miles SW of Swadlincote off the A444

Linton is a charming and restful village, within 'The National Forest', which is mainly agricultural since the closure of the Coton Park colliery.

Rosliston

5 miles SW of Swadlincote off the A444

Rosliston was recorded in the *Domesday Book* as Redlauseton , an Ango-Saxon name meaning farm of Hrolf. Rosliston is part of the National Forest and there are way-marked walks, a wildlife hide and childrens play equipment.

The church of St Mary the Virgin is mainly 19th century but the 14th century tower with its broach spire still remains.

Coton-in-the-Elms

6 miles SW of Swadlincote off the A444

Mentioned in the *Domesday Book* as Cotune, it got its name from the elm trees which bordered every road into the village until they were obliterated by Dutch Elm disease. As befits a village with this much charm and character, Coton-in-the-Elms offers several quality eateries and inns.

Netherseal

6 miles S of Swadlincote off the A444

Netherseal is a picturesque village on the banks of the river Mease, overlooking Leicestershire. 'Seal' means forested and Netherseal was recorded in the *Domesday Book* as a wooded area on

New Inn

2 High Street, Woodville,
Derbyshire DE11 7EH
Tel: 01283 217553
e-mail: mcmcgrl@aol.com

The **New Inn** is an impressive building located right on Woodville's main street. Woodville is a tranquil village found by exiting at junction 22 of the M1 and taking the A511 towards Ashby-de-la-Zouch, then continuing on towards Burton on Trent, past the town of Swadlincote, until – after about two miles – you reach Woodville.

The inn dates back to the late 18th century and has the distinction of having been the first pub bought by Bass brewers, back in 1843. The warm-coloured brickwork combines with the inn's original feature windows and pretty porch to create a very pleasing aspect. Inside, the inn is well laid out with a spacious bar and dining area, carpeted throughout to add to the cosy atmosphere. The bar area to the rear has recently been completely refurbished.

This excellent place has been family-run for over 30 years, and present licensees Glen and Michelle have been at the helm since the year 2000. They have placed their own stamp on the place, and the bar is well stocked with a range of beers, spirits, wines and soft drinks together with two real ales – Bass and Marstons Pedigree – two ciders and a range of lagers on offer.

If you're looking for a bite to eat, there's a comprehensive menu that offers reasonably priced dishes in hearty portions, with hot and cold dishes at lunchtime Monday to Friday and in the evenings Wednesday to Saturday. The traditional Sunday carvery has two sittings (midday and 2 p.m.); booking is advised. There's also a carvery on Wednesday and Friday evenings, while Thursday hosts themed food evenings and on Saturday there's a full à la carte menu.

The inn also boasts an unusual feature in its bowling green, and there is nothing nicer on a summer evening than, glass in hand, watching a bowl roll towards the jack. If you're keen, there's every chance you could get a game yourself!

the edge of the Ashby Woulds. It was once a mining community with a two-shaft colliery and several related industries. The mining industry has long gone and the centre of Netherseal village is now a conservation area with many listed buildings including the 17th century almshouses.

Appleby Magna

5 miles S of Swadlincote off the A453

The attractive village of Appleby has three pubs, a church, a handful of shops and a school, originally designed by Sir Christopher Wren. Originally agricultural, it has become a commuter village for the nearby towns. The centre of Appleby around the historic medieval Moat House is a Conservation Area. The house, the moat and its fields on either side are scheduled as an Ancient Monument.

Measham

3 miles S of Swadlincote off the A453

Just over the border into Leicestershire, Measham is well worth that short step over the county boundary. It is large enough to be lively yet retains the air of a lovely rural retreat. It also boasts some lovely 16th, 17th and 18th century buildings. The tiny Measham Museum opened in 1992. There is a collection of artefacts, pictures, letters and documents recording the history of the village through the eyes of two generations of local doctors covering nearly a century as well as items relating to the coal mining, terra-cotta and pottery industries. Mining was recorded in this area as early as the 13th century. There is also a display of Measham ware, traditionally associated with the canal people. All kinds of tea and table ware were made in the characteristic dark brown glaze covered in shiny sprigs of flowers and birds. Measham museum's earliest teapot is dated 1886 and the last known date of manufacture is 1914. They were sold by Mrs Annie Bonas from her shop in the High Street.

Donisthorpe

3 miles SE of Swadlincote off the A444

Donisthorpe is a famous old mining village right on the Derbyshire-Leicestershire border. Its inhabitants are justly proud of the village's industrial and historical heritage. The old colliery, the pit railway and the old British Rail line closed down by the 1960s. Left behind is a proud history and a tranquillity unknown in the days of the mines.

Moira

6 miles SE of Swadlincote off the A444

Moira Furnace Museum is based in a 19th century iron blast furnace. There are interactive displays and information on how the furnace worked and its influence on the local economy and the lives of the workers.

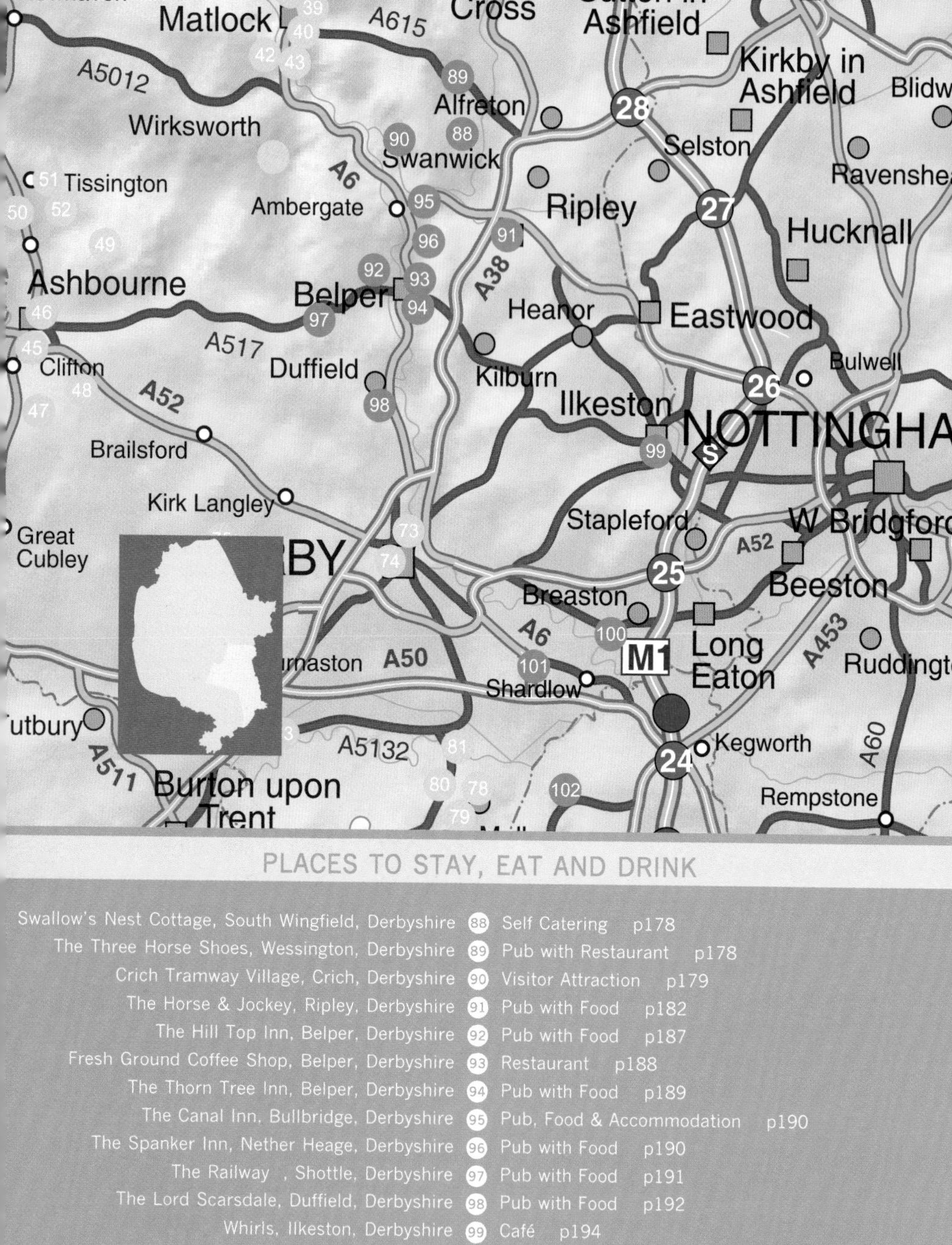

PLACES TO STAY, EAT AND DRINK

Swallow's Nest Cottage, South Wingfield, Derbyshire	88	Self Catering	p178
The Three Horse Shoes, Wessington, Derbyshire	89	Pub with Restaurant	p178
Crich Tramway Village, Crich, Derbyshire	90	Visitor Attraction	p179
The Horse & Jockey, Ripley, Derbyshire	91	Pub with Food	p182
The Hill Top Inn, Belper, Derbyshire	92	Pub with Food	p187
Fresh Ground Coffee Shop, Belper, Derbyshire	93	Restaurant	p188
The Thorn Tree Inn, Belper, Derbyshire	94	Pub with Food	p189
The Canal Inn, Bullbridge, Derbyshire	95	Pub, Food & Accommodation	p190
The Spanker Inn, Nether Heage, Derbyshire	96	Pub with Food	p190
The Railway , Shottle, Derbyshire	97	Pub with Food	p191
The Lord Scarsdale, Duffield, Derbyshire	98	Pub with Food	p192
Whirls, Ilkeston, Derbyshire	99	Café	p194
The Coach & Horses, Draycott, Derbyshire	100	Pub with Food	p201
The Harrington Arms, Thulston, Derbyshire	101	Pub with Restaurant	p202
Donington Collection, Castle Donington, Derbyshire	102	Visitor Attraction	p204

Denotes entries in other chapters

5 The Amber Valley and Erewash

This chapter encompasses the regions of Derbyshire going by the picturesque names of the Amber Valley and the eastern part of the area known as Erewash. These two regions cover the eastern and southeastern parts of Derbyshire respectively. The Rivers Amber, Derwent and Trent run through this part of the county. Though the scenery is perhaps less dramatic than the popular Peak District, in which most of north Derbyshire lies, there are ample opportunities to enjoy pleasant walks in the extensive grounds of many of the estates.

The southeast area of Derbyshire has been heavily influenced by the two towns of Derby and Nottingham. Originally small farming communities, many of the villages grew at the time of the Industrial Revolution and they can, in many cases, be characterised by rows of workers' cottages. However, notwithstanding this there are some interesting and unique buildings to be found in this corner of Derbyshire.

While a lot of the area did not escape from the growth of Derby and Nottingham, several villages remain, their centres almost intact, and, in particular there is Ockbrook, the site of a Moravian Settlement. Unlike the area to the west, there are no great stately mansions, except for one, Elvaston Castle, which, along with its extensive grounds, is an interesting and delightful place to explore. Dale Abbey is another of the region's attractions, a now ruined abbey founded here by Augustinian monks in the 13th century.

The Derwent Valley

Alfreton

This historic town dates back to Saxon times and, despite local legends to the contrary, Alfred the Great was not immortalised in the naming of the place. It would have belonged to a Saxon noble of the name of Alfred at some time and was named 'Aelfredingtune', but there is nothing to suggest that King Alfred was based here. In the *Domesday Book* it is recorded as 'Elstretune'. This attractive former coal mining town stands on a hill close to the Nottinghamshire border. The town benefited from the philanthropy of Robert Watchorn, a pit boy made good, who emigrated to America, became Commissioner of Immigration and made his fortune, much of which was used to rebuild the southern part of Alfreton. Along the charming High Street can be found the George Hotel, a fine Georgian building that looks down the length of the High Street. There are also a number of other 18th century stonebuilt houses. The parish church of St Martin is large and has an impressive fine western tower. The ground floor of the church dates back to the 1200s.

Among the many splendid old buildings in Alfreton, the most impressive is **Alfreton Hall**, the centrepiece of an attractive public park. In soft mellow stone, the Hall was built around 1730, with 19th century additions. Owned until fairly recently by the Palmer Morewood family, owners of the local coal mines, it is now used as an Arts and Adult Education Centre. The park is quite extensive, boasting its own cricket ground and a horse-riding track around its perimeters. In **King Street** there is a house of confinement, or lock-up, which was built to house lawbreakers and catered mainly for the local drunkards. The close confines of the prison with its two cells, minute windows and thick outer walls must have been a very effective deterrent.

The market at Alfreton was granted, in 1251, to Robert de Latham and Thomas de Chaworth, to be held on a Monday, together with a fair for three days at the festival of St Margaret. There is still a bustling market and Afreton attracts visitors from quite a radius to its busy town centre.

The Amber Valley

Around Alfreton

South Normanton

2 miles east of Alfreton off the B6109

Normanton, meaning the farm of the north men or 'Northwegans' was a small holding belonging to William Peveril at the time of Domesday. Now a large, busy industrial village, it grew from a largely agricultural settlement with some tanning, framework knitting and small scale coal mining. The village was transformed after the opening of 'A Winning' colliery in 1871 and 'B Winning' in 1875, by the Blackwell Colliery Company. By the 1881's 'A Winning' had the largest output of coal in Derbyshire and employed around 500 men. Terraced houses were built to accommodate the growing population, which doubled in the ten years from 1871 to 1881. Like many Victorian industrialists the Blackwell Colliery Company took a paternalistic attitude to its workforce, providing a reading room, library, tennis courts and playing fields as well as a cottage hospital. South Normanton Colliery closed in 1952, B Winning in 1964 and A Winning in 1969.

The present population is around 8000. Despite the unemployment caused by the closing of the coal mines, the community spirit, typical of mining villages continues. The village centre, around the old market place has moved to a new market area and housing covers the site of Jedediah Strutt's birthplace. New industries have taken over with the expansion of industrial estates around the village.

St Michaels Church dates from around the 13th century but most of the present building is 19th century. It contains a monument to a Robert Ravel who lived at the nearby Carnfield Hall, an early 17th century stone mansion built by the Revell family.

Oakerthorpe

1 mile W of Alfreton off the B6013/A615/B5035

At Oakerthorpe Nature Reserve, subsidence from the Oakerthorpe coal mine has created a marshy area, which is now a nature reserve managed by Derbyshire Wildlife Trust.

South Wingfield

2 miles NW of Alfreton off the A6

Above the village, on the rise of a hill, stand the graceful ruins of the 15th

Wingfield Manor

Swallow's Nest Cottage

Park Cottage, 39 Manor Road, South Wingfield, Derbyshire DE55 7NH
Tel: 01773 833615 Mobile: 07867 602401
e-mail: wetton.antiques@bushinternet.com

Set in the picturesque village of South Wingfield, **Swallow's Nest College** is a magical and supremely comfortable retreat set just a few miles from Alfreton.

Sleeping four to five people, this excellent barn conversion has been tastefully renovated to offer guests the best of old world and new: beamed ceilings, stripped pine floors, hand-painted traditional furnishings and superb linens and drapes, ensuring guests' every comfort. Facilities in the cottage include a fully fitted kitchen, superb double bedroom and a second twin bedroom, and shower room with WC.

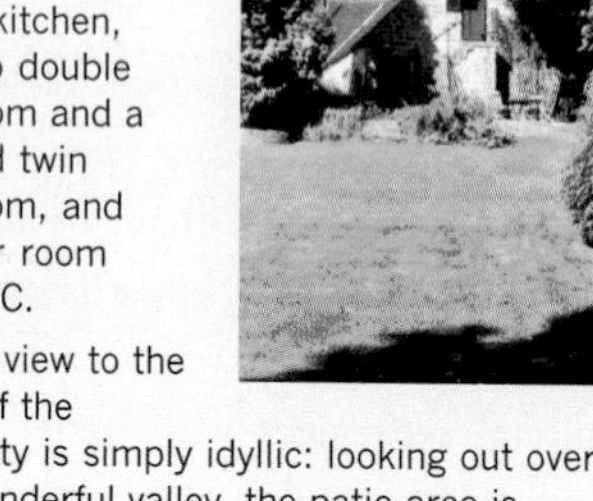

The view to the back of the property is simply idyllic: looking out over the wonderful valley, the patio area is equipped with furniture and a barbecue.

There are excellent walks in the surrounding countryside, sights and attractions such as Chatsworth House, Bakewell and the many delights of the Peak District within easy reach, and a good inn nearby.

Three-night minimum. No pets. No smoking.

The Three Horse Shoes

The Green, Wessington,
Derbyshire DE55 6DQ
Tel: 01773 834854

Found in the village of Wessington on the A615 Matlock-to-Alfreton Road, **The Three Horse Shoes** is an outstanding public house and restaurant. Dating back to the late 1600s, this former coaching house once had a blacksmith's to the rear and was a well-known stop for buying and selling horses, right up to the early 20th century.

Experienced owners Scott and Tonia and their family arrived in 2003, and with hard work and expertise have given the place a new lease of life and a fine reputation for food and ale. There are two real ales from the Hardy & Hansons Brewery.

Quality bar meals are served Tuesday to Saturday 12–2, Tuesday to Thursday evening (5.30–8.30) and Sunday lunchtime (12.30–5) Upstairs, Brownies Restaurant serves a range of excellent dishes Friday and Saturday evenings from 7 to 9 p.m. The menu includes tempting meals such as Derbyshire beef steaks, seared tuna loin Niçoise, Barnsley chop and fettuccini of oyster mushrooms, fresh basil and pistachios with parmesan cream. Membership in Peak District Cuisine ensures good local produce in all dishes.

century **Wingfield Manor**. Built by Ralph Lord Cromwell, the manor house was used as Mary Queen of Scots' prison on two separate occasions in 1569 and 1584 when she was held under the care of the Earl of Shrewsbury. The local squire, Anthony Babington, attempted to rescue the Queen and lead her to safety but the plot failed and, instead, led to them both being beheaded. One of the less well-known of Derbyshire's many manor houses and mansions, the history and architectural interest provided by the ruins make it one of the more fascinating homes in the area. A wander around the remains reveals the large banqueting hall with its unusual oriel window and a crypt which was probably used to store food and wine. Whatever its use, it is a particularly fine example and rivals a similar structure at Fountains Abbey. High up in the tower can also be seen a single archer's slit, built the opposite way round so that only one archer was needed to defend the whole tower. The ruins have been used as a location for a number of film and TV productions, including *Peak Practice* and Zeffirelli's *Jane Eyre*.

Crich

6 miles SW of Alfreton off the A6

Probably best known as the village of Cardale in the TV series *Peak Practice*, this large village, with its hilltop church and market cross, is also the home of the **National Tramway Museum** (see panel below). Referring to itself intriguingly as 'the museum that's a mile long', it offers a wonderful opportunity to enjoy a tram ride along a Victorian Street scene. The signposts, stone flags and gas lamps are all original and come from such diverse places as Liverpool, Oldham and Leeds. Today, in many towns and cities, trams are making a come back, but here the

Crich Tramway Village

Crich Tramway Village, Nr Matlock,
Derbyshire DE4 5DP
Tel: 0870 75 TRAMS (87267)
Fax: 01773 854320
e-mail: enquiries@tramway.co.uk
website: www.tramway.co.uk

Crich Tramway Village offers a family day out in the relaxing atmosphere of a bygone era. Explore the re-created period street with its genuine buildings and features, fascinating exhibitions and most importantly, its trams. Unlimited tram rides are free with your entry fee, giving you the opportunity to fully appreciate the Village and surrounding countryside.

Journey on one of the many beautifully restored vintage trams, as they rumble through the cobbled street past a traditional police telephone known as the 'TARDIS', the Red Lion Pub & Restaurant, exhibition hall, workshops, children's play and picnic area, before passing beneath the magnificent Bowes Lyon Bridge. Next it's past the bandstand, through the woods, and then on to Glory Mine taking in spectacular views of the Derwent Valley.

River Amber

Museum gives visitors the opportunity to view the real thing. As well as those shuttling up and down the mile-long scenic route, there is an exhibition, which contains not only trams but much more besides, including some wonderfully colourful fairground organs. Throughout the year the museum holds many special events and, with their policy of no hidden extras, this is a great place to take all the family for a fun day out. The Museum stands on the site of a quarry that was owned by the great engineer, George Stephenson, who also owned the railway that carried the stone down the steep incline to his lime kilns alongside the Cromford Canal.

Back in the centre of the village is the tower of **Crich Stand**, a local landmark that looks rather like a lighthouse. In fact this is the Regimental Memorial for the Sherwood Foresters erected in 1923. It stands almost 1,000 feet above sea level and from its viewing gallery, on a clear day, it is said that seven counties can be seen. A lantern is lit in the tower at night and the regiment still holds an annual pigrimage to the tower on the first Sunday of July. A climb to the top certainly offers some fantastic views. This large, straggling village, which retains its medieval market cross, was also a flourishing knitting centre at one time; the telltale 18th century cottages with their long upper windows can still be seen. The part-Norman parish Church of St Michael has a built-in stone lectern, which, though common in Derbyshire, is rare elsewhere in the country.

Whatstandwell

4 miles SW of Alfreton off the A6

This tiny village, of which it has been said 'the loveliness of the English countryside is always here,' was once owned by the monks of Darley Abbey. It nestles in the valley of the River Derwent. The highest hill surrounding the village is crowned by a War Memorial tower with a beacon that shines over Nottinghamshire and Derbyshire. Up across the valley is **Shining Cliff**, and along the village's steep lanes lie greystone cottages and farmhouses, built from the stone of its own quarries and merging gently into the background of woods and cliff. Florence Nightingale knew and loved the village, and took a keen interest in the local community.

Fritchley

3 miles SW of Alfreton off the A610

This quiet hamlet was, during the 19th and early 20th centuries, an important meeting place for Quakers. A flourishing community survives today. Here also can be seen the remains of a pre-Stephenson tramway that was built at the end of the 18th century to carry stone to the lime kilns at Bull Bridge.

Ambergate

6 miles SW of Alfreton off the A6

Where the River Amber joins the mighty Derwent, Ambergate is on the route of the National Heritage Way, a 55 mile walk along the Derwent valley. A marvellous bridge crosses the Derwent. The village itself is surrounded by deciduous woodland, including the fine **Shining Cliff Woods**, an important refuge for wildlife. The railway, road and canal here are all squeezed into the tight river valley, and the railway station, standing 100 feet above the road, was one of the few triangular stations in Britain. Built in the late 19th century, the church of St Anne was a gift to the village from the Johnson family of the Ambergate Wire Work. Inside the church there is a marble figure depicting an angel protecting a child from a serpent; this was the creation of a Belgian sculptor who sought refuge in Ambergate during the First World War.

Swanwick

2 miles S of Alfreton off the A38

Swanwick is an old Derbyshire village, which grew into a thriving industrial centre over the 18th and 19th centuries. Coal mining and stocking manufacture had provided work for centuries, but it was the arrival of the Butterley Company, the largest coal, iron and engineering concern in the East Midlands in the late 18th century that changed the face of Swanwick. Despite the fact that it has lost much of its original industries, Swanwick has doubled its size to around 5000 during the 20th century, no doubt due to its easy access to the motorway and the large towns and cities nearby.

Riddings

2 miles S of Alfreton off the A38/ A610

Riddings, was first recorded in the 12th century as Ryddynges, meaning a clearing in the grove. Now a tranquil village, Riddings has twice been the scene of important discovery. In the mid-1700s, 800 precious Roman coins were uncovered here. The second time was in the mid-1800s, when James Oakes, a colliery proprietor and ironmaster, discovered a mysterious liquid flowing on his property. He called in the assistance of his brother-in-law,

Lyon Playfair, one of the most brilliant practical scientists of his day. Playfair found the liquid to be petroleum - then an unknown product commercially, although it had been known as *naphtha*, 'salt of the earth', from Biblical times.

Playfair summoned the help of his friend James Young, who soon after he came to Riddings approached Playfair in dismay to show him that the oil was in a turbid condition. Playfair recognised at once the presence of paraffin, and instructed Young to extract enough paraffin to make two candles - the first paraffin-wax candles ever produced. With one candle in his left hand and the other in his right, Playfair illuminated a lecture he gave at the Royal Institution. From these small beginnings date the enormous petroleum industry and the rich trade in paraffin and its wide range of by-products. Young, known thereafter as Paraffin Young, earned himself a fortune, and when the knowledge of his work spread about a worldwide search for petroleum began. Thus were sown the seeds of the motor car and the aeronautical industries, and all the activities depending on the internal combustion engine.

Ripley

Ripley is an old industrial Derbyshire town, mentioned in the *Domesday Book* as Ripelie. Once a typical small market town, Ripley expanded dramatically during the Industrial Revolution when

The Horse and Jockey

68 Cromford Road, Ripley,
Derbyshire DE5 3FP
Tel: 01773 742310

Located on the outskirts of Ripley – following the town centre direction off the roundabout A38/A610, it's the first pub on your left, **The Horse and Jockey** is a convivial and welcoming inn with real ales, good food and real hospitality.

Tenants David and Maria are new to the pub but have previous experience in the trade; they bring a wealth of enthusiasm to providing all their guests with a high standard of service and quality.

The pub is open every session Monday to Thursday and all day Friday to Sunday. There are three real ales to try – Greene King IPA, Marstons Pedigree and a changing guest ale – together with a full range of lagers, cider, stout, wines, spirits and soft drinks.

Food is served at lunch (12–2) daily and at dinner (5–7) Monday to Friday. Guests choose from the menu or specials board from a range of hearty favourites expertly prepared by the pub's qualified chefs.

great use was made of the iron, clay and coal deposits found nearby. The town's Butterley ironworks, founded in 1792 by a group of men, which included renowned engineer Benjamin Outram, created the roof for London's St Pancras station. Outram's even more famous son Sir James enjoyed an illustrious career that saw him claimed Bayard of India, and earned him a resting place in Westminster Abbey.

Steam Train from the Midland Railway Centre

The village church was erected in 1820 to stem the tide of rebellion and 'irreligion' that swept the area in the hard years after the Battle of Waterloo, when the local weavers and stockingers rebelled against their harsh living conditions. The insurrection saw three rebels brought to the scaffold and drove some into exile, and became a 'cause célèbre' throughout the nation.

Near to the town is the **Midland Railway-Butterley**, which is a railway museum to delight railway buffs or families looking for a diverting day out. There are working steam trains running along a line from Butterley to Riddings, through a 35-acre country park, which provides the habitat for an abundance of wildlife from herons to foxes as well as picnic areas for visitors. There is a Victorian railwayman's church, the 'Tin Tabernacle, rescued from the railway village of Westhouses, which will be developed into a Victorian Street Scene. There is a working signal box, a collection of locomotives and farm and industrial machinery. As well as a model railway there is the Butterley Park Miniature Railway, a 3.5-inch and 5-inch gauge line with a circuit of approximately one sixth of a mile. The line is fully signalled using miniature examples of traditional railway signals controlled from a miniature Midland Railway signal box. The museum is open every weekend throughout the year, and most school holidays.

Around Ripley

Pentrich

1 mile N of Ripley off the A610/ B6013

Mentioned in the *Domesday Book* as Pentric, this hilltop village with its brownstone gabled houses is very charming. Its sturdy church is approached via a picturesque flight of 48 steps. The Normans built the lower part of the church tower, the top of the tower was constructed in the 15th century, as were the battlements and most of the windows. A striking stained-glass War Memorial window created in 1916 depicts the warrior saints of England and France and a figure of St Michael.

Pentrich is famous historically as the site of the last revolution of England, which took place here in 1817. A small band of half-starved weavers, labourers and stockingers met and made plans for a march on London. The rebels' attempted riot was soon quelled. The trial of nearly 50 of them lasted 10 days. They were accused of high treason. A few were pardoned, 11 sent to Australia for life, three to Australia for 14 years and three were hung, drawn and quartered at Derby Gaol. The poet Shelley witnessed the scene and described the despair of the relatives and the disturbance of the crowd as the men were beheaded. The executioners were masked and their names were kept secret. The block is still to be seen in Derby Prison. The 1821 Census recorded a decrease of a third in the population of the parish because the Duke of Devonshire's agents had destroyed many of the houses after the insurrection.

Lower Hartshay

2 miles W of Ripley off the A610

Lower Hartshay was on Ryknield Street, an important Roman military and trade route from the Fosse Way in Gloucestershire to the north. The line of Ryknield Street through Ripley, Pentrich and Lower Hartshay can still be seen and makes a pleasant walk with splendid views. Lower Hartshay was still on a main route for traffic until the 1970s. Now by-passed by the major trunk roads, it is a pleasant and tranquil backwater.

Heage

1 mile W of Ripley off the B6013

Heage was on the ancient pack horse route from Derby to Chesterfield and the old turnpike road passed through here. The village has no obvious centre and is scattered along the roads and lanes with some small estates of modern housing. The main occupation for centuries would have been farming and coal mining. Morley Park has been worked for coal and ironstone since 1372. The remains of bell-pits were discovered during recent opencasting. On Morley Park are the remains of two cold blast coke iron furnaces built by Francis Hurt in 1780 and the Mold Brothers in 1818, the older furnace was probably the first of its kind in Derbyshire. There was also some framework knitting and weaving.

The Parish Church of St Luke has a medieval East window, the only part of the original church to survive a ferocious storm in 1545, the chancel was built in 1645-1661 and the main part of the church in 1886.

The oldest domestic building in the village is Heage Hall Farm, once the

Heage Windmill

home of a branch of the Pole family. Crowtrees Farm was built in 1450 with three good crook beams and was refurbished in 1712.

Heage Windmill is situated west of the village between the villages of Heage and Nether Heage. It is a Grade II listed tower mill and the only one in Derbyshire to retain its six sails and fan tail and machinery. Standing on the brow of a hill, overlooking the village of Nether Heage, it is built of local sandstone and is over two hundred years old. It has been restored to full working order and is open to the public at weekends and bank holidays.

Denby

2 miles S of Ripley off the A38/B6179

Denby was mentioned in the *Domesday Book* as Denebi, which means village of the Danes. Ryknield Street runs through the village.

Denby Pottery, one of the biggest attractions in Derbyshire not far from junction 28 of the M1, off the A38 towards Derby on the B6179, has a fascinating history. Derbyshire has a long tradition of stoneware pottery, closely associated with the natural clay deposits of the county. From a number of small buildings on the site of the clay bed, Denby Pottery was established in 1809. By 1994, classic ranges such as Imperial Blue and Regency Green were proving to be best sellers, and the Pottery had earned a reputation for the quality and

Denby Pottery

durability of its wares. The business took on a new lease of life as the Visitor Centre was added - it now welcomes nearly 300,000 visitors a year. The site offers a chance to see the latest in ceramic technology. At the Factory Shop, seconds and discounts start at 20 per cent off the RRP. The Cookery Emporium offers cookery demonstrations and has in stock over 3,000 kitchen gadgets, supplies and equipment. There are tours on offer as well, including a full tour of the pottery or the Craftsmen's Workshop Tour. Refreshments are available at the comfortable restaurant on-site. A factory shop for Dartington Crystal can also be found at this superb attraction.

As well as pottery, coal and iron have made Denby its name, though it remains an unspoilt retreat. A mile from the Pottery Visitor Centre, in Denby's oldest part, is its little church, set amid a lovely churchyard filled with trees. The church's round arches and pillars date from the late 12th century, while the chancel with its sedilia, piscina and aumbry is from the 14th century. The altar table is 17th century, and from the 20th century come the church tower and the spire, the fine porch with its stone roof, and the eight-sided font.

One of Denby's most famous sons was John Flamsteed, born here in 1646. A poor boy, he went on to become the first Astronomer-Royal at the then-new Observatory at Greenwich. Benjamin Outram, the railway engineer was also born here.

Codnor

2 miles SE of Ripley off the A610

Codnor's surrounding billowy fields and woods make it easy to forget the coal and iron which have made this part of Derbyshire famous. Once it was a great park of nearly 2,000 acres, and the ruins at the gateway to Codnor were once a mighty castle, feudal home of the influential Grey family. Richard Grey was one of Henry III's loyal barons. Edward II visited another Richard here after fighting the rebels at Burton-on-Trent. Another was sent by Henry V to bring Hotspur's son from Scotland, while Henry, the last of them, busied himself with alchemy, in a vain attempt to change base metals into gold.

It is thought that the Greys built their castle with two courts, four enormous round towers and a great gateway. By the time the Zouch family sold it in the mid 1600s it was already beginning to decay. All that survives today is a length of boundary wall of the upper court, parts of the dividing wall and of the defending towers, and the odd doorway, window and fireplace, still standing tall and overlooking the Erewash valley into Nottinghamshire.

Heanor

3 miles SE of Ripley off the A608

The hub of this busy town centres on the market place, where the annual fair is held, as well as the twice-weekly market, which takes place on Fridays and Saturdays. Away from the bustle of the market are the **Memorial Gardens**. This peaceful setting always promises a magnificent spread of floral arrangements, herbaceous borders and shrubberies.

Coal mining was once the dominant industry, but since all the pits have closed the scarred landscape has been reclaimed and restored. To the south of Heanor is the **Shipley Country Park**, on the estate of the now-demolished Shipley Hall. In addition to its magnificent lake, the Country Park boasts over 600 acres of beautiful countryside, which should keep even the most enthusiastic walker busy. Well known as both an educational and holiday centre, there are facilities for horse riding, cycling and fishing. This medieval estate was mentioned in the *Domesday Book* and, under the auspices of the Miller-Mundy family it became a centre for farming and coal mining production during the 18th century. Restoration over the years has transformed former railways into wooded paths, reservoirs into peaceful lakes, and has re-established the once-flowering meadows and rolling hills, which had been destroyed by the colliery pits. Here also can be found the American Adventure, a busy theme park with over a hundred thrill rides, gun fights, special events and boat trips on the lake.

The River Erewash passes through the area at Langley Mill and visitors are able to enjoy the restored boats, which travel to and from the 200-year-old canal basin.

The ancient Parish Church of St Lawrence dates back to the 12th century, though little of the old church remains after rebuilding in 1868. The 15th century tower is still intact.

Belper

Belper is a small, attractive market town 8 miles north of Derby. In 1740, the population of Belper was around 500. It grew rapidly at the beginning of the 19th century due to the industrial development of cotton mills. However the origins of the town go back much further than the Industrial Revolution. It was mentioned in the *Domesday Book* as 'Beau Repaire', the beautiful retreat;

in 1964 the remains of a Roman kiln were found here and its football team is called 'the nailers', for the nail makers who worked here when the area was part of the Royal Forest.

Famous for its cotton mills, the town is situated alongside the **River Derwent** on the floor of the valley. In 1776, Jedediah Strutt, the wheelwright son of a South Normanton farmer, set up one of the earliest water-powered cotton mills here to harness the natural powers of the river to run his mills. With the river providing the power and fuel coming from the nearby South Derbyshire coalfield, the valley has a good claim to be one of the cradles of the Industrial Revolution. Earlier, in 1771 Strutt had gone into profitable partnership with Richard Arkwright, to establish the world's first water-powered cotton mill at Cromford. Strutt and his son, William, retained the North Mill at Belper in 1872 when the partnership with Arkwright was dissolved, having added another at Milford in 1780. Great benefactors to Belper for 150 years, the Strutt family provided housing, work, education and even food - from the model farms they established in the surrounding countryside.

Over 300 years later the mills are still standing and, along with them, are some unique mill-workers' cottages. To discover more about the cotton industry, the influence of the Strutt family on the town and of Samuel Slater, Strutt's apprentice who emigrated to America in

1789, built a mill there and went on to become 'the Father of American manufacturers', a visit to the **Derwent Valley Visitor Centre** is a must. The oldest mill still surviving is the two-storey **North Mill** at Bridgefoot, near the magnificent crescent-shaped weir in the Derwent and the town's main bridge. Built in 1876, the mill has cast-iron columns and beams, and hollow tile floors which provided a warm-air central heating system. It is now the visitor centre. The massive, neighbouring redbrick **East Mill** was constructed in 1912, but now is largely empty. A Jubilee Tower in terracotta was erected on the mill site in 1897 to mark Queen Victoria's 60th anniversary on the throne.

Derwent Valley

Train travellers through Belper are among those treated to a glimpse of George Stephenson's mile-long cutting, walled in gritstone throughout and spanned by no fewer than 10 bridges. When completed in 1840 it was considered an engineering wonder of its

The Thorn Tree Inn

21 Chesterfield Road, Belper,
Derbyshire DE56 1FF
Tel: 01773 823360

The Thorn Tree Inn is a cosy and comfortable inn that boasts the best in hospitality and well-kept ales. The interior is a happy marriage of classic and modern, with traditional features and a light and airy feel enhanced by the tasteful décor and furnishings.

Open Monday to Thursday from 5 p.m., Fridays and Saturdays from 4 p.m. and all day on Sundays (from midday), the accent is firmly on ale here. There are four real ales to enjoy here - Greene King IPA, Abbot and rotating guest ales – together with a good selection of lagers, cider, stout, wines, spirits and soft drinks. If you're peckish, there are a range of freshly-made cobs available.

Susan and Bob Starman are lovely hosts who offer all their guests a warm welcome – you are guaranteed an enjoyable pint and relaxed ambience at this friendly and traditional Derbyshire inn.

To get to this fine inn, take the A609 out of Belper and then the B6013 (signposted Heage). The inn is a short distance along here, on your left.

THE CANAL INN

30 Bullbridge Mill, Bullbridge, Belper,
Derbyshire DE56 2EW
Tel: 01773 852739

In the village of Bullbridge, found half a mile off the A610 Ambergate-to-Ripley Road, **The Canal Inn** is a superb place that dates back to the mid-1800s. Situated close to the famous Cromford Canal, the inn is well known for its food and hospitality. Tenants David and Lorraine and their friendly staff know how to make every guest feel welcome. Lorraine does the cooking and her meals are really delicious. Served Monday to Saturday at lunch (12.00 – 2.30) and dinner (Monday to Thursday 6 – 9.30 p.m., Friday and Saturday 6 – 10 p.m.), and for most of the day (midday until 8.30 p.m.) on Sundays, booking is advised at all times. The menu and specials boards boast a range of tempting meals ranging from hearty grills to a choice of vegetarian dishes.

To drink there are two real ales from the Hardy & Hanson's brewery together with a good selection of lagers, wines, spirits and soft drinks.

This fine inn also offers two guest bedrooms, perfect to use as a comfortable base while exploring the many sights and attractions of the area.

THE SPANKER INN

Nether Heage, Belper, Derbyshire DE56 2AT
Tel: 01773 853222

Hidden away in the tranquil village of Nether Heage, four miles southwest of Alfreton off the A6/A38, **The Spanker Inn** is one of the most popular and esteemed public houses in Derbyshire, renowned for its atmosphere, superb food and good selection of ales.

The inn takes its rather unusual name from the favourite whippet of the first innkeeper back in 1760. The dog was named Bonny but was known as 'a real spanker' in the racing parlance of the day because she was such a good racer who had won many trophies in her day.

Leaseholders Susan and John have been here since 2001 and have made a great success of the inn. John is a professional chef and creates delicious cuisine at lunch (daily) and dinner (Monday to Saturday). The extensive menu boasts a range of excellent dishes such as a selection of steaks and mixed grills, lamb madras, breaded plaice, salmon and broccoli bake, chicken and bacon wraps, vegetarian dishes and a children's menu. Booking is advised at all times, and essential on Sundays.

day. There are also some lovely waterside walks in this bustling little town. Among Belper's other interesting buildings are the **Christ Church**, a lofty, spacious house of worship built in 1849, the parish church of St Peter with its pinnacled west tower (1824) and Chapel of St John the Baptist in The Butts, dating from 1683. A monument to George Brettle can be seen in St Peter's Church - **George Brettle's Warehouse**, in Chapel Street, is a distinctive and elegant building created in 1834.

The River Gardens were established in 1905 and today they are a pleasant place for a stroll among the beautifully tended gardens. Rowing boats can be hired for a trip along the Derwent. The Gardens are a favourite with the film industry, having been used in Ken Russell's *Women in Love*, as well as television's *Sounding Brass* and *In the Shadow of the Noose*. The riverside walk through the meadows is particularly rich in bird life.

Around Belper

Farnah Green

1 mile W of Belper on the A517

Farnah Green is a charming hamlet on the outskirts of Belper. It has no shops but has a pleasant old country pub, which serves food.

Shottle

2 miles W of Belper off the A517

Shottle is a picturesque hamlet of a few

The Lord Scarsdale

New Zealand Lane, Duffield,
Derbyshire DE56 4BZ
Tel: 01332 841156
e-mail: lordscarsdale@hotmail.com
website: www.thelordscarsdale.com

Just a couple of minutes' drive off the main A6 in Duffield, **The Lord Scarsdale** is a handsome and welcoming public house. Leaseholders Paul and June Friend have been here since 2003; it is their first venture into the licensing trade, but they have a strong and loyal following of locals and visitors who come to sample the great food, drink and hospitality.

The interior has recently been refurbished, with the main area now offering a tasteful and very attractive place to enjoy a pint. Currently a new kitchen is being built to help Paul and June provide a better service and allow them to improve upon the 300 meals they currently prepare each week. This will also allow for a new adults-only tap room. Paul and June welcome ideas as to how their customers would like this room to look.

Most of the food can be tailored to your individual tastes and needs. If you have any special requirement please feel free to ask.

Open every session, there are always two to three real ales, with Marstons Pedigree the permanent real ale here.

Food is served Monday to Saturday at lunch (12–2) and dinner (6–9), Sundays from 12–3.30. Once a month on a Thursday night there is a theme night with the likes of French, Greek, Italian, and the chef's special fish accompanying the normal Lord Scarsdale's menus, which feature light-bites such as baguettes, wraps and jacket potatoes served together with main courses such as beef bourguignon, Moroccan lamb, pan-fried lamb's liver, Thai green curry, roasted salmon and vegetable stroganoff. Specialities include fish dishes, steaks and cuisine from around the world. June is a superb cook, and uses the freshest local ingredients wherever possible. On Sundays guests have a choice of five starters, five main courses (including a roast, a pasta dish, a fish and a vegetarian dish) and five puddings. The wine list is very good

farms, houses, a church and a chapel, surrounded by little lanes and footpaths. Unlike most of the surrounding villages it appears little changed since the 19th century. Shottle was the birthplace of Samuel Slater, the apprentice to Jedediah Strutt, who left Belper for the USA and built the first water powered cotton mill there. He is credited as the father of the Industrial Revolution in the USA and his original Slater Mill at Pawtucket is now a museum.

Idridgehay

10 miles NW of Derby off the B5023

This pleasant village is called 'Ithersee' by the locals and it lies in the valley of the River Ecclesbourne. Formerly a working rural village, it is now purely residential. Part of the village is a conservation area including the half-timbered building, **South Sitch**, dating from 1621. The apparent Elizabethan mansion, **Alton Manor**, was in fact built by Sir George Gilbert Scott in 1846, when he moved from Darley Dale because of the coming of the railway.

Milford

1 mile S of Belper off the A6

Milford was a quiet hamlet until the cotton mills came. The village's first cotton mill was built by Richard Arkwright and Jedediah Strutt using stone transported from nearby Hopping Hill. It was only a year later that their partnership dissolved and both industrialists went their separate ways to forge individual empires. Housing was built for the workforce some of which still remain. Although most of the mill buildings are now gone, those that remain are used by small businesses.

Holbrook

2 miles S of Belper off the A6

The Saxon name for Hobrook was Hale Broc meaning Badger Hill. The ancient Roman Portway runs through the village and one of the toll houses for the turnpike road still stands in the village. In the early 1960s two Roman kilns were discovered in the village. Holbrook was once a busy industrial village well known for framework knitters, who supplied stockings for royalty. It is now a pleasant village, with some attractive old houses, serving mainly as a commuter area for the nearby towns of Belper and Derby.

St Michael's Church was built in 1761 as a private chapel to Holbrook Hall. It was rebuilt as the parish church in 1841, but still retains the elegant classical lines of its predecessor. Holbrook Hall was built in 1681 although it looks later. The hall is now a residential home for the elderly.

Duffield

2 miles S of Belper off the A6

This ancient parish is a charming place, with Georgian houses and cottages lining the banks of the River Ecclesbourne. For such a cosy place, it seems odd that the parish church of **St**

Alkmunds is situated in isolation down by the river. It has a 14th century east tower with a recessed spire. It was much restored in the 19th century. Inside the Church there is an impressive monument dating from 1600, dedicated to Anthony Bradshaw, his two wives and their 20 children. Bradshaw was a barrister and the deputy steward of Duffield Firth, a former hunting forest between Duffield and Wirksworth. His great nephew went on to officiate over the court, which called for the execution of Charles I.

Also in the village is a large mound, all that remains of **Duffield Castle** which was ransacked and burnt to the ground in 1266. However, excavations show that it must have been a massive building, with a large keep whose walls were over 16 feet thick. Following the Battle of Hastings, in 1066, William the Conqueror awarded Henry de Ferrers, one of his chief supporters, by giving him great areas of land. Controlling his estates from Tutbury Castle in Staffordshire, Henry built a motte and bailey castle here in around 1080 and installed his son Engenulph. The de Ferrers estates passed peacefully from father to son for nearly 200 years until they were inherited by Robert de Ferrers in 1254. Only 15 years of age at that time, by the age of 27 he had managed to ruin the family name and lose the estate and titles. The two-acre site on which the Castle stood is owned by the National Trust; the interesting relics that were excavated here between 1886 and 1957 can be seen in Derby Museum.

Duffield Hall is situated at the southern edge of the village. It is an Elizabethan building, enlarged in 1870 and once used as a girls boarding school. It is now the Head Quarters for the Derbyshire Building Society.

Ilkeston

The third largest town in Derbyshire, Ilkeston received its royal charter for a market and fair in 1252. Both have continued to the present day. The history of the town, however, goes back to the days when it was an Anglo-Saxon

Erewash Museum

hilltop settlement known as Tilchestune. Once a mining and lace making centre, its history is told in the **Erewash Museum**, housed in a fine Georgian house with Victorian extensions on the High Street. It was a family home and then part of a school before becoming a Museum in the 1980s. Many original features survive including a restored Edwardian kitchen and wash house. The garden has unrivalled views across the Erewash Valley. Other fine examples of elegant 18th century houses can be found in East Street while, in Wharncliffe Road, there are period houses with art nouveau features.

Ilkeston commands fine wide views from the hillside above the valley of the **Erewash**, which here bounds the county. The town's church-crowned hilltop is a landmark that can be seen from far afield. This textile manufacturing town in a colliery district has a fine church, which has undergone many changes since it was first erected in the 1300s. It is particularly notable for its window tracery, especially in the six windows in the older part of the church. A former tower and elegant spire were destroyed by storm in 1714. The tower only was rebuilt, to be succeeded by another on the old foundations in 1855. This tower was then moved westwards in 1907, at which time the nave was doubled in length. One intriguing feature it has retained throughout all these changes is its 13th century archway. The organ is also distinguished, in that it was built from one, which came from a London church and is known to have been played by the great Mendelssohn himself.

Around Ilkeston

Mapperley

2 miles NW of Ilkeston off the A609

This historic village was first granted a market charter in 1267 and, though its old church was demolished due to mining subsidence, the modern church has some interesting stained glass windows. In the heart of Derbyshire mining country, any stroll from the village centre will take the walker past industrial remains.

To the south of Mapperley is the

former branch line of the Midland Railway which served Mapperley Colliery as well as the old raised track which is all that remains of an old tramway which ran from the Blue Fly Shaft of West Hallam Pit to the **Nutbrook Canal** further east. The Canal, which opened in 1796, carried coal from the pits at Shipley to the ironworks at Stanton and beyond. Only just over 4 miles long, the Canal had some 13 locks but it fell into disuse after the Second World War and much of it has now been filled in. The relatively new "Nutbrook Trail" for cyclists and walkers follows the old Stanton to Shipley mineral railway line more or less, parallel to the canal, from Long Eaton to Heanor. It is part of the Sustrans network of cycle ways and is very popular with both recreational users and commuters. The railway trail and the canal towpath can create a circular walk between West Hallam and Stanton Bridge. The Nutbrook Trail received grant aid from East Midlands Arts for three sculptures, which drew their inspiration from the social and industrial heritage of the Erewash Valley. The three sculptures represent vegetation found along the trail- Birch, Campion and Vetch and the collection is entitled 'Wild Weeds'.

West Hallam

2 miles W of Ilkeston off the A609

West Hallam stands on a hilltop. Its church, set between the great expanse of **West Hallam Hall** and the rectory, is approached via a lovely avenue of limes. The rector's garden has a glorious lime tree, and looks out over the valley to a great windmill with its arms still working as they have done since Georgian times. St Wilfred's Church is over 700 years old and has a very handsome tower, with a blue clock with gilt hands and figures.

The Powtrell family were historically important to the village of West Hallam. Their former home was offered as a hiding place for fugitive priests during the 16th century. One priest taken at the house was condemned to death, but after long imprisonment his sentence was commuted to banishment. Another priest, sentenced for celebrating mass at West Hallam Hall, was sent to prison and later died there. On a stone on the chancel floor of the village church is an engraved portrait of Thomas Powtrell in armour of the 15th cenutry. A magnificent canopied tomb depicts Walter Powtrell, who died in 1598, and his wife Cassandra. He wears richly decorated armour, she a gown of many folds. Around them are depicted their seven children.

One of the premier attractions in the area, **The Bottle Kiln** is a handsome and impressive brick built former working pottery, now home to contemporary art and craft. Visitors can take a leisurely look at exhibitions (changing throughout the year) of both British studio ceramics and contemporary painting in the European tradition. From figurative and descriptive to abstract, many styles and media are displayed here. In addition there is a selection of imaginative contemporary British jewellery and craftware on display in and around the old kiln. Two shops filled with jewellery, cards, gifts, objets-d'art, soft furnishings and housewares with an accent on style, design and originality can also be found at this superb site. At the Egon Ronay recommended Buttery Café, visitors can enjoy a wide choice of freshly prepared and hearty food, along with a tasty selection of teas, coffees and cakes. Visitors can also take their meals in the tranquil Japanese tea garden on fine days.

West Hallam has a well-dressing ceremony each year, normally held during the second week of July.

Horsley

6 miles west of Ilkeston on the A609

Horsley is a charming little village with a population of around 500. It has a main street lined with mature trees and a village green. The church of **St Clement and St James** is a real gem dating back to the 13th century. It has a broach spire and mid-15th-century battlements and a pretty porch with a medieval crucifix. The interior is much restored but there are some scraps of ancient glass in one window.

Morley

4 miles SW of Ilkeston off the A608

Morley is essentially a rural village with working farms around it. There are four parts to the village, Brackley Gate and the Croft, the Smithy and Brick Kiln Lane, Almshouse Lane and Church Lane.

Brackley Gates has some disused quarries and marvellous views to the north. It is now a wildlife reserve, managed by the Derbyshire Wildlife Trust. The Croft has a cluster of 17th and 18th century cottages. The 17th century almshouses in Almshouse Lane were originally provided by Jacinth Sitwell, then Lord of the Manor of Morley for '6 poor, lame or impotent men'.

The **Church of St Matthew** has a Norman nave, with the tower, chancel and north chapel being late 14th/early 15th century. It is perhaps best known for its magnificent stained glass windows. Originally in the Abbey Refectory at Dale, the windows were acquired by Sir Henry Sacheverell in 1539. There are monuments and brasses to important local families like the Sacheverell's and the Sitwell's, including one to John Sacheverell, who died at Bosworth Field in 1485 and the beautifully carved tomb chest of Henry Sacheverell, who died in 1558 and his beautiful wife Katherine Babington, who died in 1553 with its recumbent effigy and kneeling figures.

Dale Abbey

3 miles SW of Ilkeston off the A6096

The village takes its name from the now-ruined abbey that was founded here by Augustinian monks in the 13th century. Beginning life in a very humble manner, local legend has it that a Derbyshire baker came to the area in 1130, carved himself a niche in the sandstone and devoted himself to the way of the hermit. The owner of the land, Ralph FitzGeremunde, discovered the baker and was so impressed by the man's devotion that he bestowed on him the land and tithe rights to his mill in Borrowash. The sandstone cave and the romantic ruined 40 feet high window archway (all that now remains of the original abbey) are popular attractions locally and a walk around the village is both an interesting and pleasurable experience. Nearby **Hermit's Wood** is an ancient area of woodland with beech, ash, oak and lime trees. It is wonderful at any time of year, but particularly in the spring when the woodland floor is covered with a carpet of bluebells.

The village **Church of All Saints**, which dates back to the mid-12th century, must be the only church in England, which shares its roof with a farm. The church has a pulpit that dates from 1634 and the whole interior appears rather crammed with its box pews and open benches. The farmhouse was once possibly used as an infirmary for the Abbey and then as an inn. The adjoining door was blocked up in the 1820s to prevent swift transition from salvation to damnation. To the north of the village is the **Cat and Fiddle Windmill**, built in the 18th century and a fine example of the oldest type of mill. The stone roundhouse is capped with a box-like wooden structure which houses the machinery and which is fitted onto an upright post around which it can rotate to catch the wind.

Stanley

3 miles SW of Ilkeston off the A609

Stanley is a pleasant little rural village, whose main industry was coal mining until the closure of Stanley colliery in 1959.

All that is left of **Stanley's chapel** that was here over 800 years ago is a Norman priests' doorway, now in the wall. Some of the buttresses and a small lancet date from the 1200s. The font dates back to the 1300s, and the pulpit from the 17th century. A brass tablet on the floor by the pulpit is dedicated to Sir John Bentley of Breadsall, who was buried here 20 years before the Civil War.

Stanton by Dale

2 miles S of Ilkeston off the B6002

Stanton-by-Dale is mentioned in the *Domesday Book* and derives its name from the nearby stone quarries. The houses in the village are mainly 18th and 19th century brick or stone cottages built to house the workers of the Stanton Ironworks, which still continues to provide employment as Stanton PLC. The village pump, erected in 1897 to commemorate Queen Victoria's jubilee, had fallen into a sad state of dilapidation. It is now repaired, completely renovated and returned to its original green and gold. The village church of **St Michael and All Angels**, is 13th century in origin but there is a fine modern stained glass window depicting Stanton Works.

Sandiacre

4 miles S of Ilkeston off the B6002

Sandiacre is situated on the border with Nottinghamshire. Although it has been all but incorporated into the ever-expanding Nottingham conurbation, it maintains many village features including a picturesque 14th century church up a narrow lane at the top of a hill. In the churchyard four stones remain of the remarkable Charlton family. One was an MP as far back as 1318. Sir Richard was slain on Bosworth field. Sir Thomas was Speaker in 1453. Edward was a commissioner in the Civil War.

Risley

4 miles S of Ilkeston off the B5010

This small village has once again become a quiet backwater now that the main Derby to Nottingham road bypasses it to the south. Apart from ribbon building along the former main road, Risley consists of no more than a small group of old buildings, but they are unique and well worth a visit. In 1593, Michael Willoughby started to rebuild the village church. Although small, even by the standards of the day, it is charming and essentially Gothic in style. In the same year his wife founded a school and, although none of the original school houses exist, those seen today date from the early 18th century and were constructed by a trust founded by the family. The central school building is a perfect example of the Queen Anne style and acted as both the school and school house, with the boarders sleeping in the garrets. The trustees still maintain this wonderful building, along with the Latin School of 1724, the English School of 1753 and another School House built in 1771.

Ockbrook

4 miles SW of Ilkeston off the A52

This quiet village close to, but hidden from, the busy main road between Derby and Nottingham, is quite a place and well worth a visit. The old part of Ockbrook was established by Occa an Anglo Saxon, around the 6th century but the village is unusual in that, in the mid-18th century, a Moravian Settlement was founded here when a congregation of the Moravian Church was formed. The Settlement has several fine buildings, including The Manse, built in 1822, and the Moravian Chapel. Within the Settlement there is also a girls boarding school. Historical research has discovered that Ockbrook may have been a Pagan religious site well before **All Saints' Church** was built. It became the parish church in the mid 1500s and its most interesting features include a

Saxon font, the 12th century tower, some fine windows and the oak chancel screen dating from around 1520. This is farming country and many of the ancient hedgerows remain, sustaining all manner of wildlife that has disappeared from many other areas. Several old farm buildings also remain, including an impressive 17th century timber-framed building at Church Farm. Little but the ground floor however, remains of **Ockbrook Windmill**, one of only 10 windmill sites extant in Derbyshire.

Borrowash

6 miles SW of Ilkeston off the A6005

Close to the River Derwent, this once quiet place, separated from its neighbour, Ockbrook, by the main Derby to Nottingham road, has developed into a commuter village. Pronounced 'borrow-ash', the village has lost its railway station and canal, which was filled in during the early 1960s. P H Currey designed the small redbrick church of **St Stephen** in 1899. The interior features a low, 18th century ironwork chancel screen, believed to be the work of Robert Bakewell of Derby.

Spondon

5 miles SW of Ilkeston off the A52

This village, with many Georgian brick houses, is now almost engulfed by Derby, but the older parts can still be picked out. The church, damaged by fire in 1340, was completely rebuilt and has also undergone restoration work in 1826 and again in the 1890s. Nearby is **Locko Park**, the privately owned ancestral home of the Drury-Lowe family since 1747. The present Hall was built by Francis Smith in the mid 1700s, and since then it has been given an Italian appearance. Today, the Hall houses one of the largest private collections of Italian paintings in Britain. The chapel is earlier than the Hall, having been built in 1669. Way back in medieval times a leper hospital stood here.

Breaston

5 miles S of Ilkeston off the A6005

On the southern borders of the county, close to Nottinghamshire and Leicestershire, Breaston occupies the flat countryside near the point where the River Derwent joins the River Trent before continuing on its long journey to the North Sea. The mainly 13th century **Church of St Michael** boasts the 'Boy of Breaston' - a small, chubby-faced child immortalised in the 13th century by the mason of the nave arches. He has smiled down on worshippers and visitors for the past seven centuries. The story has it that this boy would come in and watch the masons at work while the church was being built. The master mason decided to make the child part of the church, so that he could always have a good view of it!

Coffins had to be carried to neighbouring **Church Wilne** for burial up until the early 1800s, as there was no burial ground at Breaston until that time. For this reason the footpath over the fields of Wilne continues to be known by villagers as the 'Coffin Walk'. The now drained Derby Canal passed through the village at one time. The basin where the narrowboats were turned can still be seen.

Draycott

7 miles S of Ilkeston off the A6005

Having strong connections with the Nottingham lace trade, Draycott's **Victoria Mill** was built in 1888 and was established as one of the most important lace factories in the world. The four-storey building, with its green-capped ornamental clock tower, still dominates the Draycott skyline though it is now the home of an electrical component manufacturer. Draycott House, designed by Joseph Pickford, was built in 1781. It remains a private residence.

Elvaston

8 miles SW of Ilkeston off the B5010

Elvaston is gathered around the edge of the **Elvaston Castle** estate, home of the Earls of Harrington. The magnificent Gothic castle seen today replaced a 17th century brick and gabled manor house; part of the original structure can be seen on the end of the south front. Designed by James Wyatt, the castle was finished in the early 19th century but, unfortunately, the 3rd Earl died in 1829 and had little time to enjoy his new home.

The Coach and Horses

1 Victoria Road, Draycott,
Derbyshire DE72 3PS
Tel: 01332 872483

Located in Draycott, a former lace-making village on the A6005, halfway between Derby and Long Eaton, **The Coach and Horses** is a former coaching inn dating back to the 1730s. Draycott Mill, with its green-capped clocktower, dominates the immediate area and was built in 1888; today it is a luxury apartment building with 120 flats.

The inn is a fine old building with many period features, run by husband-and-wife team Paul and Caroline Bainbridge, who have been here since 1996 and who have, during that time, turned the inn into one of the most popular in the area.

The interior is welcoming and cosy, with thick old walls that keep the inn warm in winter and cool in summer, and an ideal place for a meal or drink. The bar offers two real ales – Bass and a rotating guest ale – along with a good range of lagers, stout, cider, wines, spirits and soft drinks.

The food is best described as traditional and hearty, and all dishes are home-cooked. Guests choose off the menu and specials board from a range of freshly prepared and tasty meals and snacks. Booking required for Sunday lunch at this popular and convivial inn.

Elvaston Castle

It is, perhaps, the grounds, which make Elvaston Castle famous today. They were originally laid out and designed for the 4th Earl by William Barron. Barron, who was born in Berwickshire in 1805, started work in 1830 on what, at first, appeared to be an impossible task. The 4th Earl wanted a garden 'second to none', but the land available, which had never been landscaped, was flat, water-logged and uninspiring with just two avenues of trees and a walled kitchen garden (but no greenhouses or hot houses). First draining the land, Barron then planted trees to offer shelter to more tender plants. From there the project grew. In order to stock the gardens, Barron began a programme of propagation of rarer tree species and, along with the tree-planting methods he developed specially to deal with Elvaston's problems, his fame spread. The gardens became a showcase of rare and interesting trees, many to be found nowhere else in Britain. Barron continued to work for the 5th Earl, but resigned in 1865 to live in nearby Borrowash and set up his own nursery. Now owned by Derby County Council, the gardens, after years of neglect, have been completely restored and the delights of the formal gardens, with their fine topiary, the avenues and the kitchen garden can be enjoyed by all visitors to the grounds, which are now a Country Park.

As well as fine formal gardens and the walled kitchen garden, there are gentle woodland walks and, of course, the man-made lake. However, no visit to Elvaston would be complete without a

walk down to the **Golden Gates**. Erected in 1819 at the southern end of the formal gardens, the gates were brought from the Palace of Versailles by the 3rd Earl of Harrington. Little is known of the Gates' history, but they remain a fine monument and are the symbol of Elvaston. Around the courtyard of the castle can be found a restaurant as well as an information centre and well-stocked gift shop. All manner of activities take place from the castle, which can provide details.

Shardlow

9 miles SW of Ilkeston off the A6

There was a settlement at Shardlow at the time of the *Domesday Book*, when the area belonged to the Abbey of Chester and the village was known as Serdelov. Shardlow was once an important port on the river Trent and a horse drawn ferry was used to cross the river. This was replaced in 1760 by a toll bridge and the stone giving the toll charges can still be seen on the roadside approaching the modern Cavendish Bridge. This replaced the old bridge, which collapsed in 1947. After 1777, when the **Trent and Mersey Canal** was opened, Shardlow became a canal port, one of only a few in the country. With Liverpool, Hull and Bristol now linked by water, the warehouses here were quickly filled with heavy goods of all descriptions that could be carried at half the cost of road transport and with greater safety. Many of the homes of the canal carriers and their warehouses survive to this day and the port is now a modern marina, linked to the River Trent, and filled with all manner of pleasure barges. Many of the old cottages in Shardlow were swept away by 1960s development but some were saved when much of the canal side was designated a conservation area in 1978. There are still some fine houses remaining that were built by the wealthy canal merchants. Broughton House, built in the early part of the 19th century is just one example.

The outstanding **Shardlow Marina** covers 46 acres, of which the Marina itself covers 12 acres, set in beautiful rolling countryside. The marina has moorings for up to 365 boats, with berths available for up to 70-feet narrow and wide-beam boats.

Aston-on-Trent

9 miles S of Ilkeston off the A6

Aston stands on the River Trent, marking the border between Derbyshire and Leicestershire. Aston's **All Saints Church** is mainly Norman, though also boasts parts of a Saxon cross with beautifully interlaced carving. The cross is built into the outer wall of the south aisle. There is an octagonal font dating from the 1200s inside the church, and a moving, early 15th century alabaster tomb chest of a husband and wife holding hands, she with a small dog at her feet.

Aston Hall dates from 1753; much enlarged over the centuries, it was originally a fine Georgian mansion with no fewer than five bays and central Venetian windows.

Castle Donington

10 miles S of Ilkeston off the A6

Castle Donington (pronounced Dunington) is just over the Leicestershire border on a hill above the Trent River. The castle from which Castle Donington takes its name is now merely a mound on the northern edge of the village. It was built in the 11th or 12th century, demolished in 1216, rebuilt later that century and was finally demolished in 1595. The oldest part of the church of **St Edward, King and Martyr,** dates back to 1200 but it was probably built on the site of an older Saxon church. The spire, rising to a height of 160 feet, is a landmark for miles around.

A 17th century stone farmhouse in the centre of Castle Donington is now a museum tracing its fascinating history. **Donington Park museum** (see panel) on the edge of the racing circuit boasts the Grand Prix collection of more than 130 vehicles from motor racing history, most in working order. Vehicles on show include Ascari's Ferrari, Jim Clark's Lotus 23 and Nigel Mansell's Williams.

The Donington Grand Prix Collection

Donington Park, Castle Donington,
Derby DE74 2RP
Tel: 01332 811027 Fax: 01332 812829
e-mail: enquiries@doningtoncollection.co.uk
website: www.doningtoncollection.com

More Grand Prix cars, under one roof, than anywhere else in the world. Driven by more famous names than you could possibly imagine! It's all at the **Donington Grand Prix Collection**, located at Donington Park, the World famous Grand Prix circuit, in Leicestershire, containing over 130 exhibits within five halls, depicting motor sport history from the turn of the 1900s to the present day.

The Collection now features the World's largest collection of McLaren Formula One cars on public display. An incredible array of cars are on display including the only complete collection of Vanwalls, BRMs, Ferrari, Jordan, Williams and also those driven by Tazio Nuvolari, Sir Henry Segrave, Stirling Moss, Damon Hill, Nigel Mansell and many more! Plus there's the World's biggest collection of helmets including those worn by Mansell, Senna, Coulthard, Nuvolari and Ascari.

The Collection is the work of Tom Wheatcroft, who for over 40 years has collected the cars which reflect his love of the sport which started when, as a young boy, he himself witnessed the amazing spectacle of the awesome Mercedes Benz and Auto Unions, in the pre war Donington Grands Prix. During the War, the circuit was taken over by the War Office and became the biggest base in the country for military vehicles. After the War, the circuit became neglected, and it was Tom Wheatcroft, by this time a very successful builder, who bought the circuit in the early 1970s, and racing returned there in 1977.

Among the faciliteis here are a restaurant, picnic area and a comprehensive range of gifts and souvenirs on sale.

Long Eaton

7 miles SE of Ilkeston off the A52

Long Eaton, straddling the Derbyshire and Nottinghamshire border, has a history that goes back earlier than the 7th century. Lying close by the River Trent, the name came from the Anglo Saxon 'Aitone' meaning town by the water. Visited by the Romans and settled by the Danes, this medieval village remained undisturbed for centuries. A national census of 1801 recorded that only some 504 people lived here.

It was the machine age that transformed Long Eaton from a small market town into a boom town by the mid-19th century. The arrival of the railway in 1847 triggered the expansion, and the hosiery and lace making factories, escaping the restrictive practices in nearby Nottingham, brought employment for many and wealth for some. By the 1870s the population was recorded at over 3,000; it then doubled in the following 10 years. In 1915 construction began on the National Shell Filling Factory sited just over a mile away from Long Eaton's ancient market place. A staggering 19 million large shells were filled to aid the war effort, and it was not until there had been some 19 explosions at the plant, the worst with a death toll of 140, that the operation ceased. The lace industry, forever associated with this area, gave way to furniture, narrow fabrics and electrical wiring manufacture which reflected the interests and activities of a stream of entrepreneurs drawn to the town. The most famous of these men was Ernest Tehra Hooley - lace maker, property dealer, builder, benefactor and company director. Hooley was responsible for the flotation of such well-known names as Dunlop, Raleigh, Humber and Bovril before he went bankrupt.

Sawley

8 miles SE of Ilkeston off the B6540

Situated close to the county border with both Nottinghamshire and Leicestershire, Sawley is an attractive village standing on the banks of the River Trent. Over 1,000 years ago a small collective of monks boated down the Trent from Repton to the green meadows of Sawley. Parts of the church they built remain in the edifice between the road and the river. Much of the church is 14th century, with 15th century tower and spire and much 15th century timbering. The chancel arch is Saxon. The interior boasts an impressive group of monuments, a 600-year-old font, a 500-year-old screen, a Jacobean pulpit and 17th century altar table.

In the late 1400s the Bothes (or Booths) settled at Sawley in a house of which some of the timbers remain in the cellars of **Bothe Hall**, near the church. Sawley's most noted son was John Clifford. Born here in 1836, he became one of the most powerful voices of Non-conformity, known as 'the greatest Free Churchman of his day'.

PLACES TO STAY, EAT AND DRINK

The Miners Arms, Brimington, Derbyshire	103	Pub with Restaurant	p211
The Odd Couple, Unstone, Derbyshire	104	Pub with Food	p212
The Royal Oak , Barlborough, Derbyshire	105	Pub with Food	p215
The White Hart, Calow, Derbyshire	106	Pub with Restaurant	p218
Hardwick Inn, Hardwick Park, Derbyshire	107	Pub with Restaurant	p222
Bateman's Mill Hotel, Old Tupton, Derbyshire	108	Hotel	p226
The Old Poet's Corner, Ashover, Derbyshire	109	Pub with Restaurant	p228
The Famous Red Lion, Stonedge, Derbyshire	110	Pub with Food	p230
La Bistro Chameleon, Chesterfield, Derbyshire	111	Bistro	p230
Cow Close Farm, Cutthorpe, Derbyshire	112	Self Catering	p231
The Angel Inn, Holmesfield, Derbyshire	113	Pub with Food	p233

Denotes entries in other chapters

6 Derbyshire Coal Mines

This area of northeast Derbyshire and the District of Bolsover, with the Peak District to the west, South Yorkshire to the north and Nottinghamshire to the east, centres around Chesterfield. This was the heart of the county's coal mining area, and many of the towns and villages reflect the prosperity the mines brought in Victorian times. Sadly, the vast majority of the collieries are now closed; there was for a while a period of decline, but visitors today will be surprised at the wealth of history and fine architecture to be seen throughout the region. Geologically this area makes up one of Derbyshire's four distinct regions, with sandy coal east of Derby and Chesterfield and a band of magnesium limestone around Bolsover and Whitwell.

Sometimes overlooked, this part of Derbyshire is well worth exploring, and there are many new and interesting sights and attractions to discover. The ancient custom of well-dressing is just as popular and well executed here as elsewhere in the county, plus there are curiosities such as a 'castle that isn't a castle despite its battlements, a church clock that has 63 minutes in an hour and an Italian-style garden in the grounds owned by a famous English family', according to the North East Derbyshire District Council. The area boasts two exceptional Norman churches, at Steetley (near Creswell) and Ault Hucknall.

Despite appearances that many of the places in and around Chesterfield only date from the Industrial Revolution, the area is rich in history. From medieval times this has been an area of trade and the weekly markets were an important part of the local economy. Though some

The Peak District

have been lost over the years, these traditional centres and meeting-places remain.

Chesterfield

This friendly, bustling town on the edge of the **Peak District National Park** grew up around its open-air market, which was established over 800 years ago and claims to be England's largest. As the town lies at the crossroads of England, the hub of trade routes from all points of the compass, the town's claim seems easily justified. Life in Chesterfield has revolved around this market since the town's earliest days. It was earning Royal revenue in 1165, as the Sheriff of Derbyshire recorded in the Pipe Rolls and, in that year, the market earned the princely sum of £1 2s 7d for the Crown. The Pipe Roll of 1182 also mentions a fair in Chesterfield. Such fairs were large markets, usually lasting for several days and drawing traders and buyers from a much wider area. Chesterfield's formal charter, however, was not granted until 1204, but this charter made the town one of the first eight free boroughs in the country. Escaping the prospect of redevelopment in the 1970s, the markets are as popular as ever and are held every Monday, Friday and Saturday, with a flea market each Thursday.

The town centre has been conserved for future generations by a far-sighted council, and many buildings have been saved, including the Victorian **Market Hall** built in 1857. The traditional cobbled paving was restored in the Market Place, and New Square was given a complete facelift. There are several Tudor buildings in the heart of Chesterfield, most notably the former Peacock inn which is now home to the **Peacock Heritage Centre** and the tourist information office - built in 1500 for the wealthy Revell family, who later moved to Carnfield Hall near Alfreton. The black-and-white timbering in Knifesmithgate, however, was built only in the 1930s, to resemble the famous rows in Chester.

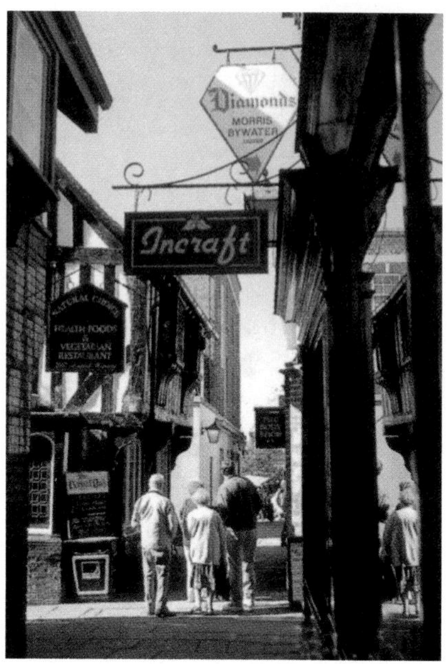

Chesterfield Shambles

Visitors to the town are drawn to a peculiarly graceful spire reaching high into the skyline; twisting and leaning, it is totally confusing to the eye. Recognised as one of Chesterfield's landmarks, the **Crooked Spire** of St Mary and All Saints' Church has dominated the skyline for so long that local folk have ceased to notice its unusual shape. Superstition surrounds it, and sadly the real story to its unusual appearance has been lost over the years. The truth probably lies in the wake of the Black Death during the 14th century, when the people of Chesterfield were building their beautiful new church and awe-inspiring steeple. Many must have fallen to the plague and, among them, skilled craftsmen who knew how to season wood. The survivors built the spire out of green timber, which, over the years, has distorted under the heavy lead covering. However, some stories say it was the Devil, who, pausing for a rest during one of his flights, clung to the spire for a moment or two. Incense from the Church drifted upwards and the Devil sneezed, causing the spire to twist out of shape.

This magnificent spire rises to 228 feet and leans 9 feet 4 inches from its true centrepoint. It is eight-sided, but the herringbone pattern of the lead slates trick the eye into seeing 16 sides from the ground. The Crooked Spire is open most Bank Holidays and at advertised times; the church, the largest in Derbyshire, is open all year, Monday to Saturday 9 a.m. to 5 p.m. (9 a.m. to 3 p.m. January and February), and Sundays at service times only.

Opposite the Church is **Chesterfield Museum and Art Gallery**, home to exhibitions depicting the story of the town, from the arrival of the Romans to the first days of the market town, the industry of the 18th century and the coming of the 'Father of the Railways', George Stephenson. The Art Gallery displays paintings by local artists such as Joseph Syddall (who lived at nearby Whittington).

In the heart of Chesterfield, **The Spread Eagle** stands opposite the new shopping mall in Beetwell Street. The premises date back some 400 years and once had stables to the rear - the archway where the carriages and carts used to pull in can still be seen. Once upon a time prisoners would be held in

Chesterfield Cathedral

the cellars here when the police station cells were full. The old police station used to stand across the road, in what is now the library, and an underground tunnel linked the two buildings.

Chesterfield Canal

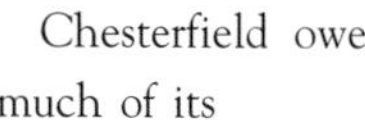

Chesterfield owes much of its prosperity during the industrial age to the great railway engineer George Stephenson. His home, Tapton House, lies just outside the town and it was to here that he retired and carried out his experiments in horticulture. Buried in Holy Trinity Church, where one of the windows was created in his memory, his death, in 1848, was announced by one local newspaper with the headline 'Inventor of Straight Cucumber Dies'.

Perhaps surprisingly, Chesterfield is home to one of the earliest canals in the country, the Chesterfield Canal. After seeing the success of the Bridgewater Canal in 1763, the businessmen of Chesterfield, which was at the start of its rapid expansion, looked to link the town with the River Trent via Worksop and Retford in Nottinghamshire. Construction work began in 1771, just a year before its builder, James Brindley, died while surveying the Caldon Canal. The biggest engineering project along the length of the new canal was the Norwood Tunnel, which took four years to build. The Tunnel was officially opened on 9 May 1775. It was 2,884 yards long, 9 feet 3 inchess wide, and 12 feet high. The entire canal was officially opened in 1777. The most famous item carried on the canal was stone to rebuild the Houses of Parliament in the 1840s. The stone was loaded into canal boats at Dog Kennels Bridge, carried to West Stockwith, and transferred to Trent sloops for the journey to Westminster, via the Humber, North Sea, and Thames. In October 1907 the roof of Norwood Tunnel collapsed, cutting the canal in two. Coal cargoes from Shireoaks colliery continued until the Second World War, but after that there was little boat traffic apart from brick cargoes from the kilns at Walkeringham. All the working boats on the Chesterfield Canal were horse-drawn until, by 1962, virtually all the boat traffic had gone. The whole length of the Canal is in the process of restoration and is open to walkers and, though some sections border onto busy roads, much of the waterway runs through quiet and secluded countryside. The Chesterfield Canal Trust runs boat trips on the canal, and one of the boats has wheelchair access.

Finally, although the custom of tap-dressing took place in Chesterfield in the 19th century, it was not until 1991 that the tradition, this time of well-dressing, was revived. Initially with help from local experts from Holymoorside, the Chesterfield dressers are developing their own styles and customs and, while the well-dressing at the Peacock Centre takes its inspiration from buildings, their colleagues at St Mary and All Saints Church follow the theme of the stained glass windows within the church.

Around Chesterfield

Sheepbridge

3 miles N of Chesterfield off the A61

Dunstan Hall, below Newbold Moor, was built in the 17th century and extended in the 18th century. In an excellent parkland setting, the Gothic style park railings mirror the Gothic revival details that were added to the Hall in 1826.

Whittington

3 miles NE of Chesterfield off the B6052/A61

During the 17th century, **Revolution House** was part of an alehouse called the

The Miners Arms

217 Manor Road, Brimington,
Derbyshire S43 1NS
Tel: 01246 234870

The Miners Arms is a superb village inn that is well worth seeking out. To reach it, follow the A619 (Worksop Road) out of Chesterfield to Brimington, then from the centre follow the road around the one-way system as if you were heading back to Chesterfield, turning left into Manor Road. The inn is about three-quarters of a mile down this road on your left.

Named for the many miners who used to work in the area, this convivial, family-run pub is open every session weekdays and all day Saturday and Sunday, serving two real ales from the Burtonwood Brewery range together with draught Burtonwood Mild, lagers, cider and stout, and a good range of wines, spirits and soft drinks.

Tempting home-cooked food using the freshest ingredients is available weekday evenings (5 – 8), Saturdays 12 – 8 and Sundays 12 – 2.30. Food-themed evenings are held once a month on a Saturday. There is a no-smoking area and a lovely outdoor decked area. During the lifetime of this edition an extension is to be added to incorporate a no-smoking restaurant and toilet facilities for guests with disabilities.

The Odd Couple

799 Sheffield Road, Unstone, Chesterfield, Derbyshire S41 9EQ
Tel/Fax: 01246 455784
e-mail: diatoddcouple.com@fsmail.net

Standing on the Unstone Road, found off the main A61, **The Odd Couple** is a spacious and impressive inn. Formerly called The Railway Inn, the premises date back about 150 years.

Diane Wharmby has been the leaseholder here for two years, and has been in the trade since 1996. She and her friendly staff offer all their guests a warm welcome and real hospitality.

Open all day, every day for ale, the two real ales available are Timothy Taylor Landlord and a rotating guest ale. The bar area is comfortable and handsome, boasting a wealth of polished wood, open fire, exposed beamwork and other classic features.

Excellent food is served Monday to Saturday at lunch (12 – 3) and dinner (5 – 9) and Sundays between 12 and 7 p.m. Guests choose off the printed menu or the specials board, which can include up to eight main courses daily. The menu includes home-made and tempting dishes such as Scottish steak pie, braised lamb, salmon fillet and vegetable cannelloni. Friday and Saturday nights are steak and grill night, where a range of hearty meals such as Scotch rump steak, t-bones, minted Barnsley chop and more are featured. There are also two carveries a week: Sundays until 4 and midweek on Wednesday evenings from 5.30 until 7.30. In addition to all this, there are also special themed evenings held monthly and featuring, for example, Chinese cuisine.

Booking advised on Sundays. The no-smoking dining area seats up to 40. Cosy and clean with an understated elegance, it's a relaxed place to enjoy your meal. There's also a handsome patio area to the front of the inn. Children welcome.

Once a month there's live entertainment to be had on a Friday evening from 9 p.m. This convivial inn is also happy to host private luncheons and functions for up to 40 people.

Revolution House, Whittington

Cock and Pynot ('pynot' being the local dialect word for magpie). It was here that three local noblemen - the Earl of Devonshire, the Earl of Danby and John D'Arcy - met to begin planning their part in the events which led to the overthrow of James II in favour of his daughter Mary and her husband, William of Orange. The Glorious Revolution took place later in the same year, November 1688, and it was in the year of its 250th anniversary that this modest house was turned into a museum. Both the 100th and the 200th anniversary of the Revolution were keenly celebrated at the Revolution House; the inhabitants of Whittington and Chesterfield being proud that they had provided the venue where the plot was hatched to overthrow the Catholic King James.

Revolution House, a tiny cottage with thatched roof, flower border and charming garden gate which belies its rather incendiary name, is now open to the public and features period furnishings and a changing programme of exhibitions on local themes. A video relates the story of the Revolution and the role which the house played in those fraught and dangerous days.

Despite the growth of Chesterfield, Whittington has managed, on the whole, to retain its village centre, though one of its best buildings (apart from Revolution House), Manor Farm, was demolished in the 1970s. However, the farm's barns still survive and can be found to the west of St Bartholomew's Church.

Eckington

6 miles NE of Chesterfield off the A616

This large, sprawling village built of local Derbyshire stone, lies close to the Yorkshire county border. The name Eckington is of Saxon origin, meaning the township of Ecca. In medieval times it was a small but important settlement, whose main occupations were farming and then mining. Since the decline of coal mining in the late 20th century several light industries have become established and much farmland has been lost.

The parish church of **St Peter and St Paul** dates from the year 1100 and still retains the original Norman doorway. In a field at the back of the church, near the river, stands the Priest's Well where the parish priest used to draw water as did the travelling people, who used the field as a camp until the 1930s.

The Sitwell family had their home close by; **Renishaw Hall**, situated midway between Eckington and neighbouring Renishaw, was built by George Sitwell in 1625 after he had re-established his fortune with the success of the Renishaw Iron works. The massive house was greatly transformed under the first baronet, Sir Sitwell Sitwell, and in the grounds can be found the world's most northerly vineyard. The Sitwell family and, in particular, Dame Edith, Sir Sacheverell and Sir Osbert, have, over the years, become famous for their literary leanings - perhaps there is something in the wine that promotes success in this field! The Hall is also said to be haunted by a number of ghosts, though few houses of any great age seem to escape the interest of some form of poltergeist. In particular there is the little boy in pink, known as the Kissing Ghost because it seems that this is just what he likes to do to any guests at the Hall. The grounds of the village Rectory, a handsome late Georgian building, are also worth a second glance. Though not laid out by the Reverend Christopher Alderson, he set about improving them in the late 18th century. A magazine of the time said that the Reverend 'was so renowned as a garden improver that he was employed at Windsor as well'.

Renishaw Hall, Near Eckington

Renishaw

6 miles NE of Chesterfield off the A616

The village lies close to the Sitwell family home and was the site of the family iron works, which helped to re-establish their fortune.

Staveley

4 miles NE of Chesterfield off the A619

Staveley lies to the south of the great **Staveley Iron Works** and has its fair share of large 20th century housing estates. However, this is not altogether a modern village and has some fine earlier structures, including its 13th century church dedicated to St John the Baptist and **Staveley Hall**, built in 1604 and now the District Council Offices. The name of Frecheville is one that crops up from time to time in this part of Derbyshire, and the church has a selection of tombs and monuments to the family. As well as the tomb-chest of Peter Frecheville, dating from around 1480, there is also an early 16th century monument to Piers Frecheville. In the Frecheville Chapel is a memorial to Christina Frecheville, who died in childbirth in 1653.

Barlborough

7 miles NE of Chesterfield off the A619

Lying close to the county borders with both Nottinghamshire and Yorkshire,

this village still retains its manor house. Lying just north of the village centre, **Barlborough Hall** (private) was built in 1584 by Lord Justice Francis Rodes to plans drawn up by the designer of Hardwick Hall, Robert Smythson. Those who visit both houses will notice the strong resemblance. As well as building houses, Rodes was also one of the judges at the trial of Mary, Queen of Scots. The Hall is supposed to be haunted by a grey lady, said to be the ghost of a bride who received the news of her groom's death as she was on her way to the 12th century village church. Barlborough Hall should not be confused with **Barlborough Old Hall**: this is an easy mistake to make as Barlborough Old Hall is actually the younger of the two! Built in 1618, as the date stone over the front door states, the Old Hall is of a large H-plan design and has mullioned windows.

Although there is a lot of new development, particularly around Barlborough Links, the village also boasts some fine old stone houses with pantile roofs. The village **Church of St James** dates from the beginning of the 13th century, though it was heavily restored in 1899. Among the medieval work extant is the four-bay north arcade. The church contains the effigy of a grieving woman. This is said to be Lady Furnival, who died in 1395. The monument was probably brought here from Worksop, where she is buried.

The custom of well-dressing was started anew in 1975 when the Young Wives' Group produced a modest picture to dress the village well for St James' Day (25 July). From such humble beginnings, well-dressing in Barlborough is now an annual event that coincides with the church flower festival.

Clowne

7½ miles NE of Chesterfield off the A616

This small town has grown up around the county's coal mining industry though, away from the centre, the part-Norman Church of St John the Baptist can be seen. It is now mainly residential, but retains its own identity and sense of community. It is well known locally for its dazzling Christmas Lights display.

Creswell

9 miles E of Chesterfield off the A616

Once a sleepy hamlet nestling amid peaceful farming country, the character of Creswell was irreversibly changed at the end of the 19th century. It was then that Creswell Colliery was opened, and now the village is one of the biggest in the county. There is also a village within a village here as, between 1896 and 1900 a model village of houses and cottages was built. The Model Village was built by the Bolsover Colliery Company in 1896 to house the workforce at the Creswell Colliery. Everybody who lived on the Model worked in the coal mine. It remained as housing for miners until the mid 1980s when the houses were let on the open market. The houses were neglected, repairs were not done and the area became run down. Now with the help of a Lottery Grant, the central park has been almost restored to its original Victorian state with newly planted trees and shrubs, seating and play areas. Many of the houses around the park have been restored and renovated and more will be restored in the next phase. The restored Model Village is an excellent example of Victorian social housing for working families.

Lying close to the Derbyshire-Nottinghamshire border, the limestone gorge of the **Creswell Crags** is well worth seeing. Formed thousands of years ago by the erosion of a river which cut through the limestone, this rock, which is porous and subject to erosion underground as well as on the surface, contributes by its very nature to the forming of natural chambers. The subterranean movement of water created a vast network of caves, which were subsequently exposed. Used by Neanderthal man as shelters while out hunting, tours can be taken from the visitor centre, where there is also a display of artefacts found in the area. Testimony to the artistry of the later inhabitants of these caves was the discovery of a bone carved with the head of a horse, which is about 13,000 years old, and can now be seen in the British Museum. The largest cavern, Church Hole Cave, extends some 170 feet into the side of the gorge; it was here that hand tools were found.

Not far from the village and close to the county border with Nottinghamshire is **Steetley Chapel**, thought by many to be the most perfect specimen of Norman architecture in Europe. Whether this is so or not, the elaborate chapel has a rare and unique beauty. Having lain derelict for many years after being desecrated during the Commonwealth, the Chapel of All Saints was restored in the 1880s and at this time some of the wonderful carvings to be seen in the porchway were re-created. Luckily much of the interior remains intact, having survived the test of time. It remains a mystery as to why such a small building should be given such elaborate decoration in the mid-12th century.

Whaley

8 miles E of Chesterfield off the A632

The **Whaley Thorns Heritage Centre**, situated in a disused school, tells the story of human activity in the area from the Stone Age to the present day. In particular there are displays illustrating the history of coal mining in this region of Derbyshire and, since the decline of the industry, the efforts that have been made to restore the area to its natural state.

Bolsover

7 miles E of Chesterfield off the A632

The approach to Bolsover from the north and east is dominated by the splendid, sandstone structure of **Bolsover Castle**, which sits high on a

The White Hart

Top Road, Calow, Chesterfield,
Derbyshire S44 5TE
Tel: 01246 232650

Pete Cuckson and Alan Lucas are the friends and business partners who took over at the excellent **White Hart** inn in February 2004. It's their first venture into the business, but their enthusiasm and attention to offering great service and hospitality have made the place a real success. Ably assisted by Alan's partner Ann, this fine inn offers great food, drink and atmosphere.

Set in Calow, adjacent to the A632 Chesterfield-to-Bolsover Road, the inn dates back to the early 19th century. A restaurant was added in the 1970s. The interior is handsome and comfortable, and there's a wealth of bygone memorabilia on display – plates, brasses, old-fashioned fishing implements and more. Warm polished woods make up the bar surround and ceilings, while the décor and furnishings are traditional, comfortable and attractive.

Open all day every day for ale, there are always two to three real ales available – Marstons Pedigree, Banks and a rotating guest ale – together with a good selection of lagers, cider, stout, wines, spirits and soft drinks.

Food is served Tuesday to Sunday and Bank Holidays at lunch (12 – 2.30) and dinner (5.30 – 9). The restaurant seats 65 – and is justly popular, so booking is advised at all times. Guests choose from the menu and specials board from a range of tempting and hearty dishes such as salmon fillet, fish and chips, calamari, Cajun chicken, steaks, mixed grills, pies, roast of the day, vegetable lasagne, stuffed roast peppers and main-course salads. Excellent bar snacks – baguettes, scampi, onion rings, jacket potatoes and more – are also available throughout the day. Everything from the starters to the puddings is expertly prepared using the freshest ingredients, and the chef is happy to cater for special dietary requirements.

Entertainments at this convivial inn include live music on Friday and Saturday evenings, a music quiz Sunday nights and a general knowledge quiz Tuesday night.

Children welcome.

limestone ridge. A castle has stood here since the 12th century, though the present building is a fairytale 'folly' built for Sir Charles Cavendish during the early 1600s on the site of a ruined castle. By the mid-18th century much of the building had been reduced to the ruins seen today, though thankfully the splendid keep has withstood the test of time.

Pevsner remarked that not many large houses in England occupy such an impressive position as Bolsover Castle, as it stands on the brow of a hill overlooking the valley of the River Rother and Doe Lea. The first castle at Bolsover was built by William Peverel, illegitimate son of William the Conqueror, as part of his vast Derbyshire estates. Nothing remains of that Norman building. Now owned by English Heritage, visitors can explore the Little Castle, or Keep, which is decorated in an elaborate Jacobean celebration with wonderful fireplaces, panelling and wall paintings. The series of remarkable rooms includes the Vaulted Hall, the Pillar Room, the Star Chamber, the Elysium and the Heaven Room. Sir Charles' son, William, was responsible for the eastern range of buildings known as the Riding School, an impressive indoor area built in the 17th century, and the roofless but still impressive western terrace. The ruins of the state apartments are also here to be discovered. The whole building later descended to the Dukes of Portland, and it remains a strangely impressive place. However it is threatened by its industrial surroundings. The legacy of centuries of coal mining beneath its walls is subsidence.

The town itself is industrial, dominated for many years by coal mining, however it was once famous for the manufacture of buckles. The Hudson Bay public house across the road from the castle recalls in its name the fact that it was originally built by Peter Fidler, a Bolsover man, who was a distinguished surveyor with the Hudson Bay Company in Canada during the 18th century. A Peter Fidler Society exists in Canada to this day. Bolsover's oldest public house is probably The White Swan, and is said to have served as the moot hall from the Middle Ages to the early 19th century. Bolsover was granted its market charter by Henry III in 1225.

Naturally, the parish **Church of St Mary's** in Bolsover holds many monuments to the Cavendish family, but it seems amazing that the Church has survived when its recent history is revealed. Dating from the 13th century, the church's monuments include two magnificent tombs to Charles Cavendish, who died in 1617, and Henry Cavendish, who died in 1727. Destroyed by fire in 1897, except for the Cavendish Chapel, St Mary's was rebuilt, only to be damaged again by fire in 1960. It has since been restored. Buried in the churchyard are John Smythson and Huntingdon Smythson, the 17th century architects probably responsible for the design of the rebuilt Bolsover Castle.

Scarcliffe

8 miles E of Chesterfield off the B6417

Scarcliffe, recorded as Scardeclif in the *Domesday Book*, takes its name from the escarpment of magnesium limestone on which the village stands. It was settled in Roman times evidenced by the collection of Roman coins found near the village in 1876. The church in this little village is Norman and contains a most magnificent monument of a woman holding a child in her arms. Dating from the 12th or 13th century, the effigy is probably that of Constantia de Frecheville, who died in 1175. Known in Scarcliffe as Lady Constantia, a bell is tolled in her memory around Christmas. During the industrial revolution coal mining was the main industry and the Lancashire, Derbyshire and East Coast Railway cut through the previously agricultural land including a tunnel between Scarcliffe and Bolsover. The Langwith Colliery closed in 1978 and the railway has long gone.

Poulter Country Park, created from the old colliery spoil heaps, provides scenic walks with excellent views of the surrounding countryside.

Heath

5 miles SE of Chesterfield off the A617

To the north of Heath, overlooking the M1, are the ruins of what was one of the grandest mansions in Derbyshire, **Sutton Scarsdale**. Built in 1724 for the 4th Earl of Scarsdale, to the designs of Francis Smith, the stonework of the previous Tudor manor house was completely hidden behind the Baroque splendour of the new hall. The magnificent Italian plasterwork can now be seen at the Philadelphia Museum, in Pennsylvania, and demolition of the back of the house has revealed some Tudor brickwork. At the beginning of the 20th century Sutton Scarsdale was owned by a descendent of Sir Richard Arkwright, the famous industrialist. It is this gentleman that D H Lawrence is supposed to have chosen as the inspiration for his character of Sir Clifford Chatterley in the novel *Lady Chatterley's Lover*.

Also close to Heath is the National Trust-owned **Stainsby Mill**. With its machinery now restored to illustrate the workings of a 19th century water-powered corn mill, Stainsby is well worth a visit. Though there has been a mill here since medieval times, the buildings seen today date from 1849 when the then new machinery was first fitted. The large (17-feet) cast-iron waterwheel, which because of its particular design is known as a high breast shot, not only provided power to turn the millstones but also for lifting sacks, cleaning the grain and sieving the flour. Open between the end of March and the end of October, visitors can watch the operations from a viewing gallery.

Ault Hucknall

6 miles SE of Chesterfield off the A617

The strange name of this village probably means 'Hucca's high nook of land', and this pleasant place, standing on a ridge close to the Nottinghamshire border, is home to the magnificent Tudor house, **Hardwick Hall**. 'More glass than wall', it is one of Derbyshire's Big Three stately homes alongside Chatsworth and Haddon, all three glorious monuments to the great land-owning families who played so great a role in shaping the history of the county. Set in rolling parkland, the house, with its glittering tiers of windows and crowned turrets, offers quite a spellbinding sight. Inside, the silence of the chambers strewn with rush matting, combined with the simplicity of the white-washed walls, gives a feeling of almost overwhelming peace. The letters E S can be seen carved in stone on the outside of the house: E S, or Elizabeth of Shrewsbury, was perhaps better known as Bess of Hardwick. This larger-than-life figure had attachments with many places in Derbyshire, and the story of her life makes for fascinating reading.

She was born in the manor house at Hardwick in 1520. The house stood only a little distance from the present-day Hall and was then not much more than a farmhouse. The young Bess married her neighbour's son, Robert Barlow, when she was only 12. When her young husband, himself only 14, died a few months later she naturally inherited a great deal of property. Some 15 years later she married Sir William Cavendish and, when he died in 1557, she was bequeathed his entire fortune. By this time she was the richest woman in England, save for one, Elizabeth, the Queen.

The Gallery at Hardwick Hall, with its gorgeous lavender-hued tapestries, has, in pride of place, a portrait of this formidable woman. The portrait depicts a personage who could be mistaken for Elizabeth R, and it seems only right to compare the two. First the 'Virgin' Queen who commanded so forcibly the men around her yet never married, and then Bess, who married and survived four husbands. Bess began the building of the house in 1590, towards the end of her life and after her fourth lucrative

Hardwick Hall

Hardwick Inn

Hardwick Park, Chesterfield,
Derbyshire S44 5QJ
Tel: 01246 850245 Fax: 01246 856365
e-mail: batty@hardwickinn.co.uk
website: www.hardwickinn.co.uk

Hardwick Inn can be located not far from Chesterfield, on the edge of the Hardwick Hall estate, which has a long history going back many hundreds of years. At the end of the 16th century, the manor house was home to Elizabeth, Countess of Shrewsbury, known throughout the land as Bess of Hardwick. It is thought that Bess built the present inn for one of her faithful servants, on the site of an older hostelry. Constructed of locally-quarried sandstone, the mellow building retains to this day many original features including the leaded windows and handsome

gables. In 1959 Hardwick Hall, its surrounding park and woodland, and the inn were transferred into the care of the National Trust. The NT continues to be responsible for the care and preservation of the estate.

When you step over the threshold there is a feeling of stepping back in time. The traditional, historic feel has been retained while the atmosphere is at the same time friendly and comfortable – the perfect place to enjoy some fine food and drink.

There are two bar areas, three family rooms where children are welcome, and also meeting rooms available for hire. In winter the whole area is kept snug and cosy with open coal fires. It will come as a relief to most to know that there are no slot machines or juke boxes to be found here, just quiet relaxation.

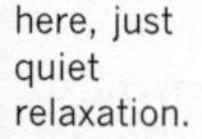

The Batty family have run the inn since 1928; present licensees Peter and Pauline Batty have been here since 1982. The Batty's pride themselves on providing friendly, conscientious service to all their customers, old and new. They stock a first-class range of drinks with five real ales available (Theakstons, Ruddles, Marstons and Speckled Hen varieties, to name a few), over 200 malt whiskies and a superb and extensive wine list, together with lagers, cider, stout and soft drinks.

The restaurant is open Tuesday to Sunday lunch 12.00noon-2pm. and Tuesday-Saturday evening 7.00pm-9.00pm, while bar meals are available Monday to Saturday from 11.30am-9.30pm, Sunday 12noon-9.00pm. Head chef Paul Booth creates exquisite dishes using the finest and freshest ingredients. The wide-ranging menu of home-cooked dishes includes steak-and-kidney pie (a dish the inn is justly famous for), casseroles, fish dishes, grills and much more, all expertly prepared and presented. Booking advised at all times.

marriage to George Talbot, sixth Earl of Shrewsbury. It stands as a monument to her wealth and good taste, and is justly famous for its magnificent needlework and tapestries, carved fireplaces and friezes, which are considered as among the finest in Britain.

Though Bess is the first person that springs to mind with regard to Hardwick Hall, it was the 6th Duke of Devonshire who was responsible for the Hall's antiquarian atmosphere. He inherited the property in 1811 and, as well as promoting the legend that Mary, Queen of Scots stayed here, he filled the house with furniture, paintings and tapestries from his other houses and from Chatsworth in particular.

As well as viewing the Hall, there are some wonderful grounds to explore. To the south are the formal gardens, laid out in the 19th century and separated by long walks lined with yew. One area has been planted as a Tudor herb garden and is stocked with both culinary and medicinal plants used at that time. Down in the southeastern corner of the garden is the small Elizabethan banqueting hall, used as a smoking room by the 6th Duke's orchestra, as they were not allowed to smoke in the Hall. There is also, to the back of the house, a lake and lime avenue. Owned by the National Trust, Hardwick Hall is a must for any visitor to Derbyshire and is certainly a place not to be missed. The parkland, which overlooks the valley of the Doe Lea and the M1, is home to an impressive herd of Longhorn cattle among the stag-headed oaks. The ruins of Hardwick Old Hall (English Heritage) also stand in the grounds, and are the interesting remains of Bess's former Tudor mansion.

The village **Church of St John the Baptist**, situated on a back lane, is one of the finest in Derbyshire. Overlooking Hardwick Hall's beautiful parklands, with the square towers of Bess of Hardwick's great house in the distance, the battlemented church exterior does not prepare visitors for its dark, mysterious interior, which reveals the church's much earlier origins. There are many Norman features, including the north arcade, nave and the narrow arches holding up the rare crossing tower. There is more Norman work in the plain capitals of the north arcade.

There are several interesting tombs in the church, such as the large and detailed wall monument just below the east window to the first Countess of Devonshire, dating from 1627. On the floor in front is a simple black slab commemorating the influential and renowned philosopher Thomas Hobbes - author of *The Leviathan* and *De Mirabilibus Pecci: Concerning the Wonders of the Peak* (the latter being one of the first accounts of the Seven Wonders of the Peak) - who died at Hardwick. A much simpler table in the north aisle commemorates Robert Hackett, a keeper of Hardwick Park who died n 1703. It reads: 'Long has he chas'd/ The red and fallow deer/But death's cold dart/At last has fix'd him here.'

Winsick

2 miles S of Chesterfield off the A617

This charming hamlet is just a short drive from the centre of Chesterfield but retains a tranquil rural feel.

Wingerworth

3 miles S of Chesterfield off the A61

The village was settled in Anglo-Saxon times, and is recorded in the *Domesday Book*, as a community of fourteen households. It expanded after the Middle Ages although until the 20th century the population never exceeded 500. The Hunlokes were the dominant family in Wingerworth from the reign of Queen Elizabeth I until 1920, acquiring nine-tenths of the land in the parish and becoming lords of the manor. The grand mansion of Wingerworth Hall, which they built in the early 18th century, was demolished in the 1920s. Olave, Lady Baden-Powell, first Chief Guide, was born here in 1889. The village church, although it retains some Norman and 13th century work has had many additions. A tower was added around 1500 and a substantial extension in 1963.

Grassmoor

3 miles S of Chesterfield off the B6038

Originally named Gresmore ('Grey Copse') according to parish records of 1568, the main employment in the village was for many years coal mining, at Grassmoor Colliery. The first shaft was sunk in 1846 and officially opened in 1880 by Mr Barnes. The colliery closed in 1970. The site of the colliery is now a country park and the start of a pleasant walk called the **Five Pits Trail**, a popular trail running between Grassmoor and Tibshelf, with 8 miles of traffic-free walking and cycling. Originally created in 1971, the paths have been recently re-surfaced. There are many picnic sites along the way past the sites of the old pits, along the line of some of the old railways. Almost all traces of the pits have disappeared, although the head gear remains at Holmewood pit.

Pilsley

5 miles S of Chesterfield off the B6039

The Herb Garden in Pilsley, featured on the BBC TV programme *Country Gardens*, is one of the foremost gardens in the country. Consisting of four display gardens, the largest is the Mixed Herb Garden, boasting an impressive established parterre. The remaining three gardens are the Physic, the Lavender and the Pot Pourri, each with its own special theme and housing many rare and unusual species. Areas of native flowers and wild spring bulbs can be enjoyed from March to September. On the grounds there is also a lovely tea room serving such delicacies as lavender cake, rosemary fruit slice and cheese and herb scones.

Tibshelf

6 miles S of Chesterfield off the B6014

Tibshelf is a large, former coal mining village, with a population of around 3300. There had been coal mines here for over 650 years until the last two pits, Long pit and Bottom pit, closed 70 years ago. In 1891 over 2000 men were employed in the village mines. Stretching from here north, to Grassmoor, the Five Pits Trail is a scenic route, which passes the old collieries at Tibshelf, Pilsley, Alameda, Williamthorpe and Grassmoor. At first the idea of exploring these old coal workings may not appeal, but since their reclamation by Derbyshire County Council this is now an interesting and entertaining seven mile walk. Suitable for walkers, cyclists and horse riders, the Trail is quite lovely, and offers some splendid views.

With the closure of the pits, which had been largely developed since the middle of the 19th century, the land had fallen into disuse. With the help of the Countryside Ranger Service, Derbyshire County Council manages the Trail and there is also a great deal of support from local groups who have contributed much time and effort to bring this land back to life. The clearing of paths and the addition of plantations, ponds and meadows has ensured that many species of wildlife have been encouraged to return here. Wild plants to look out for include the bush vetch, meadowsweet and the corn poppy. At one time these lovely wild flowers could be seen in abundance in many of Derbyshire's fields and hedgerows.

The church of St John the Baptist has been much restored over the centuries but it still retains an impressive 14th century tower.

Clay Cross

5 miles S of Chesterfield off the A61

This busy market town, situated on a

Clay Cross Church

Bateman's Mill Country Hotel and Restaurant

Mill Lane, Old Tupton, Chesterfield,
Derbyshire S42 6AE
Tel: 01246 862296 Fax: 01246 865672
e-mail: info@batemansmill.co.uk
website: www.batemansmill.co.uk

Bateman's Mill Country Hotel and Restaurant is a handsome and gracious establishment with excellent food, drink and accommodation. The mill was built in 1831, and used to process corn for the local community right up until the 1930s. Named for the Bateman family, tenants here from the 1880s, this superb hotel and restaurant is owned by John and Maggie Roberts, who arrived in July of 2004 and, ably assisted by their son Steven, have made a great success of the venture. John is a professional chef who has worked at the Savoy and Dorchester hotels. Head Chef Robert Moakes and the kitchen team produce fabulous food focusing on a range of local and international dishes. Using the freshest ingredients and locally-supplied produce wherever possible, the menu boasts a range of classic and modern dishes such as roast loin of lamb, confit of Gressingham duck, gratin of asparagus, chicken and scampi ragout, and much more, certain to please every palate.

Excellent food is available at lunch (12 – 2.30) and dinner (6.45 – 9.30) daily. Booking required Thursday to Saturday evenings and for Sunday lunchtime. Guests can dine throughout the bar or in the upstairs no-smoking restaurant, which seats 60. Children welcome.

To drink, there are real ales from the Hardy & Hanson's brewery group, together with a full range of lagers, cider, stout, wines, spirits and soft drinks.

Bateman's also plan to host a wine club and special food- and drink-themed evenings – please ring for details.

There are eight lovely ensuite guest bedrooms, four on the ground floor. The rooms differ in size, but all are spacious, supremely comfortable and welcoming. The tariff includes breakfast, and there are special weekend breaks. Guests can also stay on a dinner and B&B rate if they wish.

During the lifetime of this edition, an adjacent building will be converted into a bakery and patisserie, and cookery demonstrations and courses will be held – please ring for details.

This superb hotel is also happy to host and cater for weddings and other personal celebrations, with space for 20 to 60 diners.

high ridge, is largely a product of the Industrial Revolution. It developed after coal was discovered in the area, when George Stephenson was building a railway tunnel. It grew from a small farming community into an industrial town dominated by the Clay Cross Company. The Company also provided schools, churches and housing. An impressive monument consisting of two large wheels with the inscription "In memory of all North East Derbyshire Miners who lost their lives working to keep the home fires burning and the wheels of industry turning", takes pride of place in the High Street. In 1972 the town earned the title "the Republic of Clay Cross", when the leftwing councillors, including David and Graham Skinner, both related to Dennis Skinner, MP for Bolsover, would not implement the terms of the Tory Housing Finance Act. The Clay Cross Rebels, as they became known, refused to put up council house rents by £1 a week. After a bitter dispute with the Government, which divided the community, they were surcharged, bankrupted and disqualified from office.

Stretton

6 miles S of Chesterfield on the A61

Stretton village lies close to Ogston Resevoir, which covers an area of over 200 acres and is a favourite place for sailing. The man-made lake is overlooked by the romantic Ogston Hall, which dates from the 16th century and was the ancestral home of the Turbutt and Revell families. The house was altered extensively in 1768, and then modernised and 'medievalised' during Victorian times.

Brackenfield

7 miles S of Chesterfield off the A632

This village was known as Brackenthwaite in the Middle Ages, a name that means 'clearing in the bracken'. Like Clay Cross, Brackenfield is known today primarily for its proximity to the Ogston Reservoir, created in 1960 by damming the River Amber at the south end of the valley. The site of the former Ogston Mill was submerged under the rising waters. Hidden in the surrounding trees is the ruin of the former **Trinity Chapel**. The church is mentioned in the *Domesday Book*, but was abandoned when the new church was built in 1856. An ancient screen was removed from the chapel and brought to the new church.

Ashover

6 miles SW of Chesterfield off the B6036

Viewed from the southern rocky ridge known as **The Fabric** (apparently because it provided the fabric for much of the local building stone) and with the monolith of **Cocking Tor** in the foreground, Ashover can be seen as a scattered village filling the pleasantly wooded valley of the River Amber. The name of this village means 'ash tree

The Old Poets' Corner

Butts Road, Ashover, Chesterfield,
Derbyshire S45 0EW
Tel: 01246 590888
website: www.oldpoets.co.uk

The Old Poets' Corner is a great place situated in the very handsome village of Ashover, found four miles northeast of Matlock off the B6036.

Owners Kim and Jackie arrived here in June 2004. Kim is a chef by trade and has many years' experience in the trade.

Open every session Monday to Thursday and all day Friday, Saturday, Sunday, Bank Holidays and on Ashover Show Day, this excellent Free House boasts no fewer than seven real ales. Regulars include Old Poets Ale, Ashover Gold and Abbot Ale, together with rotating guest ales. There's always a strong dark available, along with a selection of rough and smooth ciders. Together with this there are lagers, stout, wines, spirits and soft drinks.

Food is served Monday to Saturday at lunch (12 – 2) and dinner (6 – 9 summer; 6.30 – 9 winter), and on Sundays there's a carvery served between 12 and 3.30 p.m. Guests choose off the printed menu or specials board, and can dine throughout the inn or in the separate no-smoking bistro, which seats 28. Booking required Friday and Saturday evening and for Sunday lunch. Kim and the inn's other chef, Mick Foster, create a range of delicious dishes – specialities include home-made pies, home-made lasagne, and spicy dishes such as chillies and authentic curries, together with a range of hearty favourites such as steaks, lamb, haddock, vegetarian dishes and more.

Living up to its name, the second Tuesday of the month is poets' night – guests come to listen to local poets or share poetry of their own. Every other Sunday night from 8.30 is folk night, and every three weeks (usually on Friday or Saturday nights) there's live rock or blues music.

The inn is also happy to host two annual beer festivals, in October and late spring. October's festival features 25 real ales to sample; in spring it's held outdoors in a marquee, and features even more real ales to try.

By the spring of 2005 this excellent inn will also have ensuite accommodation – please ring or visit their website for more details.

slope' and though there are, indeed, many ash trees in the area, many other varieties including oak and birch also flourish. Ashover was a flourishing industrial town in the past. As well as lead mining, which dated back to Roman times, there was nail making, lace, ropes, stocking weaving and malting. One part of the village is called the Rattle because of the sound of the looms rattling in the making of stockings. The main occupation now is farming.

Ashover lies just outside the boundary of the Peak District National Park but it still captures the typical character of a Peak village. At the heart of the largest parish in northeast Derbyshire, the village is chiefly constructed from limestone and gritstone, which were both quarried locally. The ruined shell of **Eastwood Hall**, once a large fortified Elizabethan manor house, also lies in the village. Owned, over the years, by several prominent Derbyshire families, including the Willoughbys, the house was blown up by the Roundheads during the Civil War. The ropes were said to be the longest and strongest in the country. The industries, with the exception of quarrying and fluor spar have all died out and the work is now chiefly farming.

Ashover

The Crispin Inn, next to the interesting parish **Church of All Saints**, claims to date from the time of Agincourt, 1415. However, it is far more likely that, like many other buildings in the parish, it dates from the 17th century. The inn's name reflects one of Ashover's traditional trades: St Crispin is the patron saint of shoemakers and cobblers. The church, with its 15th century tower, houses the alabaster tomb of Thomas Babington and his wife, said by many to be the best in Derbyshire. There are also some handsome brasses. What is surprising is the lead-lined Norman font, described by Pevsner as 'the most important Norman font in the country', the only lead-lined font in this area that is so well known for its mining.

Holymoorside

3 miles SW of Chesterfield off the A632

Surrounded by the attractive moorland and lying in the picturesque valley of the River Hipper, this scattered village has grown into a popular residential area for the nearby towns. The custom of

The Famous Red Lion

Darley Road, Stonedge, Chesterfield,
Derbyshire S45 0LW
Tel: 01246 566142 Fax: 01246 591040
e-mail: info@thefamousredlion.com
website: www.thefamousredlion.com

The Famous Red Lion is a large, friendly place with bags of style and charm. The interior dates back to the 17th century and boasts many original features.Open all day every day guests can experience some of the finest quality home cooked food in the area. Meals are served daily 12.00-9.00 (12.00-9.30 on Saturdays). Thursday night hosts an International Cuisine all you can eat buffet and Sunday's showcase the best in local produce with one of the most popular Carvery's around.Guests can expect a comprehensive selection of ales (including two cask ales), wines and soft drinks and these can be enjoyed in the bar or in the garden, weather permitting, with its unrivalled views of the surrounding countryside.

well-dressing in the village was revived in 1979 after a gap of about 80 years. Two wells are dressed, a large one and a smaller one for children, on the Wednesday before the late summer Bank Holiday in August.

The dressers follow the tradition of Barlow, where only flowers and leaves are used and not wool, seed and shells, though they do not stick to biblical themes. In 1990 the well-dressing depicted a scene commemorating the 50th anniversary of the Battle of Britain, one of their most spectacular dressings to date, and won the dressers pictures in the national press.

La Bistro Chameleon

370 Chatsworth Road, Chesterfield,
Derbyshire S40 2DQ
Tel: 01246 277344
website: www.la-bistro-chameleon.co.uk

Situated adjacent to the A619, approximately one mile west of Chesterfield town centre towards Baslow, **La Bistro Chameleon** is an excellent French restaurant well worth seeking out. Owned and run by Amanda and Carl Fuller since 2003, the restaurant has been refurbished to the highest standard of comfort and quality. Occupying two floors plus the basement-level wine bar, this gracious and handsome establishment has a relaxed and welcoming ambience.

Head chef Andrew Wilson is a master of his craft, creating a range of mouth-watering dishes for the menu and specials board, including chargrilled fillet of Scottish beef with ratatouille, seared pork with cardamom-scented carrots, crisped leeks and apple-and-grain mustard, roast duckling breast, maize-fed chicken and baked red onion filled with Mediterranean vegetables and buffalo mozzarella. Everything on the menu is expertly prepared and presented. The wine list is excellent.

Open Tuesday to Saturday for dinner, this excellent venue also caters for small parties and functions, and hosts regular wine-tasting evenings – please ring for details.

Old Brampton

3½ miles W of Chesterfield off the B6050

Situated on a quiet road above a wooded valley, Brampton retains both its medieval church and also its manor hall from the 16th century. The church of **Saints Peter and Paul** is of interest for its battlemented walls, short octagonal spire and Norman doorway and window. Also worthy of note is the large cruck barn, probably the largest in Derbyshire, to be found at **Frith Hall Farmhouse**.

Cutthorpe

4 miles W of Chesterfield off the B6050

Before the Second World War the well-dressings in this village, which take place on the third Friday in July, had no religious links. After the war the custom died out, but was revived again by three people from nearby Barlow, in 1978. The three dressed wells are blessed during a service of thanksgiving for the pure water.

Near the village are the three **Linacre Reservoirs**, set in the attractive wooded Linacre Valley. Built between 1855 and 1904, until recently they supplied water to Chesterfield. Today the area is home to many species of fish, waterfowl, mammals and plant life, and is considered one of the most important ecological sites in the area. There are very pleasant walks, nature trails and fishing, and a scenic picnic area.

Barlow

3 miles NW of Chesterfield off the B6051

Barlow is mentioned in the *Domesday Book*, and was the home of Robert Barlow, the first of Bess of Hardwick's four husbands. Although situated outside the limestone area, Barlow has been dressing its main well for longer than most. It is not known for certain when the custom began in the village, though it is known that, like Tissington, the well here provided water throughout the drought of 1615; this may have marked the start of this colourful practice.

Another theory suggests that the tradition in Barlow could date back to the days of Elizabeth I's reign, as the church register of 1572 states that the festival of St Lawrence was celebrated. Whatever the origins of the well-dressings in the village, it is known that they have continued, unbroken even through two World Wars, throughout living memory. The wells are dressed during the second week of August every year.

West of the village, **Barlow Woodseats** are not as uncomfortable as they sound for this is the name of an irregular gabled 16th century house, also called Woodseats Hall (private), which has a cruck barn in its grounds. Home to the Mower family - Arthur Mower was the agent to the Barlow family in the 16th century, and kept a truly remarkable diary from 1555 to 1610. All 52 volumes are now kept in the British Museum. He records the death of Bess of Hardwick in 1608, recalling her as 'a great purchaser and getter together of much goods' and notes that she 'builded Chattesworth, Hardwick and Owlcotes'.

For those interested in Norman churches, there is another in Barlow. At first sight, however, **St Laurence's Church** may appear to be Victorian, but this was the work of enthusiastic remodelling in the 1860s. The interior reveals the true Norman features - the doorways leading from the nave and the short chancel - and there is also a fine alabaster slab in memory of Robert Barley, who died in 1467, and his wife. (The village was originally known as Barley, and the family took their name from it, later changing it to Barlow.) Bess's husband Robert Barlow is also buried here.

Holmesfield

3 miles NW of Chesterfield off the B6054

Holmesfield is an attractive suburb of Chesterfield with its own flavour and rural tranquillity. The parish church of St Swithin was built in 1826 on the highest point of the village, giving spectacular views both north and south.

Dronfield

5 miles NW of Chesterfield off the A61

An important market town which has since developed industrially, there are some fine 17th and 18th century

The Angel Inn

Main Road, Holmesfield, Dronfield,
Derbyshire S18 7WT
Tel: 0114 289 0336
e-mail: theangelinn@amserve.com

Situated three miles northwest of Chesterfield off the B6054, there's been a pub on the site where **The Angel Inn** now stands since the early 1700s. This latest incarnation dates back to 1953. Leaseholders James and Ruth and their four-year-old daughter Charlotte took over here in December 2003, after Ruth had worked here for many years – James and Ruth met here, and it had been their local for years when they were given the opportunity to run it, which they jumped at.

The interior is attractive and comfortable, with a traditional lounge and dining area and a very modern bar area. Open Tuesday to Sunday and Bank Holidays, there are three real ales – Timothy Taylor Landlord plus two rotating guest ales – together with a good range of wines, spirits, lagers, cider, stout and soft drinks. Quality food – lamb's liver and onions, roast of the day, chicken curry, vegetarian cannelloni, Thai fish cakes and more – is served Tuesday to Sunday at lunch (11.30 – 2) and dinner (6 – 8.30). Booking is advised at weekends.

buildings in the town's conservation area. Centred around the Peel Monument, the church and the cruck barn, **The Hall** here is also worthy of a second glance as it has an attractive balustrade and a fine Queen Anne façade. In front of the early 18th century Manor House, now the home of the town library, is a highly elaborate Town Cross. Erected in 1848, it commemorates the repeal of the Corn Laws.

The prosperity of Dronfield in the early years of the Industrial Revolution was such that an unexpectedly large number of mansions were built in and around the town. Of those that remain today, **Chiverton House**, built in 1712, and Rose Hill, dating from 1719, are worthy of note.

To the east of the town can be seen a large group of 19th century coke ovens, once a common sight in this part of Derbyshire. The 48 seen here, arranged in two groups, were part of the Summerley Colliery complex; the tall engine house also survives.

TOURIST INFORMATION CENTRES

ASHBOURNE

13 Market Place
Ashbourne
Derbyshire DE6 1EU
Tel: 01335 343666
Fax: 01335 300638
e-mail: ashbourneinfo@derbyshiredales.gov.uk

BAKEWELL

Old Market Hall
Bridge Street
Bakewell
Derbyshire DE45 1DS
Tel: 01629 813227
Fax: 01629 814782
e-mail: bakewell@peakdistrict-npa.gov.uk

BURTON UPON TRENT

Coors Visitor Centre
Horninglow Street
Burton upon Trent
Staffordshire DE14 1YQ
Tel: 01283 508111 or 508112
Fax: 01283 517268
e-mail: tic@eaststaffsbc.gov.uk

BUXTON

The Crescent
Buxton
Derbyshire SK17 6BQ
Tel: 01298 25106
Fax: 01298 73153
e-mail: tourism@highpeak.gov.uk

CHESTERFIELD

Rykneld Square
Chesterfield
Derbyshire S40 1SB
Tel: 01246 345777 or 345778
Fax: 01246 345770
e-mail: tourism@chesterfield.gov.uk

DERBY

Assembly Rooms
Market Place
Derby
Derbyshire DE1 3AH
Tel: 01332 255802
Fax: 01332 256137
e-mail: tourism@derby.gov.uk

GLOSSOP

The Gatehouse
Victoria Street
Glossop
Derbyshire SK13 8HT
Tel: 01457 855920
Fax: 01427 855920
e-mail: info@glossoptouristcentre.co.uk

LEEK

1, Market Place
Leek
Staffordshire ST13 5HH
Tel: 01538 483741
Fax: 01538 483743
e-mail: tourism.services@staffsmoorlands.gov.uk

MACCLESFIELD

Macclesfield
Town Hall
Macclesfield
Cheshire SK10 1DX
Tel: 01625 504114 or 504115
Fax: 01625 504116
e-mail: Informationcentre@macclesfield.gov.uk

MATLOCK

Crown Square
Matlock
Derbyshire DE4 3AT
Tel: 01629 583388
Fax: 01629 584131
e-mail: matlockinfo@derbyshiredales.gov.uk

MATLOCK BATH

The Pavillion
Matlock
Derbyshire DE4 3NR
Tel: 01629 55082
Fax: 01629 56304
e-mail: matlockbathinfo@derbyshiredales.gov.uk

RIPLEY

Town Hall
Market Place
Ripley
Derbyshire DE5 3BT
Tel: 01773 841488 or 841486
Fax: 01773 841487
e-mail: touristinformation@ambervalley.gov.uk

SHEFFIELD

Visitor Information Point
Winter Garden
Sheffield
Tel: 0114 2211900
e-mail: visitor@sheffield.gov.uk

INDEX OF TOWNS, VILLAGES AND PLACES OF INTEREST

A

B

N

O

P

R

S

LIST OF ADVERTISERS

A

B

C

D

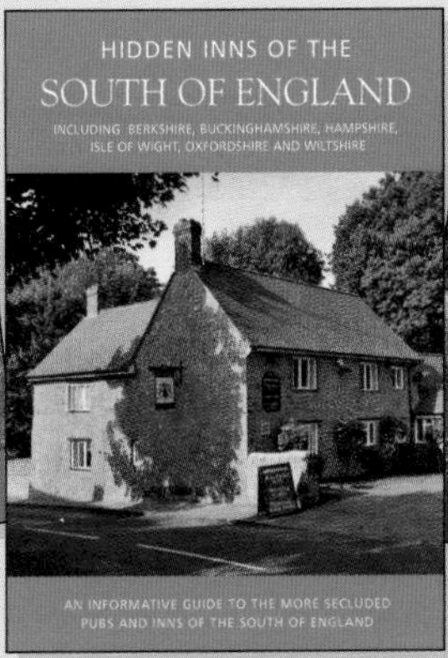

HIDDEN PLACES ORDER FORM

To order any of our publications just fill in the payment details below and complete the order form. For orders of less than 4 copies please add £1 per book for postage and packing. Orders over 4 copies are P & P free.

Please Complete Either:

I enclose a cheque for £ [   ] made payable to Travel Publishing Ltd

Or:

Card No: [   ] Expiry Date: [   ]

Signature: [   ]

Name: [   ]

Address: [   ]

Tel no: [   ]

Please either send, telephone, fax or e-mail your order to:

Travel Publishing Ltd, 7a Apollo House, Calleva Park, Aldermaston, Berkshire RG7 8TN

Tel: 0118 981 7777 Fax: 0118 982 0077 e-mail: karen@travelpublishing.co.uk

	Price	Quantity
Hidden Places Regional Titles		
Cambs & Lincolnshire	£8.99	....
Chilterns	£8.99	....
Cornwall	£8.99	....
Derbyshire	£8.99	....
Devon	£8.99	....
Dorset, Hants & Isle of Wight	£8.99	....
East Anglia	£8.99	....
Gloucs, Wiltshire & Somerset	£8.99	....
Heart of England	£8.99	....
Hereford, Worcs & Shropshire	£8.99	....
Highlands & Islands	£8.99	....
Lake District & Cumbria	£8.99	....
Lancashire & Cheshire	£8.99	....
Lincolnshire & Notts	£8.99	....
Northumberland & Durham	£8.99	....
Sussex	£8.99	....
Yorkshire	£8.99	....
Hidden Places National Titles		
England	£11.99	....
Ireland	£11.99	....
Scotland	£11.99	....
Wales	£11.99	....

	Price	Quantity
Hidden Inns Titles		
East Anglia	£7.99	....
Heart of England	£7.99	....
Lancashire & Cheshire	£7.99	....
North of England	£7.99	....
South	£7.99	....
South East	£7.99	....
South and Central Scotland	£7.99	....
Wales	£7.99	....
Welsh Borders	£7.99	....
West Country	£7.99	....
Yorkshire	£7.99	....
Country Living Rural Guides		
East Anglia	£10.99	....
Heart of England	£10.99	....
Ireland	£11.99	....
North East	£10.99	....
North West	£10.99	....
Scotland	£11.99	....
South of England	£10.99	....
South East of England	£10.99	....
Wales	£11.99	....
West Country	£10.99	....

Total Quantity [   ]

Post & Packing [   ] Total Value [   ]

READER REACTION FORM

The *Travel Publishing* research team would like to receive reader's comments on any visitor attractions or places reviewed in the book and also recommendations for suitable entries to be included in the next edition. This will help ensure that the *Hidden Places series of Guides* continues to provide its readers with useful information on the more interesting, unusual or unique features of each attraction or place ensuring that their visit to the local area is an enjoyable and stimulating experience. To provide your comments or recommendations would you please complete the forms below and overleaf as indicated and send to:

The Research Department, Travel Publishing Ltd,
7a Apollo House, Calleva Park, Aldermaston, Reading, RG7 8TN.

Your Name:

Your Address:

Your Telephone Number:

Please tick as appropriate:

Comments ☐ Recommendation ☐

Name of Establishment:

Address:

Telephone Number:

Name of Contact:

READER REACTION FORM

Comment or Reason for Recommendation:

READER REACTION FORM

The *Travel Publishing* research team would like to receive reader's comments on any visitor attractions or places reviewed in the book and also recommendations for suitable entries to be included in the next edition. This will help ensure that the *Hidden Places series of Guides* continues to provide its readers with useful information on the more interesting, unusual or unique features of each attraction or place ensuring that their visit to the local area is an enjoyable and stimulating experience. To provide your comments or recommendations would you please complete the forms below and overleaf as indicated and send to:

The Research Department, Travel Publishing Ltd,
7a Apollo House, Calleva Park, Aldermaston, Reading, RG7 8TN.

Your Name:

Your Address:

Your Telephone Number:

Please tick as appropriate:

Comments ☐ Recommendation ☐

Name of Establishment:

Address:

Telephone Number:

Name of Contact:

READER REACTION FORM

Comment or Reason for Recommendation:

....

....

....

....

....

....

....

....

....

....

....

....

READER REACTION FORM

The *Travel Publishing* research team would like to receive reader's comments on any visitor attractions or places reviewed in the book and also recommendations for suitable entries to be included in the next edition. This will help ensure that the *Hidden Places series of Guides* continues to provide its readers with useful information on the more interesting, unusual or unique features of each attraction or place ensuring that their visit to the local area is an enjoyable and stimulating experience. To provide your comments or recommendations would you please complete the forms below and overleaf as indicated and send to:

The Research Department, Travel Publishing Ltd,
7a Apollo House, Calleva Park, Aldermaston, Reading, RG7 8TN.

Your Name:

Your Address:

Your Telephone Number:

Please tick as appropriate:

Comments ☐ Recommendation ☐

Name of Establishment:

Address:

Telephone Number:

Name of Contact:

READER REACTION FORM

Comment or Reason for Recommendation: